Over the Top

Cover illustration of the 1919 edition of *The Wonder Book of Soldiers.*

Over the Top

THE GREAT WAR AND JUVENILE LITERATURE IN BRITAIN

Michael Paris

PRAEGER

Westport, Connecticut
London

Library of Congress Cataloging-in-Publication Data

Paris, Michael, 1949–
   Over the top : the Great War and juvenile literature in Britian / Michael Paris.
     p. cm.
   Includes bibliographical references and index.
   ISBN 0–275–97518–5 (hardcover : alk. paper)
   1. English literature—20th century—History and criticism. 2. World War, 1914–1918—
Great Britain—Literature and the war. 3. Children—Books and reading—Great Britain—
History—20th century. 4. World War, 1914–1918—Great Britain—Juvenile literature—
Historiography. 5. Children's literature, English—History and criticism. I. Title.
PR478.W65P37 2004
820.9'358—dc22   2004012614

British Library Cataloguing in Publication Data is available.

Library of Congress Catalog Card Number: 2004012614
ISBN: 0–275–97518–5

First published in 2004

Praeger Publishers, 88 Post Road West, Westport, CT 06881
An imprint of Greenwood Publishing Group, Inc.
www.praeger.com

Printed in the United States of America

The paper used in this book complies with the
Permanent Paper Standard issued by the National
Information Standards Organization (Z39.48–1984).

10 9 8 7 6 5 4 3 2 1

All illustrations are from the Michael Paris Collection

Contents

Illustrations

Acknowledgments

I am grateful to the Scouloudi Foundation, Institute of Historical Research, London, for financial assistance to research this book. I would also like to thank Peter Buitenhuis, Mick Gornell, John Walton, and Wendy Webster for their assistance and advice.

Introduction:
Only the Glory . . .

... Another picture was Lady Butler's "Charge of the Light Brigade." A wonderful picture of British Hussars and Lancers sabring the Russians ... The famous "Thin Red Line" picture—a colourful print of the Battle of Alma. These all hung in my nursery. Everything was glory to me. . . . a child has not seen war. I did not know how many of the noble six hundred died or that those fine English chargers starved in the snows of the Crimean winter. I knew nothing of Florence Nightingale, only glory. . . . I heard the clink of their spurs and the clash of steel, of bits and accoutrements. Only glory . . .
                              —Stuart Cloete, A Victorian Son[1]

Writing of the experience of France during the Great War, the cultural historian Stephane Audoin-Rouzeau explained the following:

Children were fully integrated into the war. In all the combatant nations childhood was the target for intense propaganda designed to bring the young whole-heartedly into the war. They too had to be "mobilised." Many means of instruction were employed to promote this mobilisation, but their themes and objectives converged to form a cultural universe specifically for the consumption of young people, including the very youngest.

The author goes on to point out that "books, illustrated magazines, toys and games" were all employed to interpret the world conflict for the young.[2] This was equally true of Britain, where such propaganda was directed at boys and young men, particularly through specially commissioned literary justifications for why Britain was at war, and through exciting fictionalised accounts of the fighting. These were intended to promote an understanding of the conflict and to "mobilise" the nation's youth. For Britain, though, the mobilisation of the young had special meaning, for alone of the European Powers, the British relied upon an army of volunteers for the first two years of the war. Thus such war stories formed a significant part of the propaganda campaign intended to persuade young men to play their part in the war effort. Yet historians of the popular culture of the war have seemingly lost sight of this wealth of material in their preference for continually revisiting war stories by authors who were a part of an elite literary establishment, such as H. G. Wells, Rudyard Kipling and John Buchan.[3]

Curiously, many studies of the literature of the Great War have ignored the war years altogether, preferring to focus on the post-1918 period, and especially the bitter, antiwar literature of disillusionment, which began to emerge in the mid-1920s and which has come to almost dominate our collective memory of the war, often, as military historians have claimed, to the detriment of studies of the "real" war of history.[4] It is not the intention here to join with that debate but simply to note that the vast bulk of popular war literature has been neglected in favour of these later works—the canon of Great War literature. However, what needs to be borne in mind is that the anguished memoirs and novels of the disillusioned were written, not only to reveal the horrors of war their authors had encountered on the Western Front, but equally in protest that victory had neither marked a return to the secure, comfortable Edwardian summer of 1914 nor delivered the shiny new world—the land fit for heroes—promised by the politicians. The literature of disillusionment, then, was as much an attack on postwar Britain as it was a condemnation of modern warfare. But it was also an indictment of the sanitised, romantic, and glamorised images of war that had permeated prewar and wartime literature—a powerful and influential aspect of the "old lie" that sold notions of patriotism, duty, and the nobility of sacrifice to young men and which had persuaded them that war was romantic and exciting.[5]

This book, then, examines those old lies as they were manifested in the popular histories and fictional war stories published during the years of conflict, and which were intended to persuade young Britons to enlist for the Great Adventure. These novels and stories, approved by parents, teachers, and school governors, were extremely popular and were consumed by a vast audience of young readers. Yet they have been almost completely ignored or, at best, noted only in passing in the cultural/literary histories of the war as scholars hurry on to revisit yet another overworked classic from the accepted cannon. But this literature was important, not simply because the exciting images of the war it presented and the patriotic sentiment it aroused encouraged readers to enlist, but also because such heroic and romantic representations offered a patriotic interpretation of the war which endured until the Second World War, even withstanding the onslaught of post–1918 antiwar literature. Until 1939, and in some instances even later, such fictions could be found in bookshops, their bright covers still proclaiming the war as heroic adventure, as they lay alongside the anguished anthems for doomed youth. Yet patriotic novels had not suddenly emerged in 1914 when Britain found itself engaged in a major European war, but had long been established as a popular sub-genre of the adventure story—a patriotic response to Britain's military adventures across the world and a vibrant justification of British imperialism.

From its development during the early nineteenth century, children's literature had formed a part of the socialisation process, offering instruction, guidance, and role models for the behaviour, values, and attitudes that society deemed worth promoting among the young. This literature offered the young the opportunity to make sense of their world, and popular adventure stories written for young males provided a means through which the great events of the day could be interpreted, particularly the struggle to maintain imperial preeminence. Adventure fictions, generally written for boys and young men aged between 10 and 18 years, were intended to inculcate patriotism, manliness, and a sense of duty to Crown and Empire among readers. Such stories, as Kelly Boyd has pointed out, were principally an exploration of the character of the hero and his response to challenges set by the author, and clearly intended to provide role models through which the young male could negotiate his way to manhood.[6] However, from the 1880s, a new sub-genre of the adventure mode became popular, the war story specifically written for younger readers. War fictions, based on past conflicts or contemporary imperial struggles, were largely the creation of George Alfred Henty, an ex-soldier and war correspondent. Beginning with an exciting and bloody tale of the Indian Mutiny, "Times of Peril," published in the January 1880 issue of the serial paper *Union Jack*, Henty quickly gained a reputation for enthralling action novels that reflected the aggressive masculinity of an age of almost incessant imperial warfare. His success inspired a host of imitators, and the Henty style almost dominated the world of boys' fiction, as fellow authors adopted not only his formulaic approach to the war story but also his almost mystical belief in the righteousness of the Empire and sense of purpose.

Henty himself had inherited much from earlier writers of adventure fiction like W. H. G. Kingston and R. M. Ballantyne—ideas about manliness and Britain's imperial destiny, for example, but he added to them his own romanticised view of war, developed through his experience as a war correspondent for the London *Standard*. Henty based his fiction on personal observation, on contemporary reports by war correspondents, and on popular histories. Continually short of money, he wrote prolifically in order to solve his financial problems, but he also wrote with another purpose in mind—for he "was determined to 'teach patriotism,' to inspire a belief in the manifest destiny of the Anglo-Saxon race and to offer 'bright personal examples of morality' and duty."[7] He wanted to show young men how to behave; as his friend and biographer George Manville Fenn recalled, Henty wanted his boys to be bold, "straightforward and ready to play a young man's part, not to be milksops. He had a horror of a lad who displayed any weak emotion and shrank from shedding blood, or winced at any encounter."[8] Henty, then, an advocate of imperialism and chivalric manliness, bound these qualities into an idealised portrait of the imperial warrior, the instrument through which the Empire had been created and the frontiers held secure. Influenced by contemporary historical views, he saw British history as a series of inevitable wars that had created Greater Britain, believing that future generations must stand ready to wage unceasing warfare to safeguard that heritage. In 1885 he clearly articulated these views in the preface to his novel *St. George for England.*

It is sometimes said that there is no good to be obtained from tales of fighting and bloodshed—that there is no moral to be drawn from such histories. Believe it not, war has its lessons as well as peace. You will learn from tales like this that determination and enthusiasm can accomplish marvels, that true courage is generally accompanied by magnanimity and gentleness, and that if not itself the very highest of virtues, it is the parent of almost all the others, since few of them can be practiced without it. The courage of our forefathers has created the greatest empire in the world around a small and in itself insignificant island; if this empire is ever lost, it will be by the cowardice of their descendents.[9]

Henty valorised the defenders of empire—not just generals and officers but, like Kipling, the rank and file as well. In *Through Three Campaigns* (Chitral, Tirah, and Ashanti), he rebuked the British public for ignoring their warrior sons fighting on the forgotten frontiers of empire.

Our little wars attract far less attention among the people of this country than they deserve. They are frequently carried out in circumstances of the most adverse kind. Our enemies, although ignorant of military discipline, are, as a rule, extremely brave, and are thoroughly capable of using the natural advantages of their country. Our men are called upon to bear enormous fatigue and endure extremes in climate; the fighting is incessant, the peril constant. Nevertheless they show magnificent contempt for danger and difficulty, and fight with valour and determination worthy of the highest praise. . . . The country has a right to be proud indeed of the prowess of both our own troops and of our native regiments.[10]

According to Henty, martial prowess and love of fighting had always been a characteristic of the British race. When Nita, the heroine of *A Soldier's Daughter,* suggests that it is peculiar that men should be so fond of fighting, her companion, Lieutenant Charlie Carter of the Indian Army, explains,

It is; I have often wondered over it many a time. All savage races love fighting, and certainly our own people do. If there were a great war, hundreds and thousands of men would volunteer at once. I am afraid this instinct brings us very near the savage. I think no other nation possesses it to anything like the same extent as the British race.[11]

In Henty's fiction, then, the British were portrayed as born warriors with an inherent love of fighting, and war was indeed represented as exciting and romantic, and above all necessary to maintain the empire upon which the nation's wealth and prestige depended.

In his early novels, Henty established the formula that he would adhere to throughout his career, and which would provide a model for his successors.[12] The Henty hero was usually middle class, between 16 and 18 years old, sometimes orphaned or who has lost his inheritance, and who sets out on his travels to find fame and fortune on the frontiers of empire. He is tested, fights battles, is captured, escapes, fights more battles, gains the approval of a famous imperial warlord, and invariably makes his fortune in the process. Many of Henty's stories make use of imperial heroes like Clive, Wellington, Roberts, or Kitchener in their titles to add verisimilitude to the story,[13] but the key factor here is that it is only through the test of battle that the youthful hero achieves his reward. Henty's young heroes are sometimes the products of the great public schools, sometimes of lower birth, but all are manly, resourceful, chivalric, courageous, and intensely patriotic. In an age when imperial security depended upon a small voluntary army, Henty romanticised war and turned it into an attractive adventure that boys found enormously appealing in order to inculcate a sense of duty in his readers and the commitment to defend the empire. Through war a young man could show what he was made of, win status and wealth, and revel in his part in defending or extending the greatest Empire in the world. As every Briton's birthright was a talent for fighting, battle posed little real danger for the trueborn Briton. For boys, Henty created an exciting world where warfare provided an exciting route to manhood and played to their more primitive emotions and fantasies. In reality, of course, few young men actually wanted to make a career in the late Victorian army, but the warrior became an idealised masculine fantasy, an imaginary escape from the dull routine of everyday life. Yet at times of crisis, the conditioned response to the war story and other channels of patriotic propaganda took over, and few young men failed to realise where their duty lay—as the thousands of young recruits who flocked to volunteer during the Boer War demonstrated. Henty's successors adapted this highly successful format for their own fictions and, as we shall see, when war came in 1914 the formula, already widely adopted by storytellers, needed only minor adjustment to make it relevant for this new war.

Henty's books were popular reading for boys, but they were also approved by both parents and teachers, who presented them to their children as gifts and prizes because they reflected the spirit of the age, mirrored many of the enshrined attitudes of the later Victorians, and powerfully reinforced those

The Imperial Hero, *Chums*, 1894.

beliefs. Certainly his books had an educational content that mingled fact with pure invention, for his usual practice was to place the fictitious hero's adventures against the background of some great episode of British history—a necessary requirement in an age when many parents and teachers still believed that reading matter should be improving as well as entertaining. But Henty's fictions served a more indirect but perhaps more important purpose, for he successfully redirected the natural violence and aggression of young males into generally approved channels—imperial expansion and the defence of national interests—a legacy which later writers willingly took on.

The war stories written by Henty and his successors were but one element in what we can call the pleasure culture of war,[14] heroic and romantic representations of war that offered exciting entertainment for many Victorians and were part and parcel of the popular militarism that increasingly infected British society towards the end of the nineteenth century, and which it has been argued pushed the nation so easily into war.[15] From around midcentury, the pleasures of war had been disseminated through virtually every channel of popular culture: poetry and literature, visual illustration, theatre and pageants, music hall songs, and the reports of war correspondents, and by the last decades of the century they had, as we have seen, begun to have an impact upon the world of male childhood.[16] The pleasure culture of war was in part a spontaneous celebration of the nation's military prowess, but more importantly it was a reflection of the realities of the aggressive expansion of empire. That war could be presented as entertainment was made possible because Victorians had no direct experience of the suffering or brutality of war—the last battle fought on British soil had been in 1745—and this distancing from the realities of battle enabled Britons to enjoy the vicarious excitements of war with none of the suffering, hardship, or danger. Equally, the rediscovery of chivalry early in the century softened and romanticised the imagining of war, removing the most brutal elements of battle by imposing a strict moral code for the warrior—the so-called rules of war. Chivalry turned the act of killing into an exciting game, played according to a well-defined code of noble behaviour.[17] Thus, for most Britons, real but distant wars were little different from the exciting stories reconstructed on the stage or in the words of storytellers and ballad mongers. For most Victorians war was simply theatre and the warrior a masculine ideal. After midcentury, war was even legitimised by a crude Darwinism that preached the biological necessity of war—the means by which a dynamic and racially superior people achieved their true destiny. At the end of the nineteenth century, the poet W. E. Henley suggested as much in *The Song of the Sword*, a collection of war poetry for boys.

Sifting the nations,
The slag from the metal,
The waste and the weak
From the fit and the strong.[18]

The theme was taken further in General R. C. Hart's 1911 essay,

the means of improvement [for mankind] must be the same as in the past, namely war, relentless war of extermination of inferior individuals and nations. The process will be slower than in the past, because natural selection is hindered and thwarted by civilised man.[19]

Thus Henty and his successors, sharing such common views and driven by concerns about the danger to British imperial supremacy, had simply expanded the pleasure culture of war into the realm of adolescent entertainment. They attempted to inculcate these notions about war in boys for good reason, for the world of the late Victorians was far less secure than it had been at midcentury.

The rapid expansion of the empire after the 1870s, especially in Africa, created even greater demands upon an already overstretched British army that, unlike Continental rivals, still depended upon the voluntary principle. At the same time, the territorial ambitions of other European powers were perceived as threatening British interests, and this, combined with increasing economic competition from the expanding economies of nations like Germany and the United States, conspired to create a profound sense of unease among many Britons. By the end of the century, many believed that the territorial and economic ambitions of powerful rivals coupled with their aggressive foreign policies made a major European war a distinct possibility. Such anxieties were compounded by the army's uninspiring performance during the South African War of 1899 to 1902, when the British were hard-pressed to deal with the irregular Boer forces. Thus part of the adult approval for Henty and his successors came about because they inspired, through the war story, a sense of duty and promoted the martial spirit in British boys upon whom the security of Britain's future would ultimately depend.

These authors implicitly believed they were performing an important social function, doing their duty to Crown and Empire by preparing the youth of the nation to play their part in the inevitable struggles that would arise from Britain's imperial status and the jealousy of her rivals. Their attempts to instill the martial spirit and patriotism in British boys were powerfully reinforced by the public school ethos of duty, honour, and sacrifice, by the training received through cadet forces and, for the vast majority of boys unable to attend public school, through the popular youth organisations that emerged in the last decades before the Great War. The Boy's Brigade, the Lads' Drill Association, and many others all sought to inculcate patriotism and discipline, and all provided some form of military training. Even Baden-Powell's Boy Scout movement emerged as a result of its founder's belief that a European war was inevitable and that boys needed to be versed in the basic skills of scouting and fieldcraft if they were to be of use in this future war.[20]

At the same time, these organisations promoted the physical activities and healthy lifestyle that would counter what many prophets of doom believed was the growing problem of physical degeneration among the nation's urban population, thus creating a generation of young men who were not only psychologically but physically prepared for the great struggles to come.[21] Toys and games, especially model soldiers, war-based board games, guns, and uniforms extended the experience of battle from the written word into active opportunities to play at war. As Cecil Eby has pointed out, "for an English youth growing up in the late Victorian period, infatuation with empire, with its inevitable corollaries—the vision and paraphernalia of war—was as natural as breathing."[22] Writing in later life, William Earl Johns (b. 1893), the creator of the "Biggles" stories, provides us with a sense of just how far martial fervour had penetrated the world of adolescence by the turn of the century.

It is difficult for a boy of today to realise the enthusiasm the boys of 1900 had for anything military. Soldiers were gods. Mind you, in those days a soldier in full dress uniform was something to look at. When troops went overseas they did not creep away furtively, for security reasons, in the middle of the night. They marched through cheering crowds in broad daylight, bands playing, colours flying, flowers in their caps. We boys, decorated with as much red, white and blue ribbon as we could afford to buy, marched with them to the railway station and yelled our heads off as the train steamed out.[23]

By the early twentieth century, then, the pleasure culture of war had taught the nation that for a great imperial power, conflict was inevitable. It had imbued Britain's youth with a romantic view of war and a blind, unquestioning patriotism, and it had convinced them that battle would be little more dangerous than a hard-fought game on the pitch; the poet Henry Newbolt had told them as much in his much-quoted poem *Vitae Lampada*. Here, a British regiment, its squares broken, the colonel dead, and with jammed Gatling guns faces the Dervish army—a situation, claims the author, little different from a home match in which the house team fields its last man while still needing ten runs for victory.[24] British youth had also been taught to believe that the nation was poised on the brink of disaster: that a major war loomed and, through the popular tales of the "great war to come," that Germany posed the single most dangerous challenge to the continued well-being of the British Empire.[25] Niall Ferguson has suggested that militarist propagandists enjoyed only limited success in influencing public opinion. Most Britons, the argument goes, were invariably opposed to what they considered excessive expenditure on national defence. Compulsory military service, despite the best efforts of the National Service League and other pressure groups, was never a serious possibility, and Parliament was anxious to ensure that the military was distanced from the decision-making process.[26] Nevertheless, these much heralded but superficial trappings of antimilitarism have perhaps disguised the popular militarism that seethed beneath the surface of society. Patriotism was intense, as was the conviction that war was an acceptable method of solving international or imperial disputes. The public had considerable admiration for soldier heroes, and the nation's wars were widely supported—however questionable they might be. But the essential point here is that we need to keep in mind that the exciting and romantic images of war widely disseminated in popular culture were far more enticing and influential on the young and immature than they were on adult minds, and it might well be argued that the success of militarist propaganda embedded in the war story and in other aspects of the pleasure culture of war were clearly demonstrated when war came. In August 1914 hundreds of thousands of these young men, believing wholeheartedly that the war would be fun, rushed to the colours, anxious to leave behind the dull routine of school, university, or office. Their most often expressed anxiety was not of being maimed or killed, but rather that the war would end before they got to France and that they would miss the Great Adventure. As Ferguson has shown, the most eager and most numerous of these recruits were young, often very young, upper- and middle-class males, precisely those most likely to have been exposed to the war stories of Henty and Co.[27] The class of 1914 had been well prepared for the eventuality of war.

A number of excellent studies have been published that have examined how juvenile fiction promoted manliness, patriotism, militarism, and an imperial worldview during the later nineteenth century, but invariably they ended with the outbreak of war in 1914. Even Jeffrey Richards' admirable collection of essays surveying juvenile fictions through the nineteenth and twentieth centuries somehow skips Great War stories, except for Dennis Butts' essay on aviation fiction, which devotes some attention to war stories.[28] While those studies that have discussed Great War fictions for the young have done so in a fairly cursory manner.[29] Neither have studies of wartime popular culture been more enlightening, for their focus has also usually been on the products of high culture and rarely the sort of material intended for a mass audience, let alone young males.[30] But of course the war stories for boys did not disappear in 1914; they were published in ever-increasing numbers, and they became one of the major channels through which young readers learned about the war—what caused the conflict, how it was being fought, and what was expected of them in the present crisis. Henty's immediate successors—Captain F. S. Brereton, Herbert Strang, Percy Westerman, Escott Lynn, and Captain Charles Gilson—were joined by a younger generation of writers like Eric Woods, Rowland Walker, D. H. Parry, and Ernest McKeag, for example, who were also inspired to become propagandists for the Allied cause. And there was no battlefield to which they did not turn their attention: from the Western Front to Gallipoli and Africa, and from naval warfare in the North Sea and Atlantic to the aerial battles in the skies over Flanders. Initially, writers of juvenile fiction had very little understanding of modern warfare, and their stories were just as fanciful, just as sanitised, romantic, and unrealistic as had been their earlier stories about warfare on the North West Frontier or the

African veldt. But as the true nature of this war began to be realised after 1916, their stories did take on a more realistic edge, notwithstanding the imaginative, often incredible, adventures of their young heroes. And as the reality of the grim attritional battles of Verdun, the Somme, and Passchendaele, which cost so much and seemingly achieved so very little, became public, authors began to represent the more horrible aspects of trench warfare and the effects of modern weaponry. Nevertheless, none of these authors ever lost faith in the ultimate justice of the Allied cause or despaired at the incompetence of military and political leaders and, until the Armistice and beyond, their heroes and heroines remained faithful to their leaders and committed to the final victory, whatever the cost.

Unlike much of the overt propagandist fiction written for adults during the war years, war stories for the young written during the conflict remained in print throughout the inter-war period, and they were reinforced by the work of younger authors—often men who had themselves experienced the war at first hand in the trenches, in the air, or at sea. But these authors and their publishers were seemingly untouched by disillusionment with the war that began to emerge in the late 1920s. For authors of juvenile fiction, 1914–1918 always remained the Great War for Civilization—another glorious triumph for the British Empire. This book, then, examines how juvenile fiction, written during the years of conflict, represented the war, how it explained the causes, promoted participation, and how it portrayed the fighting on the Western Front and elsewhere, as a significant part of the unofficial, and sometimes official, propaganda effort to sell the war to boys and young men. Moreover, it considers how such fictions continued to offer an heroic and justified view of the Great War throughout the inter-war years, a view that was vastly different from the images of the war in the work of the disillusioned war poets and memoirists whose work has now come to dominate the popular memory of the war. They were, as Rosa Maria Bracco has pointed out in her study of adult wartime fiction, part of the "minor literature which attempted to rescue the war from futility"—the antithesis of the memoirs and novels of the disillusioned.[31] Thus a study of these now largely forgotten fictions offers an important perspective on a neglected aspect of unofficial propaganda during the war years, and an alternative view of how much of British society preferred to remember the Great War between the wars.

Chapter 1 examines how the war was explained and justified for young readers through popular histories and fictional narratives, and how those readers who were old enough were encouraged to volunteer for this "Great Crusade." Chapter 2 focuses on the war on the Western Front. Initially glossing over the difficulties and hardships faced by the British Expeditionary Force, war stories for the young focused on the individual's contribution to the war. Authors adopted an idealised masculine stereotype, usually an ex-public school boy, as protagonist in order to create a role model for the behaviour of those who would follow. However, the static nature of the war, the failure of Allied offensives, and the squalid conditions of the trenches resulted in many authors turning away from tales of the front line, particularly after the failure of the Somme offensive in 1916, and sought new, more glamorous battlefields with which to inspire young men. Chapter 3 explores the war in the air, a new field of combat about which most writers, initially at least, knew little. Chapter 4 examines the war outside Europe, the sideshows at Gallipoli, in the Middle East, and in East Africa. Here, of course, writers were in familiar territory, for there was little to distinguish a war against Germany's African colonies or against the "slippery" Turk, from the imperial adventures they had written before 1914. In chapter 5 we are concerned with the contribution of Britain's allies, and the part played by soldiers from Empire and Dominion. Apart from demonstrating that this was indeed a war waged by the whole empire, writers, steeped in the belief of the inherent superiority of the British, now faced the challenge of heroicising old enemies like the French and Russians. In chapter 6 we return to the Western Front for the last year of the war in order to examine how the war story had been modified by the four years of war, the growing public awareness of the realities of trench warfare, and the introduction of new methods of warfare. Unfortunately, the length of this volume precludes a detailed examination of the manner in which the war at sea was portrayed. The conclusion examines the significance and consequences of this heroic and triumphant representation of the war. Here we consider why such stories remained popular throughout the inter-war period and how their view of the conflict was reinforced by the work of a generation of younger writers, who told essentially the same story.

CHAPTER 1

Selling the War

> In all this war there is nothing for us to be ashamed of: we fight for honour. You know what honour is among schoolboys—straight dealing, truth speaking, and "playing the game." Well, we are standing up for honour among nations, while Germany is playing the sneak and the bully in the big European school. Germany must be taught to "play cricket," to play fair, to honour a "scrap of paper." A boy who behaved as Germany has done would be "sent to Coventry" by all the school.
>
> Sir James Yoxall, *Why Britain Went to War*[1]

For British boys, the First World War started, not in 1914 but in 1895 when, according to the Hamilton Edwards serial, "Britain in Arms," published in the story paper *Pluck*, a coalition of Continental powers, envious of Britain's empire, attempted to invade the British Isles. Despite some tense moments, the Royal Navy eventually succeeds in destroying the enemy fleet, while the British army under the command of the nation's most popular soldier, Lord Roberts of Khandahar, invades the Continent and deals the aggressors a lesson they will long remember.[2] "Britain in Arms" offered a new theme for the popular war stories written specifically for boys and young men: a tale of the great war to come, something new and excitingly different from the familiar cycle of stories inspired by the nation's little wars of empire. The idea of a future European war, particularly one in which Britain suffered invasion, had both terrified and fascinated adult readers since the 1870s when Sir George Chesney's controversial story of the conquest of Britain by the Prussian army, "The Battle of Dorking," had been published in *Blackwoods Magazine*.[3] Hamilton Edwards's tale of a future European war, written specifically for the younger reader, proved enormously popular: it was reprinted in *The Boys'*

Friend in 1897 and again in *Pluck* in 1899, and it persuaded the proprietor of *Pluck*, Alfred Harmsworth (later Lord Northcliffe), that he had found a theme that would not only entertain his readers, but would also encourage them to prepare for the great European war he believed was inevitable. The story inspired a flock of imitators in the boys' serial papers, and by the early 1900s even authors of reputable adventure novels were publishing exciting fictions about the great war to come for their young readers. In juvenile literature, then, the years leading to 1914 witnessed an almost endless series of fictional conflicts as Britain was invaded by the French, the Russians, the Germans, or even a coalition of the lesser powers like China, Japan, or Mongolia. On dark evenings, it was suggested, Zeppelin airships hovered above Britain's cities locating strong points and arsenals, while alien spies uncovered the nation's military secrets and foreign dreadnoughts cruised off the English coast ever ready to ambush an unwary Home Fleet.[4]

Until 1904 the creators of these stories believed France was the most likely aggressor. However, as territorial difficulties with that country were resolved through the 1904 *Entente Cordiale*, Germany became the arch-enemy in popular fiction. This both reflected what many Britons saw as the "German Problem," and reinforced the widely held belief that Germany was plotting to invade Britain. The alarmist nature of such propaganda was particularly virulent in publications from Harmsworth's Amalgamated Press which, reflecting its owner's paranoid distrust of Germany, were continually issuing warnings about the Kaiser's evil intent.[5] In the last few years of peace, many writers of juvenile fiction had begun to subscribe to the idea that Germany was actively working to undermine British power. Inspired by the scaremongering popular press and sensational fiction, many Britons cherished the belief that the Kaiser had not only infiltrated hundreds of spies into Britain, but had also managed to place large sections of the German army in British cities— invariably disguised as Swiss or Austrian waiters, or as members of the popular touring "Oompah" bands. These malicious agents of Potsdam were eagerly awaiting the signal that would send them into action to seize administrative centres, railway stations, and telephone exchanges, and thus pave the way for invasion.[6] As Robert Roberts, then growing up in Salford, later remembered,

Spy stories abounded. Germans who came here to "work," we were assured, could be spotted by a special button worn in the lapel. Each man had, we believed, sworn to serve Germany as a secret agent. With this, and innumerable myths of the same sort, the seeds of suspicion and hatred were sown.[7]

Typical of these tales of German aggression was Herbert Strang's *Sultan Jim: Empire Builder*, which combined traditional imperial adventure with a warning about Germany's territorial ambitions, and Percy F. Westerman's *The Sea-Girt Fortress*, a cautionary tale of the Kaiser's war plans, both published on the eve of war.

Herbert Ely and James L'Estrange, writing as "Herbert Strang," published their first novel in 1904 and quickly established a reputation as worthy successors to Henty; as a reviewer in the *Bookman* noted, "Herbert Strang will undoubtedly do much to fill the gap in boys' lives left by Mr. Henty."[8] The prolific Westerman, denied the naval career he desired by poor eyesight, found employment as a naval clerk at Portsmouth Dockyard. Turning to writing as a substitute for the real-life adventure he craved, he published his first novel in 1909 and, like Strang, at first followed the Henty formula of tales of imperial warfare and historical adventure. However, he quickly carved out his own niche by specialising in naval war stories. By 1912, both authors had begun to express concern about German intentions and to reflect an interest in contemporary military matters.[9] *Sultan Jim* tells the story of Jim Saltoun, a young English gold prospector in Rhodesia. Straying into a remote frontier region, he discovers a sinister Prussian, Major Schinkelstein, preparing for the takeover of British and Portuguese colonies in Africa. Needless to say, Jim foils the German plan, and Britain eventually acquires the region as a British protectorate with Jim as its first commissioner. Explicit throughout the novel is Strang's conviction that it is Germany's intention to gain an African empire at Britain's expense.[10] Interestingly, the Henry Frowde catalogue actually advertised the novel as a "tale of German aggression." In *The Sea-Girt Fortress*, the war that Strang suggests is coming actually breaks out. The novel, owing a great deal to Erskine Childers's popular 1903 story *The Riddle of the Sands*, deals with a young Briton and his friend on a sailing holiday in the North Sea. By chance they discover that Heligoland is being used as the base for the German invasion of England. Captured and imprisoned, their plight stirs up a diplomatic row, and the Germans decide to hasten the invasion. As the architect of the invasion plan tells the Kaiser, "Give us four clear days and Great Britain will be humiliated: her navy . . . destroyed . . . an aerial fleet will be able to inflict enormous damage to the docks of the east coast of England; perhaps even London may be reduced to a heap of ruins."[11] But when battle is joined, it is the German fleet that is destroyed by the Royal Navy, and the humiliated Kaiser is forced to seek terms. The novel, powerfully reinforcing the idea of a future Anglo-German war, perfectly encapsulates then-current ideas about future wars—short and decisive, with a major role assigned to the all-powerful Royal Navy. But anxiety regarding German intentions was not just confined to the paranoia of newspaper barons or the fertile imaginations of novelists; rather, it was reflected in a wider distrust of Germany among the British public and much of the political/military establishment, and it had been steadily growing since the 1890s.

By 1914 Britain had avoided involvement in Continental wars for almost a century, but at the beginning of the twentieth century the German Empire had become something of a bogeyman for the British, and not least due to the Kaiser's decision to expand the German navy. Dynamic, militarily powerful, and aggressively expansionist, Germany appeared to pose a major challenge to the continued supremacy of the British Empire. By 1900, then, and despite economic and commercial links and the ties of kinship between the British and German monarchies, a growing Anglo-German antagonism had emerged as each side continually misconstrued the other's motives.[12] Nevertheless, British governments were careful not to slip into the camp of Germany's enemies, France and Russia. Certainly, imperial tensions with France had been resolved by the *Entente Cordiale*, signed in 1904, and a similar settlement was made with Russia in 1907. Yet, despite what many Germans believed, Britain was not bound by treaties or alliances and was under no obligation to become involved in a war defending those nations against an aggressive Germany. However, the situation was actually far more complex than this. Many Britons preferred to believe that they did not need Europe, that national prestige and prosperity depended upon the Empire alone, and that there were no pressing reasons to become embroiled in Continental affairs. However, in the long term, who dominated Europe was a matter of supreme importance for Britain, as the more perceptive realised. Europe was a major focus for British trade, far more lucrative than the empire, and if a single hostile power gained hegemony in Europe, Britain could well be shut out. Particularly dangerous was the possibility of a rival naval power controlling the European coastline and dominating the sea-lanes around the British Isles. This could well isolate Britain from her empire and deny her the freedom of the seas upon which British commerce had been built. Thus the British government needed to ensure that the balance of power on the Continent was maintained. As the perceptive Foreign Office official Eyre Crowe pointed out during the crisis in the summer of 1914,

Should this war come and England stand aside, one of two things must happen: a) Either Germany and Austria win, crush France and humiliate Russia. . . . What will be the position of friendless England? b) Or France and Russia win. What would then be their attitude towards England? What about India and the Mediterranean?[13]

However, what civil servants like Eyre Crowe, the public, and even most politicians did not know was that since 1906, the military planners of both Britain and France had been discussing joint action in the event of a German invasion of France. Without cabinet approval, indeed without even discussion (except with the prime minister and secretary of state for war), the military had concluded an informal agreement that in such an event, the British would secure the left flank of the French army—a defensive line guarding the Franco-Belgian frontier. Although no treaty had been signed which guaranteed this British commitment, the French had constructed their defence strategy based upon such a premise. Thus by 1914, while some politicians and diplomats were convinced that British interest could only be served by maintaining the balance of power in Europe, the General Staff had virtually committed Britain to military support for France if that nation was faced with a

German invasion.[14] When the German attack did come and the British decided to become involved, it was in reality, as Gerard De Groot has argued,
"a conflict about empires, capitalism, trade and food."[15] But could the British
people be persuaded to rally around such an ignoble cause, especially as most
Britons had little affection for untrustworthy and unstable Europeans? That
uncertainty was resolved when the German army marched into Belgium as a
prelude to invading France, and suddenly a "war of markets became a war of
morality." The conflict now became a war "about democracy, honour, civilisation and the defence of trusted friends."[16]

Officially, the Treaty of London, signed in 1839, by which Britain guaranteed Belgian sovereignty, had been infringed by the German invasion. But
it is doubtful if this long-standing commitment to aid Belgium would have
acted as a trigger for British intervention had it not served the government's
cause. In August, the German onslaught against a neutral nation and the
alleged atrocities committed by the invader provided a noble excuse; a cause
far more righteous than the sordid business of economics, trade, and under-
the-counter military agreements. Britain could now pose as the chivalric
champion of the underdog by standing up to German aggression. Most Britons, including the Liberal cabinet, which included men of strong pacifist sentiment, were content to accept Prime Minister Asquith's justification of the
war in which Britain became a moral crusader, the champion of justice and
honour.

I do not believe any nation ever entered into a great controversy—and this is one of
the greatest history will ever know—with a clearer conscience and a stronger conviction that it is fighting, not for aggression, not for the maintenance even of its own
selfish interest, but that it is fighting in defence of principles the maintenance of which
is vital to the civilization of the world.[17]

As Bourne has pointed out, "Britain could go to war for France and appear
to do so for Belgium."[18] Thus would propagandists sell the war to the British
people.

Most people had actually taken little notice of the deepening shadow of
war spreading over the Continent after the assassination of the Archduke
Franz Ferdinand at Sarajevo in June. The situation in Ireland, where civil war
over the issue of Home Rule appeared a very real danger, seemed far more
ominous and, after all, assassinations in Europe, especially in the Balkans, were
not uncommon. Consequently the declaration of war took most Britons by
surprise, but there was little real opposition, and for many it was simply the
climax to the rampant anti-Germanism that had permeated popular politics
since the 1890s. Few had any real grasp of the complexities of British foreign
policy, but the invasion of Belgium provided a righteous rallying cry allowing
Britons to wallow in their own nobility as they championed the underdog.
With popular opinion firmly on the side of the government, then, the British

Expeditionary Force—six infantry divisions and a division of cavalry (about 90,000 men in total)—was dispatched to France under the command of Field Marshall Sir John French. The mobilisation was remarkably swift, and by 14 August most divisions were in France. On 21 August the BEF began to cross the Belgian border alongside the French towards the advancing Germans. Two days later the British and Germans met at Mons. Facing a numerically superior enemy and afraid of being encircled by a French withdrawal, the BEF fell back into France. After the German advance had been stopped on the Marne, both sides began to dig defensive positions to protect themselves from the devastating firepower of modern weaponry. Neither side was strong enough to gain the advantage, and the war settled into stalemate. By late 1914 a line of trenches, the Western Front, extended from Nieuport on the Belgian coast to the Swiss frontier. On the Flanders plain, close to the Channel ports, and further south in Picardy, the trenches were held by the men of the British Expeditionary Force. They would occupy more or less the same positions for the next four years.[19]

Although popular opinion now regards the Great War as "the prime example of war as horror and futility,"[20] in 1914 it was an immensely popular cause, and much of the public eagerly anticipated the excitement and drama that such a conflict would offer. Of course, almost no one believed it would be a long war—"over by Christmas" was the common belief, and none but the most prescient could imagine the devastation that would be wrought by modern weaponry. But while most people viewed the war as a just and noble crusade, a few did realise that it would be a very different proposition from the relatively small-scale colonial conflicts to which the nation had become accustomed. This was a war against one of the most industrially advanced and militarily prepared nations in the world, and some wondered how long popular support would last if the war was not over by Christmas and if there were no immediate victories. Britain, alone of the combatant nations, still relied on a volunteer army, so how could a steady flow of recruits be maintained if casualties were heavy? It was equally a war in which armament production would be crucial—how could the enthusiasm and production of the home front be sustained? Consequently, within the first few weeks of war, the government, concerned organisations, and private individuals, anxious to maintain public support for the war and the sympathy of neutral nations, particularly the United States, began to create a system of mass persuasion that would sell the war to the British people and the world at large, and maintain the morale of the people. As Philip Taylor has noted, for the first time the government "deployed the twin weapons of censorship and propaganda to impose a rigid control over public perceptions . . . about how and why the war was being fought."[21] With almost no experience of such matters, a government-controlled propaganda machine was quickly created that was to prove remarkably effective. For despite over four years of brutal warfare, despite casualties on an unprecedented scale, despite hardships and restrictions at home, the British people remained largely committed to the war and to fighting on until victory was eventually achieved.

The British propaganda campaign came about largely in response to the development of German propaganda, which was having a detrimental effect on Britain's cause among the neutral nations.[22] Thus the main thrust of official propaganda was directed at a foreign audience. The government was seemingly so confident of the public's commitment to the war that initially they were content to leave domestic propaganda to the press and various unofficial committees and individuals. But this was not as haphazard as it first appears. The press, while often critical of government policy over domestic issues, were by and large uncritical when it came to foreign policy. Officials at the Foreign Office were adept at manipulating news reports via personal contacts with the editorial elite of Fleet Street, and the Admiralty followed the same policy.[23] Equally, the press had discovered that popular patriotism sold papers. Literature, the music hall, theatre, and even cinema had found that the endlessly repetitive tales of daring and the valorisation of imperial adventurers were remarkably profitable—the public apparently had an inexhaustible appetite for such fare. The media's uncritical exploitation of such material reflected their own patriotism, fostered support for government policy, and whipped up jingoist sentiment among the public.[24] Domestic propaganda, then, could, initially at least, be safely left in the hands of the press and the amateur. Even recruiting propaganda—crucial for a nation that relied on the voluntary principle—was left to the War Office and the Parliamentary Recruiting Committee. Despite its official-sounding title, the committee was nothing more than an informal group of members of Parliament and public figures working on a voluntary basis, addressing meetings, producing posters and leaflets, and organising pageants and other activities.[25] But equally effective were the many private individuals and organisations that were bent on getting young men into khaki either through persuasion or through accusation.[26] One well-established and effective channel for disseminating propaganda was literature, and this was exploited by the government through the Propaganda Bureau at Wellington House, organised by Charles Masterman.

On 31 August 1914, Prime Minister Asquith invited his close friend Charles Masterman, Chancellor of the Duchy of Lancaster, to take responsibility for refuting German propaganda to the neutral nations and justifying Britain's cause. Based at Wellington House, Masterman immediately organised a conference on 2 September and invited leading authors and academics—those whom he considered the controllers of public opinion.[27] Twenty-five leading writers and academics attended the first meeting, including G. K. Chesterton, John Galsworthy, Thomas Hardy, H. G. Wells, John Masefield, G. M. Trevelyan, Gilbert Murray, and A. C. Benson. Rudyard Kipling and Arthur Quiller-Couch were unable to attend but pledged their support. Masterman's idea was that these pillars of the literary establishment should produce leaflets, pamphlets, books, and articles justifying and explaining British policy. These would be distributed through commercial publishers such as Hodder and Stoughton, Macmillan, or Thomas Nelson and Sons, as if they were personal responses from concerned individuals and not in any way orchestrated or directed by a government agency. All those recruited agreed to absolute secrecy about their connection with the government, and the committee even acquired its own literary agent, A. P. Watt. A few weeks later another 25 writers were recruited, including the popular novelists Mrs. Humphrey Ward, Arthur Pinero, and Jerome K. Jerome. But not until 1935, when J. D. Squires published his history of wartime propaganda, was the connection between these authors and the government's propaganda campaign revealed.[28] Wellington House became the "principal production and distribution centre of British overseas propaganda and working so effectively beneath its blanket of secrecy that even Parliament was largely unaware of its existence and activities."[29] The neutral nations were the main target for Wellington House material, but many of its publications were distributed in Britain as well. Literary propaganda, especially by well-known authors, had considerable impact, but proved less effective later in war, particularly once cinema had been co-opted as a channel for mass persuasion. Masterman, however, did try to ensure that what was produced under the aegis of Wellington House was based upon accurate information and measured argument rather than the rhetoric of hate that was appearing in the popular press. Inevitably some authors failed to heed this advice, and much of their work was later discredited. However, the publications sponsored by Wellington House, and which began to appear within weeks of the creation of the committee, established the precedent for literary propaganda which other authors were quick to follow.

The documentation relating to Britain's propaganda effort has not survived; it was either destroyed in 1920 or lost in the years that followed. Thus while there have been notable attempts to reconstruct the propaganda war, the whole story will probably never be known.[30] It is not known, for example, what material might have been commissioned and targeted at particular groups on the home front, or if other authors, outside the great and the good who were initially recruited, were indirectly involved with Wellington House or with the later National War Aims Committee, formed in 1917 to combat war weariness on the home front. However, because Britain relied on voluntary enlistment, recruiting was a major concern, and this meant targeting young men, and not just those approaching 18 but also younger boys who might be needed later. They needed to be told why Britain was at war, that the war was just, how it was being fought, and what part they might play in securing victory. Thus romantic, inspiring, and alluring war fictions for younger readers, which both fostered the martial spirit and the desire to "deal with" Germany, would prove vital to the war effort. Many of the authors associated with Wellington House were popular with young male readers—Henry Newbolt, John Buchan, Anthony Hope, A. E. W. Mason, Rider Haggard, and H. G. Wells, for example. Newbolt and Buchan did produce work

"In the Ranks" by Druid Grayl, *Boy's Own Paper*, 1914.

for younger readers during the war, and we know that several authors who wrote specifically for a juvenile audience were recruited by Masterman later in the war because some of their work appears in the list of Wellington House Publications made public in 1919,[31] but no evidence has survived for how these writers were recruited or what they were instructed to do. It seems likely, however, that there were many other, less exalted literary figures, either indirectly connected with Wellington House or inspired by Masterman's authors to take a stand on the war and produce their own unofficial propaganda following the parameters established by Wellington House. This study, then, is concerned with this largely unofficial propaganda specifically aimed at the young, which can only rarely be directly linked to the official literary campaign, but which nevertheless was clearly influenced by officialdom.

In 1914, the book trade, like other areas of industry and commerce, was encouraged to carry on as normal for the duration of the war by the government: "business as usual," was Asquith's directive, and there was certainly no decline in the demand for books, and especially books about the war, particularly fiction. As Peter Buitenhuis has noted, "The public appetite for stories about the war was very strong; people had a craving to know about the fighting and to see their faith in the moral and physical strength of the Allies reflected in accessible form."[32] And this was especially true for young male readers. Agnes Blackie, of Blackie and Son, one of the most successful publishers of childrens' literature, later noted,

The First World War was a quiet time, with labour and paper shortages to restrict output. Business was good in the sense that there was a demand for books by the public, and not least for children's books. It was therefore the "rewards" which saw the greatest amount of new publication, year after year.[33]

"Rewards" were of course those books selected as prizes for school achievement. Many of these were adventure stories set against the background of the European war. Interestingly, as Samuel Hynes has pointed out, war adventures written specifically for juvenile readers were not reviewed as children's books,[34] and they were in fact also read by an adult audience. It may well be that many readers, both young and old, disappointed by the lack of detail in press reports, turned to these fictions in the hope that novelists, by some mystical process, knew more than most about conditions at the Front. Certainly, many authors became extremely popular, and their books were to be found among best-selling titles. In October 1915, for example, W. H. Smith's most successful war titles included Herbert Strang's adventure story *The Hero of Liege* (published in late 1914), alongside William Le Queux's *Secrets of the German War Office* and the anonymous *My Adventures as a Spy.*[35] As memoirs and autobiographies clearly reveal, the ambition of almost every young man was to take part in the Great Adventure; but for those too young or too frail to enlist, reading about the war was the next best thing: as Huntley Gordon remembered, "our curiosity to know what it would be like to be under fire had to be satisfied from the novels of G. A. Henty, and Captain F. S. Brereton."[36] War stories, then, satisfied the curiosity of young, and not so young, readers, to know what the war was like, and positively encouraged them to take part as soon as they were able.

Most war books published for young readers were in fictional form, but there were a number of factual works that explained why the nation was at war and examined the underlying causes of the war. These were often published as multivolume series, and while never as popular as the novels written by established authors, they sold well. Nevertheless, even works of fiction often contained large sections of historical explanation and an interpretation of events during the July crisis, sometimes, as Barry Johnson has noted, to the detriment of the story.[37] Before 1914, writers of juvenile fiction had frequently drawn their inspiration from colonial wars, punitive expeditions, or epics of imperial conquest. Now, caught up in the great European struggle, they moved from these historical tales to a form of story that might well be called the newsreel novel—the fictional exploits of young men and women set against the backdrop of contemporary events. Authors who before 1914 had already established a successful formula for their stories, largely based on the Henty model, were able to adapt that formula to reflect the here and now. And they worked remarkably quickly giving their stories and novels the immediacy of newsreel. Strang's novel, *A Hero of Liege*, was on sale just four months after the events it described had taken place; Brereton's *At Grips with the Turks* and Westerman's *The Fight for Constantinople* were both published while the Allies were still fighting on the Gallipoli peninsula, and D. H. Parry published *With Haig on the Somme* only weeks after the offensive ended.[38] Few had privileged access to events, and most drew their information from newspaper accounts and the eyewitness testimony of friends or acquaintances who had been participants in the events described. The stories these authors told mirrored but simplified the official version of events, and writers were not above elaborating events to intensify the drama—an instant history, an interpretation of events excitingly packaged as heroic adventure.

Authors of juvenile fiction needed little encouragement to demonstrate their patriotism. Most had spent the decade before the war valorising the military, justifying the Empire, and attempting to instill a sense of duty in their young readers. They were the inheritors of Henty's mantle, and their writing not only offered exciting adventure, it taught valuable lessons about patriotism, duty, and the nobility of sacrifice for King and Empire. For these writers patriotism was not just a popular theme that sold books, but a deeply held conviction, a credo that informed their work. Before 1914 they had believed it their responsibility to prepare their readers for the burden of empire, and they had been remarkably successful in influencing young readers. Now, their first task was to justify the conflict—providing a simplified narrative of the complex train of events that had led the nation into a European war, to instill in their readers the conviction that Britain was in the right, and that the nation's cause was worth fighting, even dying, for. And in this endeavour they were supported by the authors of factual works specifically written to explain the causes of the war for a young audience. Such explanations varied enormously, from the patronising "play the game" rhetoric of the Parliamentarian Sir James Yoxall, quoted at the beginning of this chapter, to the detailed multivolume series by Sir Edward Parrott. The first in the field, however, was Elizabeth O'Neill's *The War, 1914: A History and an Explanation for Boys and Girls*, published in November 1914.

O'Neill specialised in writing history for the very young—her popular *A Nursery History of England* had been first published in 1912 and remained in print until the 1950s. O'Neill, whose story of the war eventually ran to five volumes, began by explaining the main events of the July crisis and emphasising how Germany had pushed a weak Austria into declaring war on Serbia and thus precipitated the European war. But for O'Neill, the root cause of the war lay in the German belief that it was England who had denied her a place in the sun. Thus the war was really the climax of German hostility towards Britain. The British, she explained, had always been peace-loving and in 1914 were desperate to preserve that peace but, echoing Asquith, she suggested that honour demanded that the promise made to Belgium be kept. Her justification for the war is worth quoting at length, for it neatly summarises how most authors dealt with war origins at that time—as a chivalric struggle against the forces of evil.

The war of 1914 was different from other wars in this, that no one but the Germans can say that Germany was in the right. The Allies, as all the world knows, were fighting for justice and right against a country and an emperor who seemed almost mad with pride. The soldiers of the Allies went out to battle not as soldiers have often gone to war, because it is the business to be done, but rather like the knights of old, full of anger against an enemy who was fighting unjustly, and full, too, of a determination to fight their best for justice and right. This is one more reason which has made the Great War of 1914 so wonderful a thing.[39]

But for O'Neill, the war was not simply a conflict about honour, it was a crusade against barbarians who had committed the most appalling atrocities. Throughout the first few months of war, detailed reports had been appearing in the popular press about the alleged atrocities committed by the German army as it advanced through Belgium. Many of these stories were later discredited, but at the time they provided vicious but effective propaganda to incite Britons to seek vengeance for these crimes against humanity.[40] And O'Neill and others writing for the young were happy to provide suitably censored accounts for their readers. The author tells us that many of the fine old Flanders churches, town halls, and libraries were destroyed or damaged, and that the Germans "seem to have taken pleasure" in their destruction. Peasants were burned in their houses, many thousands of others were made homeless, and women and girls were treated in the most horrible way—many parents, in fact, were forced to witness their little children "killed by the half-mad soldiers."[41]

O'Neill even went on to suggest that there could be beneficial effects for Britain from the war. The suffragettes, she noted, had settled their differences with the government for the sake of national unity, and even Irishmen "have forgotten their quarrels and sent their bravest men to fight for the country which they all love."[42] One almost gets a sense that O'Neill, like many others at the time, almost welcomed this "wonderful thing" as a regenerating factor for British society. For those who had begun to believe that Edwardian Britain had become over-indulgent and hedonistic, war might well be the antidote that would purify, cleanse, and revive the nation as a whole. As Michael Adams has explained,

Throughout the period, some people prescribed a little bloodletting as good for the body politic as well as for the individual. War scrubbed clean national arteries clogged with wealth and ease, produced a trimmer, fitter culture.[43]

Typical of those who held these Social Darwinist beliefs was Sir Edmund Gosse, the influential literary critic, biographer, and librarian to the House of Lords. Gosse believed that the war was the "great scavenger of thought. It is the sovereign disinfectant that . . . cleans out the stagnant pools and clotted channels of the intellect." War was the agent that would cleanse the present: not just the culture but the self-indulgent hedonism that had infected society.[44] O'Neill, then, was simply reflecting these commonly expressed beliefs. The war thus offered a chance for national regeneration, and many, especially the young, took advantage of the opportunity. In this context, it is something of a cliche to refer to Rupert Brooke and his enthusiasm for an adventure, which he believed would rescue him from the dullness of everyday life. But the simple truth is that he really did speak for most of his generation.

Robert Graves, for example, was outraged to read about the alleged German atrocities in Belgium, and even though he discounted "twenty per cent," he enlisted and began training on 11 August.[45] When the autumn term began at Charterhouse (which Graves had recently left), as Huntley Gordon later recalled, many of the senior boys were missing; they had "added something" to their ages in their determination not to "miss out on the fun."[46] Most of course, quickly discovered there was precious little fun on the Western Front, but not all these young adventurers were disappointed. Julian Grenfell, eldest son of Lord Desborough, much given to "thrashing servants" and with a passion for killing anything that moved, volunteered right away and in October 1914, after his first taste of combat, wrote home, "It's all the best fun ever dreamed of." A few days later, echoing Rupert Brooke, he added, "It's a great war, whatever. Isn't it luck for me to have been born so as to be just the right age and just in the right place."[47] For most men, the enthusiasm for war soon faded, but the initial excitement to get into the war was shared by young men from all classes. George Coppard, a Brighton elementary schoolboy, was 16 years old in August 1914. Later he recalled the outbreak of war. The news agents' placards screamed out from every corner, the military bands played martial music, and, "as if drawn by a magnet, I knew I had to enlist right away." Lying about his age, he enlisted on 27 August. A. Stuart Dolden, a solicitor's clerk in London, was forced by his employers to wait until November before joining up, and he was then "absolutely shattered" to be turned down because his chest measurement was two inches under regulation. Persuading his father to pay for a course of physical training, he was accepted several months later.[48] Such accounts could be repeated endlessly, for between August and December 1914 almost two-and-a-half million men volunteered for the New Armies.[49] Popular fictions both reflected this sense of excitement and expectation of stirring deeds, and helped set the mood of the moment.

War meant excitement! It meant active service! It meant perhaps journeying to another country; seeing strange sights and hearing unfamiliar sounds, and taking part, for all one knew, in deeds which would become historical.[50]

Nelson's magisterial history of the war, *The Children's Story of the War*, by Sir Edward Parrott, MA. LL.D, was not published until early 1915, but thereafter it became a running commentary on the events of the war as new volumes were continually added until 1918. Late in the war, a reviewer in *The Athenaeum* referred to the series as, "a readable and inspiring narrative of the war," pointing out that, "a connected and sufficiently well-explained narrative is a useful thing to put before a child—much more intelligible than newspapers."[51] Parrott, an editor at Thomas Nelson and Sons, the Edinburgh-based publisher, had written a number of school textbooks. Active in the Liberal Party, he specialised in educational affairs; in 1917 he was elected as member of Parliament for an Edinburgh constituency, and he was almost certainly known to Masterman. Although we lack any real evidence, it is likely that his history was written at the latter's instigation. Parrott offered a serial history of the unfolding drama, but he devoted the whole of his first volume to a detailed examination of the causes of the war—tracing its origins back to the Napoleonic wars—hardly exciting reading for a youthful audience. Essentially, Parrott repeated O'Neill's explanation and put the blame squarely on the Kaiser, who had led his subjects astray, and on the Prussian military.

Feeling sure . . . that Russia would not fight, that France would not resist, and that Great Britain would not interfere in what seemed to be a far-off quarrel, the Kaiser decided that "THE DAY," so long hoped for and prepared for, had come. In July of the present year he was ready to "let slip the dogs of war."[52]

A whole chapter, "Deeds of Shame and Horror," was devoted to the alleged "rape of Belgium"—"We are told of babies slaughtered, of old men hanged and burnt alive . . . and young women and girls tortured in the most horrible manner." But by 1915 when the first volume appeared, the truth of many of these atrocity stories was in some doubt, and Parrott did at least raise a cautionary note, "Perhaps all these terrible stories are not true; but no one can deny the gross cruelty of the Germans in Belgium."[53] Serial histories proved enduring but, one suspects, were more popular with parents and school prize committees than with young readers. They were still being commissioned as late as 1916, when the popular adventure writer Herbert Strang entered the field with a series of factual books about the war for young people.

Published by Hodder and Stoughton, the most interesting of these was *England and the War: A Book for Boys and Girls.* Strang had been specifically commissioned by Wellington House to produce the series, apparently the first author of juvenile fiction to be enlisted into the official propaganda campaign. The booklet proved popular and was later reissued as *Great Britain and the War.* It was available for sale at threepence; copies were also distributed free to schools and libraries. The copy in Manchester's John Rylands Library was presented by the News Department of the Foreign Office to the University of Manchester—part of a general mail shot one hopes, and not a comment on what the Foreign Office thought of standards in provincial universities! Strang's short booklet followed the usual argument that the war had come like "thunder from a clear blue sky"; that Britons had not wanted war, but had to do their duty to Belgium, and in so doing had "performed an act of friendship to France."[54] It also repeats the common argument that the British hated war. Strang, of course, was writing in 1916 when it was difficult to represent the war in the same romantic manner as in 1914. Thus he allows a slightly more realistic note to emerge when he writes of its consequences.

No one in the United Kingdom wanted war. For sixty years Great Britain had been at peace in Europe, and she desired and hoped that peace should continue. The people had grown to hate more and more the horrors of war—the waste of young lives, the ruin of happy homes, the sorrow and suffering which war inflicts upon women and children.[55]

But where Strang's book does differ from earlier explanations is that it includes a specific section on war aims—"what Great Britain is fighting for." Strang lists three principal aims: the restoration of Belgium and Serbia; the right of small nations to determine their own affairs, and finally, "for honour"—not simply that Britain's honour demanded involvement, but to teach Germany the meaning of the word. Here the author explains that Germans must learn that,

honour is as necessary among States as among individual men; and as she will only learn that lesson by suffering defeat in war, the British Empire is pledged to fight on until Germany is beaten.[56]

Strang concludes with a survey of what Britain's armed forces have achieved at sea and on land and how the home front has rallied to the cause. His final admonition is that Britain is spending the lives of her "finest manhood" and her treasure in order that "her children and the children of her allies may be free from the terror that German ambition and German ruthlessness have imposed on the world."[57]

In 1918, an extended version was published which included the events of the last two years of war. However, in 1916, the same year that *England and the War* first appeared, Strang also found time to expand some of the material into a further three volumes: *The War on Land*, *The War at Sea*, and *Our Allies and Enemies*. These slim books were highly illustrated with colour plates and line drawings and appear to have been intended for an even younger audience than his adventure stories. The first volume again offers a brief explanation of why the war came about, but with new material on German militarism. The other volumes describe how the army and navy are organised, details some of the major land and sea engagements, and summarises the contribution of Britain's allies while heaping abuse on Germany and Austria.

For Herbert Strang, as for many other authors, the root cause of the war was German militarism: the belief that might was right, that the strong should inherit the earth. In *The War on Land*, for example, the author tells us that while almost the whole world has come to hate war,

Germany alone has cherished opposite views. Her historians and philosophers have taught for generations that war is a necessity, and military service the noblest occupation. All her organising powers have been devoted to the perfection of war as a science. The result is lamentable. Conscious of her strength, she has become the bully of the world.[58]

Strang appears to have forgotten the numerous occasions in which the British had similarly bullied their way to empire. But here, the Kaiser, Wilhelm II, was of course the bullyboy in chief, the very personification of tyranny and crude militarism. Parrott had already made the bizarre suggestion that one reason why Wilhelm gave his father, Kaiser Frederick III, such a "meagre" funeral was because the latter was a peace-loving monarch, and quite unlike his grandfather, Wilhelm I, who had created the German Empire with the sword.[59] Later in the volume, the author reproduces extracts from Wilhelm's speeches which are used to demonstrate his ruthless, opinionated character.

The German people are the chosen of God. On me, as German Emperor, the Spirit of God has descended. I am His weapon, His sword, and His Vice-Regent.

There is only one master in this country. I am he, and I shall suffer no other beside me.

I consider myself . . . an instrument of Heaven, and shall go my way without regard to the views and the opinion of the day.[60]

Second only to the Kaiser as a target for the venom of the propagandists was the German Chancellor, Theobald von Bethmann Hollweg. Parrott cites the

The War on Land, by Herbert Strang, 1916.

chancellor's speeches to the Reichstag explaining the invasion of Luxembourg and Belgium as an admission of German guilt.

We are now in a state of necessity, and necessity knows no law. We were compelled to override the just protest of the Luxembourg and Belgian Governments. The wrong—I speak openly—that we are committing we will endeavour to make good as soon as our military goal is reached. Anybody who is threatened as we are threatened, and is fighting for his highest possessions, can only have one thought—how he is to hack his way through.

Thus, claims the author, "Germany began the war by a confession of wrongdoing."[61] But if the Kaiser, his chancellor, and his warlords were the chief architects of the war, all German citizens, he argued, must share some of the burden of guilt. Why, he asks, if they are not tainted with the same brush, have they permitted one man to lord it over them in this fashion and lead them into war? The answer, he explains (and here his argument appears contradictory), is because they have never known any other condition. As every German must be a soldier for one or more years, "the nation has been drilled into submission."[62] This image of the robotic, blind obedience of or-dinary Germans is a recurring image we will encounter later. In popular fic-tion, all Germans were cowed by anyone in authority, but when in authority themselves they became swaggering bullies. Escott Lynn's descriptions are typical of the manner in which novelists represented the enemy, particularly Prussians. His officers are inevitably "swaggering, bullying and insolent," and their physical appearance is equally distasteful: Lynn describes a typical pair. One is "bull-necked, red faced," the other "tall, thin and dissipated looking" with an "abnormally long neck . . . a pimply face and shock head of yellow hair."[63] The rank and file of the German army are equally unpleasant, invar-iably dull-witted, shambling, and brutal—an image that would be endlessly repeated and elaborated as the war dragged on. Propaganda for young readers, then, justified Britain's declaration of war by reviling the enemy, revealing their senseless cruelty, and the truth, justice, and nobility of Britain's case in fighting to right these obvious wrongs. Even after Germany had been de-feated, some authors found it remarkably difficult to forget the hymn of hatred they had espoused during the war. In his first postwar novel, *Tommy of the Tanks*, Escott Lynn, for example, still found it necessary to remind his readers in the foreword that, "The Great European War was entirely of Germany's making," and he then went on to point out that Germans are "loathed and despised by the whole civilised world."[64]

But lest the seemingly reasoned arguments of O'Neill, Parrott, and Yoxall failed to instill the martial spirit in young readers, a more direct literary method was employed—the adventure story that would excite and involve readers, making them anxious to share the heroic world of war inhabited by fictional heroes. Adventure fiction as recruiting agent was not new, and the inherent patriotism of British writers had, throughout the late nineteenth century, ensured that their novels had often acted as unofficial recruiting pro-paganda for Britain's colonial wars and prepared boys for future service. This seems to have been remarkably successful, for the most enthusiastic recruits in August 1914 were young, middle-class suburbanites,[65] exactly the sort of young men who had been raised on Henty and the pleasure culture of war. Thus it was inevitable that authors would respond to the crisis of 1914 in the same way. The boys' story papers, which had been so strident about the Ger-man menace and the need for boys to be prepared in the decades before 1914, were strangely silent about the outbreak of war in August. However, this was due to the fact that as future issues were prepared so far in advance of pub-lication, by the time new copy was prepared the war had been on for some considerable time and was hence old news. Only the Amalgamated Press managed to publish editorials about the war during August, and then only to crow over the paper's earlier warnings about the "Great War to Come." As we have seen, Harmsworth's boys' papers had long reflected their owner's intense Germanophobia, and serials and stories about a future war between Britain and Germany had been a regular feature. Now in 1914, when the war they had predicted had finally begun, it was time to gloat, as the editor of *The Boy's Friend* smugly pointed out,

For many years war serials have figured strongly in the *Boy's Friend* programme. For many years, through the medium of these serials, we have spoken the words "be prepared." For these we have been condemned by many people. . . . But now as I sit at my desk, the grim day has come.[66]

As we have seen, writers of adventure fiction for young readers took up the recruiter's banner almost without exception. The editor of the *Boy's Own Paper*, however, took a more practical view, advising readers who wanted to help the war effort to join the Boy Scouts, drill clubs, or gymnasiums, and to "take advantage of the opportunities to make yourself 'fit' in mind and body"; adding "this war will have done one good thing if only it results in a general bracing up of our young manhood."[67] During the first months of the war most young men of military age needed little encouragement to enlist. But propaganda was concerned with long-term recruitment, and even by the end of 1914, the number of volunteers was in decline. Thus those who had failed to respond to the initial wave of moral indignation needed further reminders. However, if the war should go into a second or even third year, boys who were now some way from enlistment age would need to be prepared to eventually take their place in the line. Some authors, then, felt the need to concentrate on propaganda that would instill a sense of righteous indignation at the barbaric behaviour of the enemy and represent the war as breathless adventure through the fictional exploits of young heroes—adventure that any normal boy would want to share. The popular boys' adventure papers took a positive role here. "The Skipper's" editorial in the October issue of *The Union Jack* explained that the publisher's office was strangely silent because so many staff members had enlisted, and then asked "how many of my readers . . . have gone to take part in making history, gone to fight in the war for freedom, liberty and honour?"[68] The papers kept up a steady stream of editorials, patriotic verse, and letters from old readers now serving in the trenches, and they ensured that the fictional characters in their stories were eager to volunteer. The editorial in the October issue of *The Captain*, for example, notes the regular procession of authors and editorial staff on their way to enlist, "the chance of getting at close grips with the enemy was 'meat and drink' to them."[69] But it was the more respectable novels by established authors that carried the most punch.

War novels were dominated by a handful of exceptionally prolific authors.

Herbert Strang and Percy Westerman we have already encountered, but equally popular were Captain F. S. Brereton, a doctor in the Royal Army Medical Corps, Escott Lynn, and Captain Charles Gilson, both infantry officers.[70] Only slightly less prolific were a second rank of writers which included Rowland Walker, who eventually served with the Royal Flying Corps; Captain Frank Shaw, a retired merchant skipper who would serve again with the Royal Navy; and R. H. Parry, a professional writer who before the war had specialised in school stories. There is a remarkable similarity about their work, particularly their first war stories. Escott Lynn's novel, *In Khaki for the King* (1915), was typical. The novel was dedicated to the following:

> Those True Britons of The Bulldog Breed who,
> In Their Country's Hour of Need, Nobly Responded
> To The Call of Arms.

Before relating the exciting adventures of his young heroes on the Western Front during the first few months of the war, Lynn, in a short preface addressed to his readers, explains that the book had been written in difficult circumstances during brief spells "off duty." "It deals," he tells us, with "ordinary youths," but ordinary lads who are today dying a hero's death in Belgium because

the civilised world is threatened by a barbaric invasion. What Attila, the ancient Hun, was to the world in the fifth century, that would Wilhelm, the modern Hun, be in the twentieth century.

He then appeals to his readers, and in so doing clearly reveals the recruiter's banner.

It is up to you boys of to-day to see that a similar danger never threatens your glorious Empire again. Those of you who have not yet donned khaki, see to it that when your are old enough you train yourselves to defend your homes, your mothers, your sisters, your country, all that you hold dear; so that should another such world scourge as Germany ever threaten us again, you will be ready at an hour's notice to take your place in the ranks . . . and so crush the monster ere it has gorged itself with the blood of innocent women and children.[71]

The story that Lynn then tells is remarkably similar to the early war novels of other popular authors—A *Hero of Liege* by Herbert Strang, *The Dispatch Riders* by Percy Westerman, *With French at the Front* by F. S. Brereton, and Charles Gilson's *A Motor Scout in Flanders*. All these writers had begun their literary careers with historical tales that owed much to Henty, but in the decade before 1914 they had also found inspiration in contemporary wars. Strang had written two novels of the Russo-Japanese War of 1904, for example; Westerman had written a tale set during the Italo-Turkish war of 1911–

1912; while Brereton had used the Balkan Wars of 1912–1913 as the background for at least one novel.[72] Several had also published tales of the great war to come. Thus they had had considerable experience in writing about modern warfare. However, when it came to the events of 1914, they all had the same story to tell. All their novels have young heroes, all ex-public school, who are on the Continent during the July crisis and the declaration of war; and all are in Belgium during the German invasion. This allows the author an opportunity to offer an "eyewitness" account of the unfolding drama, the savagery of the German army, and the courage and resourcefulness of the Belgians. Here, of course, the authors were largely repeating the standard anti-German propaganda stories that had already appeared in the press. In *The Dispatch Riders*, for example, the 17-year-old heroes, Kenneth Everest and Rollo Barrington, are touring Belgium on motorcycles while on holiday from their public school.[73] The central characters in the novels of Strang, Brereton, and Lynn are all in Germany when war begins; Brereton's Jim Fletcher is a captain attached to the embassy staff in Berlin; Strang's Kenneth Amory is in Cologne, working in a branch of his father's business; and Lynn's Oliver Hastings is studying in Cologne for a year, having just left Rugby. All have to escape from behind enemy lines when war is declared, and all finish up in Belgium where they either join the Belgian army, as in Westerman's novel, or fight as civilian auxiliaries before returning to England to enlist— or in Jim Fletcher's case to rejoin the RFC on the Western Front.

In their first stories, all these authors felt it necessary to explain why the war had come about. Lynn, typically, takes us through the July crisis though the experiences of his central character, the young Englishman Oliver Hastings, who is in Germany studying at this time. This was a common strategy for authors who used it to contrast the natural belligerence and hysteria of the German people with the calm, phlegmatic righteousness of the British. Oliver, despite being denounced as a spy, eventually returns to England via Belgium, where he helps defend the forts at Liege. Captain F. S. Brereton used much the same plot in his first novel of the war, *With French at the Front*, also published in early 1915. The story begins in Berlin on the day that war is declared. Captain Jim Fletcher, the novel's hero, is attached to the British Embassy and has to arrange the evacuation of the staff. This means a hazardous journey to the station through the hostile German crowds that surround the building. Jim emerges from the building carrying his swagger stick and calmly smoking a cigarette. As Jim walks through the crowd, the author uses the scene to compare this typically lithe young Briton with the overweight and hysterical Germans.

Jim had the head and shoulders of our islanders. A small, fair mustache set off a handsome face which was resolute and firm, and had none of the floppy stodginess so often found among the beer-drinking subjects of the Kaiser.[74]

Jim displayed no fear, refused to hurry, and never looked over his shoulder, for "he had nerves of steel." He successfully arranges the departure of the embassy staff but at the last moment is separated from his companions. After various adventures behind enemy lines he eventually manages to return to England and resumes military service at the Front.

Brereton spares us a long explanation about the crisis and reduces the war to a single cause: German aggression and ambition. This was a war for which "the Fatherland had been waiting, aye, waiting and longing," he claims, "a war they had been planning for years: a war that would make them masters of the world." The "fingers of the mailed fist were already stretched out to snatch in vast possessions."[75] But when it comes to the German advance through Belgium, Brereton adopts Lynn's comparison of modern Germans and ancient Huns.

At Louvain, the seat of Belgian universities, a city much like our Oxford or Cambridge, the Prussian hosts executed a deed as terrible as ever committed by Attila and his barbarian Huns. They burned and destroyed the city, slaughtered civilians on every side, and committed nameless atrocities. Thus the Bosches [sic] gained the name of "modern Huns," and laid up for themselves and their own people sure promise of reprisal when the tide turned.[76]

These novelists all refer to the alleged atrocities, but only Escott Lynn offers his readers a fictional eyewitness account. On his travels through Belgium, the young Oliver Hastings observes enemy soldiers clearing a village. An ancient Catholic priest, a rope around his neck, is led through the village and clubbed with a rifle butt when he stumbles. When the men of the village are lined up against a wall, a woman and her child try to halt the execution by pleading with the German officer for her husband's life. "Waste no more time," commands the German officer, "shoot her with the other cattle"—and the "half-drunken soldiers . . . sent in several volleys."[77] This plot device that allowed young Britons to be caught up in the invasion of Belgium was an enduring one and was used in many novels, stories, and serials; even as late as 1919, W. P. Shervill used it for his novel *Two Daring Young Patriots*.[78] But all these novelists found an opportunity to remind their readers that this was a war of honour—and honour appears to be the keyword for propagandists who sprinkled it liberally throughout their work. Brereton, for example, tells his readers that Britain had begun the war because of her honour, and that whatever the cost in life or treasure must see it through for, "life without honour, even for nations, is not worth living."[79]

"For the most part," suggests Richard Phillips, "Victorian girls were excluded from dreams of adventure and ignored by writers and publishers of adventure stories."[80] There were a few notable exceptions, and even a writer so obsessed with machismo as Henty could on occasion find room for women to become part of a masculine adventure, as, for example, in his novel of the

North West Frontier, *A Soldier's Daughter.* By the Edwardian period this attitude was beginning to change; several women writers entered the world of
adventure fiction and located their heroines within the adventure narrative,
often in a colonial setting. After 1914, the war opened up wider dimensions
for girls' fiction as new opportunities to serve the nation on the home front
and elsewhere emerged. Women played only minor parts in most of the fictional war stories—the hero's sister or mother might appear briefly at the
story's periphery, or occasionally a female refugee, fleeing the advancing German hordes, could become a subject for the hero's assistance—by and large,
male authors ignored women. But several women writers did attempt to give
their heroines more direct and more prominent involvement in the war. In
Angela Brazil's popular school stories set during the war, the students frequently helped to capture spies and saboteurs and did their bit for the war
effort, but these were little more than traditional school stories set against the
wider background of war.[81] However, Bessie Marchant, sometimes referred
to as the female Henty, probably the most popular and prolific writer of girls'
adventure stories,[82] produced a number of novels in which young heroines
directly engaged in the war.[83] As Nicoletta Gullace has argued, many women
saw militant patriotism as furthering their case for equality of citizenship.
Hence they undertook a variety of war work, not just because they wanted
Britain to be victorious, but also because they saw it as a means through which
they could achieve their own gender-specific goals.[84] Thus Bessie Marchant,
Brenda Girvin, and other novelists may well have been using adventure fiction
to reinforce the long-term aims of women. However, there were limitations
on how close women could get to the firing line. *Molly Angel's Adventures*,
published in early 1915, used the same plot device as many of the war novels
for boys—the young protagonist trapped by the German invasion of Belgium—but it does bring its heroine into direct conflict with the enemy. In
this case it is 13-year-old Molly Angel who, with two younger friends, are on
holiday in Belgium in the late summer of 1914. The children catch measles,
and their Bohemian parents, due to attend an art exhibition in Switzerland,
thoughtlessly leave them in the care of a Belgian friend. However, before they
can be reunited with their negligent parents, the Germans have invaded. The
children attempt to return to England, and this involves them in a number of
adventures as they try to avoid being arrested by the enemy. Eventually, Molly
meets an American, an old family friend, who manages to get the children
back to England, where they are finally reunited with their families. While
Marchant clearly has little knowledge of conditions in the occupied Belgium,
she does convey some sense of the confusion and horror of the German invasion. While attempting to reach the coast by train, the children find trav-
elling in wartime far from easy.

At every station where the train stopped the war was emphasised. The platforms were
thronged with people fleeing from the trouble that was behind. Red Cross nurses,

ambulance men, provision carriers . . . An endless throng of what might be called the by-products of war.[85]

The novel offers no descriptions of the fighting or atrocities, nor does it employ the rhetoric of hate commonplace in boys' fiction. Here the Germans are single-minded and arrogant, but not bestial. Nevertheless, Molly is revealed as compassionate, cool, and courageous in a dangerous situation, a perfect role model for young women suffering under the hardships of war. The young heroine trapped on the Continent by the outbreak of war became a device used by many later authors of girls' fiction.[86] However, in *The Cub*, the author Ethel Turner is less concerned with the excitement caused by the German invasion than with the tragedy of war. As a reviewer in *The Times Literary Supplement* gloomily noted, "war kills off the most promising lads and leaves mothers childless."[87] *The Cub* is that rare thing, a book for young readers that actually dared to ask if the human cost of the war could really be justified.

Before 1914, authors of juvenile fiction had believed it their duty to inculcate boys with a sense of duty and commitment to King and Empire. They had represented war as romantic and chivalric adventure, so that future generations would be eager to take their place in the line of battle when needed. Now, in 1914, they helped promote support for what they believed was a just and honourable war—perhaps even a war of national survival. Their strategy was to explain Britain's cause—a morally just crusade in which young men would willingly sacrifice themselves for the national cause and thus earn immortality. As we have seen, those authors young enough and fit enough did set an example by serving with the armed forces in some capacity, but exactly how they represented the grim and bloody fighting on the Western Front will form the subject of the next chapter.

CHAPTER 2

At the Front

Where are those hefty sporting lads
Who donned the flannels, gloves and pads?
They play a new and deadly game
Where thunder bursts in crash and flame.
Our cricketers have gone "on tour,"
To make their country's triumph sure.
They'll take the Kaisers's middle wicket
And smash it by clean British cricket.

Jesse Pope, *Cricket, 1915*[1]

O'Neill, Parrott, and other writers of popular histories made a significant contribution in explaining for young readers why the nation was at war. They reinforced belief in the righteousness of the nation's cause and publicised the shameful deeds of the German army in Belgium, but those readers—the nation's future defenders—were far more interested in descriptions of the fighting. As we have seen, many young men who had no experience of battle often turned to popular fiction to discover what it would be like to be in the front line and under fire. Authors like Strang, Brereton, and Escott Lynn did their best to fulfil that need in the first crop of war stories that began to appear in early 1915 and which focused on the daring exploits of fictional heroes against the backdrop of real events on the Western Front. Most novels used remarkably similar plots, and they invariably focused on the doings of upper-class heroes with a public school background. Kelly Boyd has suggested that in the period 1890–1920, the fictional heroes of the popular boys' story papers were "democratised," that the aristocratic, arrogant Victorian hero began to give way to "pit boys, engine drivers and factory lads."[2] This trend can certainly be seen in some domestic stories, but before the Great War only a handful of war stories focused on the doings of enlisted men and boys, and by and large the ex–public school officer hero remained firmly in the saddle.[3] After 1914, virtually all war fiction was dominated by officer heroes created by authors as role models and intended to persuade their less privileged brothers to take up arms and follow their example.

The imaginary stiff upper lip, masterful Englishman, as Jonathan Ruther-ford has pointed out, grew out of the uncertainties and anxieties of the late nineteenth century, when other nations were beginning to challenge Britain's economic and imperial supremacy.[4] It was at this time that the masculine ideal fashioned to serve the needs of empire appeared, an ideal that stressed the qualities of duty, service, and sacrifice. These qualities, it was believed, were most readily to be found among young men educated in the great public schools. As Edward Thring, headmaster of Uppingham, had pointed out,

The learning to be responsible and independent, to bear pain, to play the game, to drop rank, and wealth, and home luxury, is a priceless boon. I think myself that it is this, which has made the English such an adventurous race; and that with all their faults. . . . The public schools are the cause of all this manliness.[5]

It was generally considered that whatever deficiencies the schools may have had, they were far outweighed by their ability to mould character and instill in their pupils the essential qualities that defined the true Briton—exactly the qualities required to govern and expand a mighty empire. In the later nine-teenth century, under the guidance of "reforming" headmasters like Edmond Warre at Eton and H. H. Almond at Loretto, the schools also contributed those qualities required by the aggressive imperialist—unquestioning patri-otism and the martial spirit. And lest the ultimate aim of all this character building be missed, it was forcefully restated by J. G. C. Minchin at the time of the Anglo-Boer War. "In times of stress and strain," he wrote,

England can rely upon her public schools. . . . We have also learnt, through our school, to love and (if need be) die for our country. Long before the British Public at large had been fired with faith in the British Empire, one and indivisible, that was the faith in which every English public-school boy was reared.[6]

By the early twentieth century, the public schools had absorbed the middle classes—either in fact or aspiration and, through the school story (which ranged from Thomas Hughes's novel *Tom Brown's Schooldays* [1857] to the exploits of Bob Cherry and the boys of Greyfriars School in mass circulation story papers), had even begun to imbue working-class boys with a watered-down version of the public school ethos. Robert Roberts, growing up in the slums of Salford in the decade before the Great War, later recalled that many youngsters in the working class had developed an addiction for Frank Richards' school stories. . . . Over the years these simple tales conditioned the thought of a whole generation of boys. The public school ethos, distorted into myth and sold among us weekly in penny numbers, for good or ill, set ideals and standards.[7]

Thus, when war came in August 1914, it was the public school boy, the idealised masculine role model, who was expected to be first into the fight and rally the ranks, and the young men of Eton, Harrow, and the other great schools had certainly been well prepared for their role. As Geoffrey Best has shown, the public schools had groomed their pupils for just such a crisis through a curriculum that emphasised the nobility of war, the camaraderie of battle, and the eternal glory of the ultimate sacrifice. Military training provided by the school cadet corps, headmasters obsessed with martial spirit, and a procession of glamorous generals and admirals attending speech days, and extolling the virtues of war, had militarised the public schools;[8] they had ensured that young men had been taught to believe that war was romantic and exciting—a struggle little more difficult than a hard-fought match against an unruly visitors' eleven. In 1917, Henry Newbolt, a passionate defender of the public school ideal, reinforced this notion when he suggested that Eton, Harrow, Rugby, and the other great schools were the modern equivalent of the castle school where the young squires learned the chivalric code of the warrior. Clearly he believed that the games field was a contemporary version of the tilt-yard where boys learned the game of life, and honour, and how to conduct themselves in war.[9] And in 1914 public school boys went willingly, eagerly; most simply couldn't wait to get to France to embark upon the Great Adventure.

The War Office, desperate for officers for the new Kitchener armies, turned to the older public school boys, for here was a major source of young men with the right stuff and already trained for command through the schools' Officer Training Corps system. These young men could take their place in the line with only minimal further training. But recruiters also believed that public school boys were in a unique position to give a lead to the masses, that the example of their entering the military *en masse* would help overcome lower-class opposition to military service. The enthusiasm of public school boys was staggering: as Parker has noted, during the first 15 months of the war, public school boys provided junior officers for more than 570 battalions of the New Armies.[10] The example of the public school boy as enthusiastic volunteer and, if need be, as willing sacrifice in the great crusade to destroy Prussian militarism, became an endlessly repeated motif in war propaganda and particularly in adventure fiction. These propagandist stories, intended to inspire ordinary lads and to provide shining examples of endurance and courage under fire, and the immortality to be won through an honourable death, focused almost exclusively on the heroic exploits of young ex-public school officers.

In popular fictions, the public school man was instantly recognizable; it was impossible to disguise his flair, initiative, and leadership qualities, and even if serving in the ranks he inevitably become a subject for the admiration of his comrades. In Captain Brereton's *Under Haig in Flanders* (1916), for example, Roger Norman, a 17-year-old in his last year of school (and waiting to apply for a commission) believes he has killed a ruffian in a street brawl. Concerned that he might bring shame upon his family, he enlists as a private under a false name and is befriended by Bill Andrews, a "fresh-looking, honest young workman." But Roger's disguise cannot fool the observant Bill, who tells him, "You're a gent. Anyone could see that. . . . You're the stamp of chap that's made into an officer."[11] Later Bill reflects on his friend's character,

Clean look about the chap—one of the public schoolboy sort! I know 'em! And sometimes they've irritated me. But they've got grit and go, and they've made fine officers. They've shown that they can fight through difficulties, and there ain't a shadow of a doubt about it.[12]

Roger, of course, eventually earns a battlefield commission for valour and goes on to win an award for courage under fire. And the same is true in Richard Bird's story "The Schoolboy Ranker" in *The Captain* of 1915. Here young Charles Errington runs away from school to enlist, believing that his OTC training had prepared him to take part in the war, which it apparently did, for Errington is a natural leader and is soon commissioned.[13]

The heroic, honourable, and selfless public school hero was adopted by authors in the hope that their example would encourage ordinary lads, and Herbert Strang's popular novel, *Fighting with French* (1915), offers us an interesting example of how this was achieved. Young Kenneth Amory is waiting to apply for a commission when he chums up with Harry Randall, the son of a factory owner. Harry, not quite 18, is mad keen to get into the fight, but in the meantime he is trying to persuade the younger men in his father's factory to enlist, with little effect. Attending a meeting of the men, Harry and Kenneth are driven to exasperation by the workers who see little reason for going to war for the sake of Belgium. Desperately, the boys promise that if the men enlist, they will go into the ranks with them. Harry's father, worried about the "principle of social order," protests—"Destroy caste, and you'll ruin old England," he argues.[14] But to no avail, for the men make for the recruiting office and Harry and Kenneth, honour bound, follow. After action at the Front, the boys are offered commissions, and the men unanimously decide they should accept. As one of them explains,

I'm a socialist, as strong as ever I was. . . . But that ain't the point. We've got to look at things as they are, and be honest about it, and what I say is that you've had the training that makes officers and we haven't; and besides, you were born one way and we were born another, and it's no good trying to make out that chalk's as good as cheese.[15]

The boys eventually become officers and lead their faithful followers into more heroic adventures. Harry's father was clearly worrying needlessly, for breeding will always tell!

The volunteers of 1914, of whatever social class, were eager to get to France, but before they could get into battle, there was the problem of training, and few of the young men who enlisted early in the war realised just how long it would take before they found themselves in the front line. War stories had not prepared them for such delays, for few authors wasted time on such trivialities as training, preferring, like Brereton and Lynn, to create heroes who were already serving officers and could thus be dispatched straight to the Front, or like Percy Westerman's youngsters who were already in Belgium during the German invasion, and who could in some mysterious way become attached to the British Expeditionary Force—another triumph, perhaps, for British amateurism? Initially, most authors, however, subscribed to Henty's belief in the inherent fighting ability of the English, which required only a fine-tuning before duty at the Front. In Brereton's *Under French's Command*, a German spy reflects upon this natural martial ability, "[T]hese British, these Englanders, these shop people, they take young men from the counter and from the office, and drill and train them so quickly. These same soldiers of a day—youths in commerce but yesterday, and ignorant of all warfare—they fight like demons, like veteran warriors."[16] In fiction, most young Britons required little or no training at all in order to whip the Hun. In Rowland Walker's *Oscar Danby VC*, for example, the "Eagle Patrol," a Boy Scout troop camping on the Norfolk coast in August 1914, capture a German spy. As a reward, General Maxwell, the commander of the local division, promises to take them with him when he leaves for France. Getting the boys attached to the division is achieved by simply gaining their parents' consent. At the Front, the boys are employed helping Belgian civilians escape the invading Germans. While engaged in this duty, Eagle Patrol is attacked by a party of German cavalry. The Scouts, presumably well prepared for such occasions by Baden-Powell's organisation, fight off the enemy, killing or wounding a number of Germans. Being Scouts, of course, they also take care of those Germans they have wounded. "Gott in Himmel," exclaims one German, "Have we been fighting Boy Scouts? Donner und Blitz! If your Boy Scouts fight like this, what will your army do?"[17]

Clearly, then, most authors initially had little idea of what modern warfare was like, and they relied on memories of dashing cavalry skirmishes and bayonet charges more appropriate to colonial warfare than the Western Front. But this was a new kind of warfare, a war in which training, discipline, and teamwork would be essential; courage, manliness, and a belief in the inherent superiority of Britons alone would not suffice; and by 1915 some authors were beginning to confront this factor, but they still spent little time on the dull matter of preparing their young men for battle. The eponymous protagonist in Henry Newbolt's "The Adventures of a Subaltern," has had five years in the school OTC and a year at Oxford so, of course, can be commissioned and put in charge of enlisted men without any form of instruction whatsoever. Nevertheless, Newbolt does acknowledge that enlisted men need to be trained, but here it is the subaltern who "drills and instructs" the new recruits in the story, preparing them for service in France.[18] Only in Herbert Strang's *Fighting with French* (1915) do we gain some insight into the training of the new "Kitchener Armies." As we have seen, here two ex–public school boys enlist in the ranks as an example to factory workers who are reluctant to enlist. Needless to say, having seen the young gentlemen join up, the workers follow. This provides the author with an opportunity to sketch out some of the problems involved in creating the new mass armies—lack of uniforms, shortages of weapons, and temporary barracks. Nevertheless, in the novel these deficiencies are soon overcome, and the men's physical condition improves dramatically under a regime of "drill, training, PT, route marches and lectures." For their leisure hours there is a canteen and "cinema in the evening."[19] When one of the company, anxious to get to France, grumbles about the routine, Ken, one of the ex–public school chums, tells him, "We've got to work together like a football team, every man trusting every other; and that's what all this drilling and training is for"[20]—a comment curiously at odds with the individualistic acts of heroism that later feature in the novel. When the battalion is finally sent to France, the men are physically fit and confident, and they have been taught to work together as a team led by young officers who were almost exclusively the products of the public schools.

However, the static nature of trench warfare was markedly different from the colourful colonial campaigns that had provided inspiration for authors before 1914. On the Western Front there were no wild cavalry charges, and few heroic individual actions, and by 1915, and apart from the drama of the great offensives, the war had bogged down into stalemate. Combatants spent regular periods in the front line trenches, and this involved long periods where soldiers endured extreme physical discomfort, facing the constant danger of enemy snipers and artillery bombardment, interspersed with occasional highly dangerous forays into No Man's Land to renew barbed wire or to raid the enemy's trenches in pursuit of prisoners. Trench life was dangerous, but it was also boringly routine, drab, uncomfortable, and depressing. The writer R. H. Mottram later recalled his first spell in the front line.

Enormous noise. Continuous explosion. A deserted landscape. Complete immobility of everything. Men were eating, smoking, doing odd jobs but no one was fighting. A few were peering in periscopes or looking through loopholes. I tried, but could see nothing but upturned empty fields. Then suddenly there was a terrific crash which flung me yards. I picked myself up and did my best to laugh. Near by a man lay with

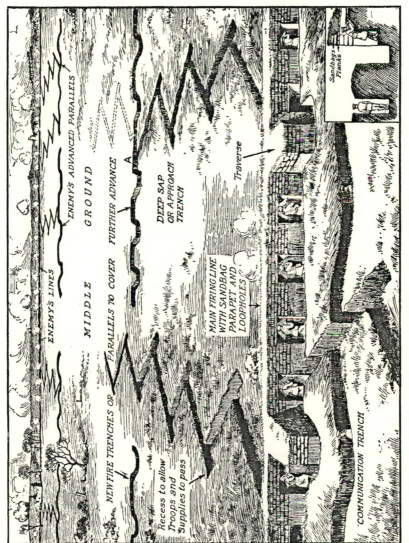

The Trench System, Sir Edward Parrott, *The Children's Story of the War*, 1915.

a tiny hole in his forehead and close to him another limped with blood pumping out of his leg. . . . That was how I first saw the war.[21]

Hardly an enticing picture to paint for young men seeking adventure on the field of honour. Thus authors were concerned to enliven this dreary, danger-ous troglodyte existence, to create an attractive and exciting image of life in the trenches.[22]

At the same time, they were anxious to persuade their readers of the essen-tial truth of their stories. Strang and Newbolt were particularly concerned that their novels were not dismissed out of hand as romantic fiction—perhaps because both authors were associated with Masterman's propaganda bureau. Thus they went to considerable lengths to establish the authenticity of their stories. In the introduction to his second war novel, *Fighting with French*, Strang admits that his first war story, *A Hero of Liege*, was little more than a "romance upon the early events of the war, when we were still under the shock of surprise and information was scanty." However, he goes on to claim the present story has been written under more favourable circumstances, and much of it is based upon personal knowledge. Yet he is careful to warn his readers that a story is not a history and that the "[R]omancer is satisfied if he is reasonably true to facts and probabilities but more than happy if his fictions . . . have also anything of stimulous and encouragement."[23] Henry Newbolt went even further in his introduction to *Tales of the Great War*, arguing that as a book is a partnership between author and reader.

My part is to give you the truth, the actual facts, well-evidenced and clearly arranged. Your part is to read them in such a way as to understand them—that is, to understand not only what happened, but how heroic and how admirable are the qualities which lie behind. . . . Feeling, then, is your part; truth is mine.[24]

Nevertheless, despite their claims to honesty and their desire to tell the truth about the fighting, they went on to weave tales of flamboyant adventure against the backdrop of real events culled mainly from distorted press reports, imbued with what they considered the spirit of young Britons at war.

Propagandists such as Strang and Newbolt with little real knowledge of conditions in the trenches relied on the reports that appeared in the popular press, and during the early part of the war, these tended to minimize the discomfort, danger, and hardships. Photographs in *The Illustrated London News* in October 1914, for example, typically showed dry, clean trenches, dugouts floored with straw, shelves stocked with domestic items, and "bomb-proof" shelters. Other images showed soldiers dozing on makeshift beds, cooking breakfast, or playing cards before going on duty.[25] By 1915, these images were beginning to change with reports about flooded trenches and the battle against mud and cold. Propagandists, however, drew their inspiration from the early images and, in an attempt to sustain a positive view of the war for recruiting

purposes, continually invoked a cosy domestic image of trench life. One curious consequence of this was that in war fiction the all-male environment of
the Western Front and the predominance of ex–public school officers turned
the front line into a sort of surrogate school,[26] where life resembled a nursery
fantasy and No Man's Land a playing field.

The intensely patriotic Henry Newbolt, champion of empire and the English public school, helped to establish this image in popular fiction with his
1915 story, "The Adventures of a Subaltern." Here, the young protagonist,
straight from his first year at Oxford, is taken up to the line for the first time.
After a winding journey through the communications trenches, he eventually
arrives at the dugouts in the front line. Later he writes home describing his
first impressions,

It's simply the world of Peter Pan's family in the underground scene. Little mud huts
about half underground and half above—made with pine-wood and mud, scattered
about among the trees, some fairly isolated, some close together, all thickly lined with
straw, and nearly all showing a thin coil of jolly-smelling smoke coming out of some
hole in the roof. Can you imagine anything more utterly romantic?[27]

The subaltern views the war as little more than an exciting escapade and
believes himself "part of a romantic novel in which English adventurers and
native tribes live in just such huts, and listen to the crack of bullets. The 'native
tribe' part of it was supplied by the odd-looking French troops which we were
relieving."[28] The war, in Newbolt's view, is altogether a jolly affair—"jolly-
smelling smoke" arises from the dugouts, and the French 75 mm gun is described as the "jolliest gun of all" while a general who visits the subaltern's
battalion is a "jolly gentlemen" who makes the troops laugh.[29] After a "spot"
of leave, the officer returns to the Front, but manages a "schoolroom big tea"
before going into the line; later, in reserve, he enjoys "first-class picnic teas
spread out on sheets in the corner of a field."[30]

In Strang's novels, the soldiers share "warm and stuffy cabins" built into
the sides of trenches and feast on "cocoa and bread and jam."[31] F. S. Brereton
paints an equally pleasant picture of life in the Front Line where good-hearted
Tommies feed on "frizzling bacon, not to be beaten anywhere, bread that
might have graced the table of the Ritz hotel, and jam that would have been
the envy of any housewife."[32] Interestingly, Brereton's reference to "the Ritz,"
may well have been taken from an ex-master's letter published in the *Salopian*
in 1914, in which the author boasted of the quality of the menu in his mess;
the *Boy's Own Paper* showed equally clean and well-built trenches with snug
dugouts where soldiers took their meals in comfort.[33] Such descriptions clearly
catered to schoolboy fantasies about secret camps in the woods, where they
feast on stolen delicacies and think up the latest "wheeze" to irritate their
masters (or the Huns). It is not coincidental that authors described the
trenches in such terms, for it was through such nostalgia for the lost days of

Henry Newbolt's view of the trenches.

boyhood that the trenches were made appealing, and this, of course, reflected the authors' own adolescent dreams.

As we have seen, it was common to link sport and war before 1914; as J. A. Mangan has pointed out, "sport became the ultimate metaphor for war and war became a 'sporting' endeavour"[34]—perhaps the most exciting sport of all. The sporting metaphor was relished by propagandists during the years of conflict and was frequently employed by authors. As A. Lochhead wrote in 1914,

> You may find your place in the battle front
> If you'd play the forward game,
> To carry the trench and man the guns
> With dash and deadly aim.
> O, the field is wide and the foe is strong,
> And it's far from wing to wing,
> But we'll carry through, and it's there that you
> May shoot for your flag and King.

Other writers maintained the fiction that the war was a sporting event.[35] Sometimes the Western Front was even more exciting than games. In a 1915 Percy Westerman novel, for example, his protagonists become involved in a bitterly fought action with the enemy. After the deadly fight in which several Britons are killed, Kenneth breathlessly declares to his chum, "It's a jolly sight better than rugby."[36] But this was not just literary invention, for many officers really did see the war in these terms. What could be more revealing, or more flamboyant, than the real-life example of young officers like Captain W. P. Nevill of the East Surreys who, before an offensive, purchased footballs for his men and offered a prize for the first man to dribble the ball across No Man's Land and into the German line?[37] In *Under Haig in Flanders*, a sergeant and his "chaps," bowl their bombs at the enemy, "as if they were cricket balls, and the beggars over there hate 'em."[38] One of D. H. Parry's young subalterns describes a hand-to-hand tussle with the Germans as "a ripping scrum," and later, on witnessing an uneven struggle between a diminutive cockney and a brawny Bavarian, the narrator tells us that "the splendid pluck with which the little man had tackled the giant appealed to [his] sporting instincts."[39] But as readers at home came to understand more about the squalor of the trenches and the anonymity of death by poison gas, high explosives, or the unseen sniper's bullet, the rhetoric of the "game of war" became less appealing.

In the comic papers, sometimes even those aimed at very young readers, the war was equally an endless source of fun, but here the characters were comedic figures and thus working class. Comics had long reflected a bellicose patriotism. "Patriotic Paul," the jingo boy hero of *Lot-O-Fun*, made his first appearance in 1908, and he usually appeared in Boy Scout uniform. In 1908 he had declared "I can't stand Germans," and in 1909 he had unmasked a German plan to invade Britain. In late 1914 Paul somehow became attached to the BEF and took on the enemy, inflicting endless practical jokes and minor humiliations on the Germans.[40] But comics equally adopted the domesticated and reassuring image of trench life—in which Tommies cultivated vegetable gardens outside the dugout, hung out their washing in No Man's Land, and cooked endless meals of "bangers and mash" on glowing braziers. In a May 1916 issue of *Puck*, for example, a trench scene featured in the comic's model series. These were intended to be cut out of the paper and assembled. *Puck's* trench is a sturdy example with deep, well-timbered dugouts, remarkably un-cluttered with the debris of fighting. Even the soldiers guarding the trench are remarkably clean and tidy and clearly have no fear of German snipers, for they stand head and shoulders above the parapet.[41] Christmas 1914, the first Christmas of the war, offered more wonderful opportunities for jolly japes. In its December 1914 issue, *The Big Comic* ran a cover strip of "Gay Gus," its trench-fighting hero. Gus and his cronies manage to acquire a Christmas tree, plant it in an unused trench mortar, and "settled down for a merry time." A scouting Zeppelin, however, intrudes on their fun. Gus sets off the mortar, and the Christmas tree brings down the German airship. Having got the better of the "Germhuns," the Tommies enjoy Christmas even more.[42] How-ever, 1915 witnessed increasingly bitter fighting, the emergence of new and horrible weapons, and the failure of the first British offensives of the war.

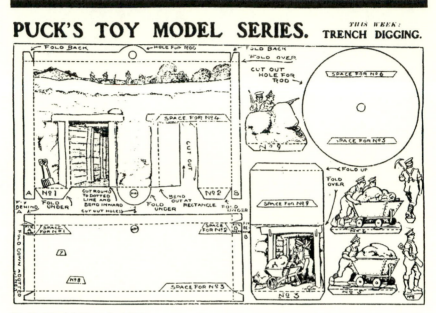

Puck's Model Trench, 1916.

Nevertheless, authors of war fiction still chose to portray the war as the Great Adventure.

The war story, with its exciting escapades and the camaraderie of the trenches, played an important part in the unofficial propaganda effort to mobilise the nation and prepare boys for future service and in spreading positive, heroic representations of the war. For a typical example of how the Western Front was represented for the youth of the nation, the early novels of F. S. Brereton, one of Blackie's most successful authors of juvenile fiction, offer a useful example. Brereton began his literary career after he retired from the RAMC after the Boer War. Despite rejoining the army in 1914, he still found time to write 12 books between 1915 and 1919—novels that dealt with almost all aspects of the war—Gallipoli, Palestine, the Eastern Front, and the Royal Flying Corps. Among these were several novels which more or less sequentially tell the story of the British experience on the Western Front.[43] Several are woven around the adventures of the young English officer Captain James Fletcher or his cousins. And it is through their eyes that Brereton re-creates the experience of war for his young readers. The first novel, *With French at the Front*, published in early 1915, opens, as we have seen, in Berlin on the day that war is declared, but after various adventures behind enemy lines, the hero James Fletcher eventually manages to return to England and resumes service in the RFC. Knowing that the Germans are massing for an offensive, he gets permission to go into the trenches facing the attack as an observer. As the "grey hordes" of the enemy advance, a young English subaltern, already wounded by a shell blast, climbs onto the parapet of the trench,

"Boys," he shouted, and at the call the men on either side sat up and cheered him. "Boys, for the sake of old England, for the sake of the regiment, you'll hold 'em.
   Fire, boys!"
   There was a choking cough, while a shudder ran down his frame. The subaltern collapsed into Jim's kindly arms, and lay white and motionless at the bottom of the trench. He was dead; another victim of the Kaiser's murderous ambition, one more count against the German nation.[44]

But his gallant example is an inspiration and the Tommies, "the thin khaki line of heroes, the cool, calm, cheery sons of Empire," fight like demons, beating back the German attack. Using the noble death of the young officer, Brereton then treats his readers to a lesson in duty and sacrifice, "It's the price we shall have to pay. . . . We'll take on our troubles like men—patiently and with courage—and we will remember." Here the war is a glorious experience, a romantic adventure, an opportunity to give one's life for the most noble of causes. British soldiers are good-humoured, plucky, eager to get into the fight, and willingly give their lives for King and Empire; a sentiment that James Clark captured so well in his widely reproduced painting *The Great Sacrifice*: beneath the Calvary, the golden youth of Britain lays dead, his features showing the contentment that comes from knowing he has done his duty.[45] *With French at the Front* is typical of the manner in which the experience of battle was represented in the early years of the war.
   The second novel of the series, *Under French's Command*, published in early 1916, deals with the events of 1915 down to the Battle of Loos, which provides the story's climax. The central character here is Norman Beamish, Fletcher's 17-year-old cousin, who is itching to get into the fight. "I tell you, Jim, it's rotten. I wish to goodness I were old enough, for I'd enlist at once and become a Kitchener," he tells his uncle. Jim's advice is to join up anyway, "Lots of fellows your age are doing their bit already and having a go at the Germans," he tells him. "Recruiting officers 'wink the other eye' when a keen, strong lad comes along."[46] Norman follows his cousin's advice but is too young for a commission, so he becomes a dispatch rider. However, his public school background has marked him out as officer material, and even during his first few weeks as a soldier he earns the respect of his comrades—"A bloomin' nob," as one of them described him. "I wouldn't mind if he was an officer this minute."[47] After completing his training, Norman is sent to the Front in 1915, where he again meets his cousin and becomes involved in the battle of Neuve Chappelle. Curiously, in the light of Brereton's view of the inherent superiority of men from public school, the author treats us to a lesson in the equality

of the trenches. Sharing a dugout with a crusty regular NCO, Norman is asked his name, to which the sergeant replies,

"Norman Beamish. . . . Swanky name, my word! Yus. Thought so." The sergeant grinned at him. "A bit of a toff at home, my lad. But out here there ain't no toffs, and swank and side don't help any fellow. We're all equal before the enemy, except of course the orfficers has to be obeyed , and deserves to be so."[48]

Escott Lynn equally promotes this idea of the equality of the trenches, telling us of a British attack where "the khaki-clad heroes, peer's son and ploughman, shoulder to shoulder, dashed out and drove the Teuton back." But while they may have been shoulder to shoulder, it was the "peer's sons" who were firmly in command.[49]

Brereton's Norman Beamish is witness to both the 1915 offensives at Neuve Chappelle and the Battle of Loos, which provides an eyewitness account for the reader. Both attacks start with "gigantic" bombardments of the German lines, a "veritable tornado" of fire on the labyrinths in which the Germans "lurked."[50] At Loos, after the bombardment lifts,

Those gallant British soldiers, those men of the old army, of Kitchener's force, and of the Territorials leaped from their trenches, when the signal was given. For a width of five solid miles they burst their way through the German first-line trenches and, over-running them . . . broke their way into the second line and exterminated its defenders . . . [and] burst like a deluge into the village of Loos. . . . German soldiers were routed out of cellars, the bayonet did its bloody work in many a garret. . . . It was all breathless work.[51]

The "much-vaunted defences of the Germans . . . were captured." If the enemy had not had other lines of defence, Brereton tells us, the Allies would have broken through and won the war on the Western Front. Here the battle is a success, with the British advancing several miles and taking over 25,000 prisoners.[52] But Brereton's account, exciting though it is, does not accord with the reality. The British artillery were desperately short of shells, and the bombardment failed to destroy the German defences. British casualties were high, over 60,000 dead. But it was, as Beckett points out, a battle fought to demonstrate support for the French and Russians, rather than part of a grand strategic plan,[53] and despite the tenacity of the army and acts of outstanding courage, the British offensive "failed to improve the general situation in any way and brought nothing but useless slaughter of the infantry."[54] Yet this was the event that Brereton suggests was the beginning of the end for Germany.

Such a fine beginning bodes well for the future, and it may be that, before these lines see the light, those efforts of the Allies may be repeated with even greater elan and determination; and, who knows? These winter months may find the Germans hurled neck and crop, out of France and Belgium.[55]

Brereton's stories are part personal adventure, part instant history, but the experiences of his young heroes were created to counterbalance the grim realities of life in the trenches for his readers. After all, who would willingly suffer the dangers, discomforts, and boredom of the Western Front? But Brereton's novels are perhaps the most unrealistic of all the fictional adventures produced during the war years. This is curious, because as we have seen, Brereton had served in the RAMC during the South African War and had returned to active service in 1914, serving in France, and later as a lieutenant-colonel seconded to the committee selecting RAMC records for the future Imperial War Museum. With his intimate knowledge of the war and his privileged access to military records, one must assume that he would have had a somewhat more realistic grasp of the nature of trench life than civilians like Strang and Newbolt. Yet his novels reveal little knowledge of the true situation in France. Barry Johnson has pointed out that despite his medical background, Brereton was "deafeningly silent about wounds and the effects of [modern] weapons."[56] Yet, as we have seen, while Brereton and other authors did not deny that the fighting often resulted in death or wounding, to expect what was essentially recruiting propaganda to catalogue the horrors of modern warfare is unrealistic. Nevertheless, as we shall see, even Brereton could not completely disguise the reality.

More justified is Johnson's claim that the author's plots often border on the absurd. In *With French at the Front*, Jim Fletcher, Brereton's protagonist, flies several reconnaissance missions for the RFC, fights with the Belgian infantry before Liege, flies more missions, takes part in a British cavalry charge that destroys a company of Uhlans, is captured, escapes to the coast, is rescued by a Royal Navy gunboat, becomes involved in a naval action, fights an aerial duel with a German "super-plane" (which he wins), and finally tracks down and kills an enemy master spy—and all within 292 pages! Equally, as Johnson notes, in all Brereton's novels "didactic surveys of the progress of the war on all its fronts frequently interrupt the story; Indeed, the extravagant fictional adventures of his heroes are often little more than pegs on which to hang such surveys."[57] But faced with the stasis of deadlocked trench warfare, authors like Brereton believed they had to enliven the unrelieved terrors of the Western Front by having their heroes undertake secret missions behind enemy lines or be dispatched on extraordinary quests to seek out spies, saboteurs, or the enemy's secret weapons. Unrealistic? Of course; but while propagandists revelled in creating deeds of pluck and daring, their representation of war was not always as sanitised as critics have assumed.

It has often been suggested that those at home were kept in ignorance about the real nature of the war, and that combatants returning from the Front were unable to tell their loved ones exactly what they had been through. Thus developed the myth of alienation between home front and fighting front that became such a significant factor in postwar memoirs.[58] Only through the memoirs, diaries, and novels of survivors, together with the revelations of those who had reported the war,[59] published after the war, did civilians come to understand exactly what combatants had been through, and this knowledge resulted in a wave of antiwar sentiment that became dominant between the wars. Yet an examination of war writing published between 1914 and 1918 casts doubt on this theory. As early as November 1914, *The Times*, for example, reported,

Trenches and always trenches, and within range of the concealed guns invisibility the supreme law. . . . Day after day the butchery of the unknown by the unseen. . . . War has become stupid. . . . The strain on the infantry is tremendous, and it is endless. . . . At the cost of thousands of lives a few hundred yards may be gained, but rarely indeed does the most brilliant attack produce anything.[60]

It was reports such as this that prompted the government to introduce more stringent censorship and attempt to control what the public read. Yet with casualty lists appearing daily in the press, it would have been impossible for those at home not to gain some insight into the real nature of this war.

Even in the sanitised tales of adventure, authors never completely disguised the realities and the manner in which this war differed from the nation's previous wars. In Escott Lynn's *In Khaki for the King*, for example, when the young Oliver returns home on leave from the Front, his father asks, "I suppose it's been fearful over there?" "Too terrible for words, Father," replies the young soldier, unable to speak of his experiences.[61] Later, Oliver's mother tells her husband, "I tremble when I think of Oliver going back [to the front]. . . . This war is so different from our previous ones: it seems as if everyone is being killed."[62] At the front during the first winter of the war, Lynn tells his readers, "The trenches were small canals of liquid mud, occasionally varied by being frozen hard. Snow, and slush, and freezing winds were the almost daily portion of the troops."[63] Nor do these authors attempt to deny that the British soldiers were dying at the Front. They certainly minimise the losses, but men are killed or wounded by unseen snipers, by explosive shells, and with cold steel in hand-to-hand fighting. They die cleanly, shot through the head or heart, and never in pain. Nevertheless, the authors did try to convey something of the chaos of battle.

The whole thing was a hideous jumble of terrifying explosions, of rattling shrapnel bullets, of puffs of smoke, and of clouds of dust and debris sent up by bursting missiles. The scene was enough, in fact, to deter the most gallant warrior from venturing to approach it closer.

Yet, concludes the author, "duty pointed ahead, that inexorable duty which attracts all of our brave soldiers."[64] And by the end of 1915, they were beginning to reflect something of the reality. At Loos, for example, Lynn admits that some British regiments were held by the enemy wire and were "mown down like grass" by the German machine guns.[65] But in fiction such set-backs were always temporary, and Lynn, like Brereton, claims the battle was ultimately successful and that the British achieved most of their goals. Yet the triumphant accounts of British achievement that Lynn, Brereton, and other authors relate are remarkably similar to the popular histories for adults written by Masterman's propagandists such as Rudyard Kipling, John Buchan, and Sir Arthur Conan Doyle. In Conan Doyle's 1916 account of the war, *A Visit to Three Fronts*, the trenches are "the most wonderful spot in the world—the front firing trench, the outer breakwater that holds back the German tide." Here, fresh-faced public-schoolboy officers and bronzed troops do their duty—quietly heroic, cheerful, resolute, and steady.[66]

A sense of duty, the respect of family, and loyalty to comrades were, of course, the key elements here, the motives for enlistment and the factors that kept men fighting long after the initial excitement had waned—not that the fictional characters of juvenile adventure stories ever lacked enthusiasm. Brereton's characters are always eager to get into the fight. In *With French at the Front*, his first war novel, Captain Jim Fletcher becomes involved in a cavalry charge against German Uhlans. Hard fighting follows, and Fletcher kills a German with his revolver, "What joy it brought him, too! Not that he loved slaying for the sake of slaying. But this was duty, this slaying of the Germans."[67] Elsewhere Fletcher describes an engagement as a "ding-dong battle," while the infantry are ever eager to get at the Huns with their bayonets.[68] And such enthusiasm is maintained throughout the series. Brereton and other authors have frequently been criticised for exaggerating Britons' enthusiasm for combat, but many soldiers did enjoy battle and the act of killing. Julian Grenfell, having nearly been shot, described how he and his comrades "yelled with laughter," and then continued, "I adore war. It is like a big picnic without the objectlessness of a picnic. I've never been so well or so happy."[69] While an anonymous Guardsman quoted by Parker claimed, "I have never in all my life experienced such a wild exhilaration as on the commencement of a big stunt [attack]. . . . The excitement for the half hour or so before it is like nothing on earth."[70] Clearly, then, some men enjoyed war, even enjoyed the killing. For others, the act of killing raised a moral dilemma, but again an appeal to duty usually resolved the problem.

The established church often used the argument that the war was a crusade against evil, against tyranny and militarism, but few churchmen went as far as the Bishop of London, A. F. Winnington-Ingram, in his 1915 Advent sermon in which the war was described as "a great crusade . . . to kill Germans: to kill them, not for the sake of killing, but to save the world . . . to kill them lest the civilization of the world should itself be killed." To be fair, as Ferguson points out, the bishop intended to make the point that the war "was an outbreak of vile passions," but few who heard it, or who later read the published version, understood such subtlety and probably accepted it at face value—a directive from a leading figure of the Anglican Church justifying the killing of Germans.[71] Juvenile fiction adopted a much simpler format—appeals to duty, or the consequences of failure. Escott Lynn relied on the old chestnut that unless the Germans are stopped, "our women and children are in danger."[72] Herbert Strang used a more personalised example. Ginger, the working man who has enlisted alongside the two ex–public schoolboys in *Fighting with French*, appears in their trench after a skirmish with the Germans looking pale. When asked what has happened, he replies, "I killed an officer chap, a nice young chap as might have been your brother. What for? What about his mother? And all those poor chaps yonder: why can't them as make wars let us alone? Men ain't made to kill each other." It is of course the well-educated Kenneth who explains the necessity for killing.

We're serving our country, Ginger. . . . It's not a question of just the present moment. We've got to think of the future. What would life be worth to our people at home if the Germans had their way? You can get nothing good without paying the price, and it *will* be good if we can teach the Germans and the world that force isn't everything, that people have a right to live their own lives without being bullied. For every man that dies, whether English or German, perhaps thousands may have a better time in days to come. That's worth fighting for, and dying for, if need be.[73]

A year later, Brereton fell back on the notion of duty as well. When Norman Beamish of the RFC rakes a German plane with his guns and kills the crew, he later tells his cousin, an experienced soldier, how awful he feels. Whereupon he's sternly told to "shut up" because it's "war, my boy. Red war, if you want to know, and this is duty. Fighting for King and Country." Norman considers this as they prepare to go into action again. "War. Yes war. . . . It might have been us. It had to be one or the other." And having rationalised this, the young man swings his gun with vigour, knowing he is morally justified.[74] The protagonists of adventure fiction are, by and large, unreflective about what they are doing—they follow orders, do their duty, and cherish an almost mystical belief in the righteousness of their cause which, as we have seen, had been powerfully established through a comprehensive propaganda campaign during the first few months of the war. However, some authors felt it necessary to reinforce these ideas from time to time, at the same time masking the brutality of war with a veneer of chivalric endeavour.

As Peter Parker has suggested, one of the most effective means of maintaining enthusiasm was to couch the war in chivalric terms, for this "gave some sense of higher purpose to the squalor and slaughter"—a sentiment that was developed in the saintly tales of chaplains and Red Cross workers at the Front in, for example, *With Our Fighting Men* by Rev. W. E. Sellers, and which strove to convince readers that God was clearly on side with the British.[75] One of the most enduring myths of the war concerned the "Angels of Mons"—a mystic figure(s) that many of the BEF believed they had seen hovering above the exhausted soldiers as they fell back before the German advance in August 1914. These angels, armoured knights or medieval bowmen (accounts varied), were seen above the battlefield and rallied the flagging spirit of the British. The myth had its origins in a story by Arthur Machen, "The Bowmen," published in *The Evening News* in September 1914. Here St. George and the shades of the bowmen of Agincourt gave their support to the hard-pressed British. Despite the author's later protestations that the story was pure invention, many people believed it to be true, convinced that the spirit of medieval chivalry was in the fight as well. Curiously, Machen later had correspondence from soldiers who actually claimed to have seen the vision.[76] The absolute conviction that God was on their side was clear proof of Allied righteousness, that their purpose was morally right, and that included killing the enemy. And this apparent proof that God was an ally was reinforced by new infusions of mystical nonsense at various times of need. In the middle years of conflict, for example, Henry Newbolt (now Sir Henry after having been knighted for inspiring public morale with his 1914 poem "The Vigil"[77]) produced several books for boys exploiting chivalric themes, intended to renew their flagging enthusiasm for the present struggle and to imbue them with the conviction that killing for such noble purpose was justified through historical example. *The Book of the Happy Warrior* retold the epic tales of Roland, Richard III, the Black Prince, and other medieval heroes. In the final chapter, "The Chivalry of To-Day," the author linked these warriors of the past with the young men of the Great War who fought daily with the Hun in France and Flanders, just another chapter in the endless struggle between good and evil. Newbolt makes this continuity clear when he argues that young men must always stand ready to take up their fathers' swords, "for so long as there remain in the world wild beasts, savages, maniacs, autocrats, and worshippers of Woden, there will always be the possibility of war."[78] But while propagandists focused on the noble endeavours of manly and chivalric warriors, the reality was very different.

On the Western Front by 1915, any notions of the romance of war were being trampled into the mud by modern, industrialised warfare. Modern weapons rendered the individual powerless when faced with the killing machines provided by an industrial society.[79] Mostly death came from the artillery shell fired from miles behind the lines, the machine guns fired by unseen adversaries, or the clouds of poison gas wafted by the breeze, and whether the individual warrior lived or died depended not on pluck, initiative, or battle skill, but on the vagaries of the machine, and on luck. In the spring of 1915, the Allies were faced with the perhaps the most inhuman and random of new weapons, poison gas—against which even the most skilled warriors were powerless.

Gas was first used by the German army at the Battle of Ypres in April 1915, in an attempt to take the British-held salient around the city. On 20 April, a German bombardment of the allied positions began—suggesting an impending attack. On the evening of the 22nd, however, an RFC pilot reported a "strange green cloud" drifting across No Man's Land towards the Allied front line. "It was the deadly poison gas chlorine, which when taken into the lungs sets up acute bronchitis and causes its victims to die in horrible agony."[80] French colonial troops were the first to be affected. Terrified by the green cloud, they fell back in panic. As Parrott describes,

> They were brave men; there was no mortal foe they were not ready to engage; but this creeping cloud that struck them down in agony was a devilish magic which they could neither understand nor resist. A horrible, unreasoning terror took possession of them, and they ran.[81]

A Canadian division behind the Front was sent up and, because the gas cloud was dissipating, managed to hold the gap in the line and prevent a German breakthrough. A second gas attack took place the following day, but the Canadians, protected by wet handkerchiefs and scarves wrapped around their faces, managed to hold on, until reinforcements could be sent up. Apart from minor gains here and there along the line, the Germans' use of gas gave them little advantage, but simply offered the Allied propaganda machine another prime example of German inhumanity. While the British press reported the incident almost immediately, they were slow to realise its propaganda potential. Under the headline "Poison Gas Used By Enemy Helps Them To Advance," the *Daily Chronicle* offered details of the attack, noting that the enemy had made use of "asphyxiating" gas and adding, "The quantity [of gas] produced indicates a long and deliberate preparation for the employment of devices contrary to the terms of the Hague Convention, to which the enemy subscribed."[82] Writing later, Parrott, however, noted that the Germans had sounded "the deepest depths of their infamy" and tried to poison those whom they could not beat in a fair fight.[83]

"Gas," as Ian Beckett has pointed out, "on its own . . . was not a decisive weapon,"[84] but it continued to be employed on a number of other occasions— including at the Battle of Loos in September 1915 when the British themselves employed gas in an attempt to break through the German line. Interestingly, in Brereton's account of the Battle of Loos, the author makes no reference to the British use of poison gas during the battle—a weapon that he obviously considered entirely inappropriate for his plucky, sporting Britons. However, this new weapon was featured in a story in *Comic Life* in June 1915 which virtually predicted the British use of gas in the coming battle. In "The Grey Gas," a young ADC is ordered by his general to assist a Canadian inventor, Mr. Abbott, in testing his new gas against the Germans. The British general is dubious about using "German methods" of warfare, but finally gives way to Abbott's belief in his new weapon and his desire for revenge. "While we are about it we may as well fight the Germans with their own weapons in the most effective way," he adds. After a night of hurried preparation, the gas is released at first light. The gas party retreat to a reserve trench and looking back see a "fearsome spectacle" for "the whole line of trench was completely lost to view in a mass of greyish foggy vapour, which welled continually and upward and rolled gradually on towards the German lines." As the British guns begin to drop their shells into the grey cloud, Abbott orders the British to take cover. Then, as he spoke, the "whole cloud caught fire and exploded with a shock that made the earth tremble." As soon as the air clears, the British move across into the enemy trenches—"no pen can tell of the sights we saw on that patch of black horror which had once been the German position," wrote the ADC. "Not a man was left with so much as a spark of life in him. Thousands of Germans lay burned, singed, blown to fragments, all dead, but slain quickly and mercifully." Abbott's gas is not poison, but rather a highly explosive agent that can be ignited by shell fire and with devastating effect.[85] Clearly, poisoning Germans was unsporting, but burning them to death was not. But what is perhaps curious about this graphic account is that *Comic Life* was intended for very young readers.

When the British really did employ gas, during the Loos offensive, it was less than successful. So rigid were the plans of the General Staff that it was used despite the absence of a favourable wind to carry it toward German lines. Consequently some British attackers were incapacitated by their own gas.[86] Loos was also the first battle in which the General Staff allowed war correspondents to visit the Front, but no mention of the British use of gas appeared in the press. Because correspondents were not in the front line they may well have been unaware of its use, but as Martin Farrar notes, even if they had been it is unlikely that the military censors would have passed such information for publication; gas was, after all, not a sporting weapon.[87] Nevertheless, it did not remain a secret for long. By early 1916 when volume four of Parrott's *Children's Story of the War* appeared, the author not only acknowledged that it had been used by the British, but justified its use.

You will remember the great gas attack of the Germans at the Second Battle of Ypres? You will remember what a shock of horror went through the civilized world when the Germans resorted to this foul weapon. We had never dreamed of sending clouds of poisoned gas against our enemies, but now we were forced to pay them back in their own coin. Many people at home thought we ought to refrain from using gas, but our generals thought otherwise, and in times of warfare their word is law. But the gas which we were now about to use was not poisoned. It was far less hurtful than that of the Germans. Men who breathed it were rendered insensible for a time; they were neither killed nor subjected to horrible torture.[88]

Parrott does note that the wind blew the gas back "momentarily" but that the British rallied and continued the attack. Thus, propagandists attempted to argue that British (or colonial) pluck, martial spirit, and gentlemanly behaviour could even counter the enemy's most fiendish weapons. But it was an argument that would prove increasingly hollow after the failure of the much heralded British offensive in the summer of 1916—the Battle of the Somme.

In early 1916, Douglas Haig, commander of the BEF, was urged by his French counterpart, Joffre, to launch an offensive against the enemy in order to relieve the pressure of the German attack upon the French at Verdun. At the same time, the British had been requested to pin down as many German units as possible in the west to assist a Russian offensive in Galicia in June. The result was a British agreement to launch an attack on the Somme at the beginning of July in conjunction with the French. Although Haig hoped for a breakthrough, he was, after the failures at Neuve Chapelle and Loos, realistic enough to see the coming struggle as part of a necessary "wearing out fight"—a battle of attrition.[89] Parrott tells us little of this, simply claiming that the Somme offensive was to "embarrass the enemy by falling upon him at a fresh point while he was deeply engaged elsewhere, and leaving him in doubt as to where he should throw his rapidly dwindling reserves of men."[90] Parrott describes how the offensive began with a great barrage of the German lines that "destroyed their batteries, blew up their ammunition dumps, and swept the ground behind their trenches so fiercely that no food or water could be sent up for days at a time."[91] But the main objective for the guns was to destroy the German wire and their frontline positions. According to Brereton this was an unqualified success: the "guns poured a tornado of bursting steel on the elaborate and often concreted defences devised by the Germans, ripping up whole miles of wire-entanglements, demolishing trenches, burrowing even to the depths of deep dug-outs and annihilating the defenders."[92]

At 7.30 A.M. on the morning of the First of July, the bombardment lifted.

Every man was very quiet; some, the veterans, looked indifferent; others merely nervous; most of the new drafts were pale and thoughtful. . . . Suddenly there was a dead silence. "They're lifting!" said the captain in a shout. He blew his whistle. . . . In an instant the men were scrambling, stumbling over the parapet. They were off.

Bernard, the central character in Herbert Strang's story, stumbles across No Man's Land, "barely conscious that the German machine guns had begun to play. . . . He did not realise that the line was sweeping forward like an Atlantic breaker," and on into the German trenches.[93] According to Brereton, sturdy British heroes "tingling with keenness" lobbed bombs at the Germans as if they were cricket balls and waited for the "off." Their advance across No Man's Land was cool, orderly, and largely successful.[94] But even in these novels, published in the immediate aftermath of the offensive, a degree of realism had begun to penetrate. D. H. Parry's *With Haig on the Somme*, first serialised in *Chums* in the autumn of 1916, describes the fight for the trenches thus,

Men stabbed and hewed and hacked at each other. Others, gripped in a tight embrace, were seen revolving in a species of grim waltz, until a chance bullet or a piece of shell ended the dance of death.

The wounded squeezed themselves against the boarded sides, the dead lay where they fell, and the living took no notice of either. If there was any shouting the guns drowned it, and the lust of slaughter was in every face.[95]

But even here the author finishes on a positive note. As the offensive drew to an end, the author notes that, "names hitherto unknown to British readers became household names. . . . To those at home who, reading between the lines, knew that at last our great and glorious armies were on the high road to victory."[96]

In reality, the first day of the Somme was one of the most disastrous days in British military history. The prolonged bombardment failed to destroy the wire entanglements or the German positions, and British troops, advancing at walking pace—as they had been ordered to do—were cut down in swathes. There were 21,000 dead and 35,000 wounded on that day alone.[97] Haig continued the offensive for another 140 days. The new Kitchener armies and the "pals battalions" were decimated. "In the industrial north of England, on Tyneside and in Ulster whole communities were plunged into mourning"; total British casualties were eventually some 400,000 men, and as Bourne notes, "their sacrifice was to little effect."[98] Despite some local successes, the Allies took little ground. However, as military historians have pointed out, apart from gaining ground, Haig also intended the battle as part of a "wearing out" strategy intended to weaken the German army, and in this aim the British were more than successful, for the German army was never quite the same after the offensive; the Somme had become "the muddy field grave of the German army."[99]

As Brereton, perhaps more aware than other authors of the realities and of Haig's attritional strategy, tells us:

[T]he Battle of the Somme found our soldiers ready and eager for conflict, and thoroughly aware of the fact that it was not ground that they were fighting for, not so much the capture of this village or that, but that they were fighting to break the strength of the German army, to drive in hard blows which should damage his strength and his "moral."[100]

The First of July, then, paved the way for later victories: it was "a triumph for the Allies and a bitter blow to our ruthless enemy."[101] The same message was to be found in the novels by Parry, Strang, and others, and in Captain Dawson's *Somme Battle Stories*, sponsored by Wellington House. Dawson was at pains to point out that,

People who try to measure the importance of the Push by the ground gained, or even by the casualties inflicted, will fall a long way short in their estimate of what it all means. The object in war is the destruction of the enemy, and the most important asset any enemy has is his spirit—the moral of his troops. Since July First our New Army has inflicted a crushing blow upon the enemy's moral.[102]

Nevertheless, even while authors were beginning to accept that this was a different kind of war from any which had gone before, they were still concerned to create battle-winning acts of individual heroism for their characters, which were the hallmark of Edwardian juvenile fiction. Thus their protagonists have adventures behind enemy lines, wage private wars against particular enemies, unmask traitors, and are sent on all manner of secret missions. This creates a curious tension between the traditional highly individualistic form of the war story and the acceptance that the Somme marked a new form of war—battles of attrition—a slogging match of heavy artillery, bombs, and machine gun bullets, where the British High Command attempted to inflict more casualties on the enemy than they themselves received, and in which the actions of individuals were of little importance.

The Somme also appeared to mark other changes as well. Fiction written during the latter part of 1916 also saw the beginnings of a move towards giving enlisted men a more significant role in the action. Earlier war novels had often included ordinary blokes, but usually for comedic purposes or to emphasise the leadership qualities of the officer hero. In stories dealing with the Somme offensive, however, other ranks from the working classes were given more a more serious role. In D. H. Parry's *With Haig on the Somme*, the working class Harry Hawke is given a far more prominent role, as is his companion in arms, Private Jim Tiddler. Parry not only acknowledges that fighting ability and heroism do not depend on social class, but also admits that the nature of warfare is changing. Significantly, Hawke is a sniper, and proud of his ability to hide out in No Mans Land and kill unsuspecting Germans: "seventeen with the rifle . . . but I've kept no tally of all I've done in wiv the bayonet," he tells his officer.[103] At the end of the novel, Hawke's fighting skills have won him the Victoria Cross. In Strang's novel of the same name, the central characters are John Barnard, an Australian private, and his two friends Sandy McPhail and Paddy O'Rourke, both recent immigrants to the Dominion. Attached to a British division on the Somme they have several misunderstandings with a cocky British officer, Captain Brian Fisher. Fisher has problems dealing with the informality of Australian soldiers, but gradually, under the pressure of combat on the Somme, these misunderstandings are cleared up and Fisher and Barnard become firm friends. As Barnard says to his officer friend at the end of the novel, "One thing this awful war is doing—bringing all sorts of opposites together, developing fellow feeling, straightening out tangles."[104] The irrepressible good humour and courage of the ordinary Tommy was also praised by Dawson in his *Somme Battle Stories*. In these sketches, almost equal attention was lavished on other ranks as on officers. Dawson relates how, on returning home on a hospital ship, a group of "bronzed, weather-worn" men of the New Armies caught his attention. "Mostly bandaged for more than one wound, they were full of laughter and good cheer. 'I almost feel sorry for the Boche,' said one. 'Not me mate,' replied his comrade, 'Seen too much of the blighter. If you'd seen the way he killed my officer, you wouldn't waste no bloomin' sorrow on him. . . . A Boche is no good till he's dead, I say.'"[105] Dawson does not completely ignore convention for it transpires that this particular soldier's dislike of the Boche stems from the cowardly killing of an admirable young British officer. But while there was some attempt to give working-class warriors a more prominent role, the officer hero continued to be the most important character in adventure fiction.

Initially the Western Front, then, despite its dangers and discomforts was, for authors of juvenile fiction, a site of adventure and heroic endeavour that offered unrivalled opportunities for exciting escapades and plucky deeds performed by young men of the public school elite. Casualties were played down—while minor characters could be killed in action or were often wounded, they were rarely crippled or disfigured and they rarely suffered from gangrenous wounds or shell shock. To that extent, these fictions sanitised the experience of war. The terrifyingly destructive power of modern weaponry was at first almost ignored; even the effects of poison gas, perhaps the most appalling weapon developed during the war, were marginalised or, it was suggested, could be overcome simply by pluck and daring. Whatever was thrown at them, the young Britons of adventure fiction never lost their commitment to fight on to victory; they remained jolly and ever eager to get to grips with the Hun. Allied offensives, particularly those at Loos or on the Somme, were portrayed as, at worst, qualified successes, and if they did not quite achieve all the objectives set by Sir John French or Sir Douglas Haig, they were at least moral victories which crushed the enemy's fighting spirit. But as the war dragged on, as the casualty lists grew, and as noncombatants at home gained some understanding of the nature of modern warfare, it became increasingly difficult to preserve romantic fantasies that trench fighting was exciting or glamorous. The introduction of conscription in 1916 made recruiting propaganda, with its exemplary upper-class heroes, virtually unnecessary, yet the war story was so deeply embedded in popular culture that it remained popular and appealed to a wide readership. At the same time, the public was becoming increasingly aware that this was a war in which men of all classes, and not just social elites, were making the supreme sacrifice. This more realistic view of the war was brought home to the public more through the visual image than through any other cultural form, and particularly through the widely seen official film *The Battle of the Somme*.

Films of the Western Front, including newsreel, had been available in cinemas from 1915 onwards. But, as Nicholas Reeves reminds us, even in April 1916, the *Manchester Guardian* was arguing that these films offered so little access to life at the Front that they might as well have been shot at home.[106] However, later that year, the government released its film record of the recent battle in Picardy, *The Battle of the Somme*, a film which presented contemporary audiences with their "first authentic images of the horror of modern war."[107] Audiences were confronted by Tommies, marching stoically into battle, going "over the top" and stumbling, shocked, exhausted, sometimes wounded, back to the reserve trenches. The film served to strengthen the public's resolve, but it also revealed something of the suffering and trauma of the war[108] and that it was the ordinary Tommy who was bearing the brunt of the fighting. These images and the growing numbers of casualties made the Western Front difficult to glamorise, and romantic representations of trench warfare became increasingly difficult to sustain. At the same time, there was a growing belief that the war would never end. This was perhaps best expressed by Frank Richards (Charles Hamilton), the prolific creator of the enormously popular school stories about Greyfriars and St. Jim's. In 1914, at the age of 41, Richards volunteered for the military but was rejected on medical grounds. He resumed his writing career, producing intensely patriotic stories for *Gem* and *Magnet*.[109] Yet by 1916, even the patriotic Richards was losing faith. In "The Patriots of St. Jim's," the aristocratic junior, Arthur Augustus D'Arcy, tells his chums in his peculiar lisping manner that the "Wah has been dwaggin' on long enough . . . our gweat statesmen are so busy lookin' aftah their jobs and salawies that they haven't weally time for weflection." "The war is a permanent institution" adds his chum Tom Merry, "Under the new law, we're going to be conscripted when we grow up, and then we shall have to take our turn in the trenches. We've got to keep ourselves fit, or we shan't be allowed to go out and get killed."[110]

By the beginning of 1917, then, forced to accept the failure of the great offensive on the Somme and the difficulty of creating daring acts of individual heroism to romanticise in this new kind of attritional warfare, many authors began to concentrate on the other theatres of war, which seemed to offer more exciting possibilities with which to inspire their young readers. Brereton, for example, focused on the Middle East, producing a series of novels about the campaigns in Mesopotamia and Palestine, as did Herbert Strang. Percy Westerman concentrated on stories of naval warfare or the sideshow campaigns in Africa, and Escott Lynn wrote tales of the war in the air—a form of warfare in which it was believed individual skill and courage were still paramount for success in battle, and one which was still largely waged by young men of the upper classes. These authors did not return to the Western Front until the last year of the war, when they had a more inspiring tale to tell.

CHAPTER 3

The War in the Air

> Nothing is more remarkable than the rapid progress, which has been
> made in the conquest of the air. In October 1897 a daring man succeeded
> in flying about three hundred yards; in October 1915 men frequently
> made flights of hundreds of miles. Twenty years ago the aeroplane was
> unknown; today it is a recognized arm of warfare. No army or navy dare
> enter upon war without its air service.
>
> —Sir Edward Parrott, *The Children's Story of the War*[1]

Although the public, military theorists, and seemingly even most generals had
little understanding of exactly how modern technology would affect land and
sea warfare in this new war, the essential principles of those forms of war had
long been established. But this was not so with war in the third dimension—
aerial warfare. In 1914, the aeroplane had been in existence for barely a decade, and the Royal Flying Corps, the British military air service, untested in
war, had been created only two years earlier. Yet while the heavier-than-air
flying machine was a relative newcomer, it had already become established in
popular culture as an icon of adventure, heroic endeavour, and weapon of war.
Long before the Wright brothers made the first flight in a heavier-than-air
machine in 1903, popular fiction had predicted the coming of the flying machine, its probable effect on world affairs, and its impact upon the future of
warfare. For the Victorians, flight was the final frontier, the ultimate triumph
of human ingenuity and technological aspiration, and some believed that the
conquest of the air would transform human affairs and bring about a new age
of peace and universal understanding. Such a vision was well expressed by the
American poet Edmund Stedman in 1879. Noting that the flying machine

would eliminate national frontiers and geographical boundaries, Stedman
went on to suggest that,

Laws and customs must assimilate when races and languages shall be mingled as never
before. . . . The great peoples of Christendom soon will arrive at a common understanding: the Congress of Nations no longer will be an ideal scheme, but a necessity,
maintaining order among its constituents and exercising supervision over the ruder,
less-civilized portions of the globe. Free trade will become absolute, and everywhere
reciprocal: no power on earth could enforce an import tariff, war between enlightened
nations soon will be unknown.[2]

For poets and prophets, then, the flying machine promised a new age for
humankind—an age of mutual co-operation and unlimited progress. But there
were others who feared that this noble invention would be claimed by the
military and appropriated for destructive purposes. In this context the novels
of the popular French novelist Jules Verne were particularly important.

It was Verne who, perhaps more than anyone else, set the scene for pre-
dictive novels of air travel and adventure. Verne, fascinated by science and
technology, had witnessed the successful flight of the Krebs-Renard airship
in 1884, and it was that which inspired him to write his novel of the conquest
of the air, *The Clipper of the Clouds* (1886), and its much-delayed sequel *Master
of the World* (1904). Robur, the inventor hero of the novels, has discovered the
secret of flight and creates a giant airship, the *Albatross*, which can be used for
rapid communication and for the furtherance of science and discovery. War
does not feature in *The Clipper*, but the destructive potential of the *Albatross*
is implicit throughout the novel. Powered by electricity, the vessel can travel
vast distances without landing, cross natural barriers and frontiers with equal
ease and hover silently above the great cities of the world, which of course
lay defenceless beneath the airship should Robur wish to attack them with
gun or explosive. Yet in 1886 the inventor was benign and his flying machine
an agent of human progress. However, around the turn of the century, Verne's
attitude towards the flying machine, indeed to technology generally, had become far less sanguine. Concerned by increasing international tensions and
the European arms race, he had come to believe that science was in danger
of being subverted by the military, and instead of new inventions becoming
agents of human progress, they would be employed for destructive purposes—
a premonition that would be borne out in 1914. In the sequel to *Clipper of the
Clouds*, Robur has lost his benign qualities and is bent upon making himself
master of the world. His airship, even more powerful than the *Albatross*, ter-
rorises the great nations and destroys an American fleet before itself being
destroyed in a great electrical storm.[3] In these novels, Verne dramatically drew
the attention of his readers to the future military potential of the flying machine and created models which other authors would build upon. Published
in book form and serialised in popular magazines, Verne's stories reached a

huge international audience and inspired many readers with his vision of the future of aviation, including pioneer airmen Alberto Santos-Dumont, Geoffrey de Havilland, and J. W. Dunne, all of whom later claimed that it was the novelist who inspired them to create their own flying machines.[4] But more than any other writer, it was Verne who created the flying machine as a romantic and exciting subject for the adventure story.

Verne's novels provided the inspiration for British authors like George Griffiths, E. Douglas Fawcett, and H. G. Wells, and for a host of less well-remembered writers, who produced novels and stories of aerial adventure for boys.[5] By the beginning of the twentieth century, then, adventure fiction involving the flying machine, and usually involving fantastic aerial vessels modeled on Verne's *Albatross*, were immensely popular; and these stories were given a new immediacy by the first successful aeroplane flight by the Wright brothers in 1903, and the subsequent rapid development of aviation throughout Europe and America. Flying meetings, air races, and cross-country flights became commonplace and an endless source of pleasure and excitement for the public, and particularly for boys and young men. In popular literature, especially in the boys' weeklies, the flying machine became a staple ingredient in adventure fiction. While many of these stories dealt with exploration, treasure hunting, and the discovery of lost civilisations in Africa or South America, others adopted the alarmist tone to be found in some adult novels by linking the flying machine and the great war that many believed was imminent. The success of the German Zeppelin airships after 1908 created a new wave of anxiety in England, for now Germany possessed the means to attack British cities, which even the much-vaunted Royal Navy was powerless to protect. Fuelled by H. G. Wells's popular novel *The War in the Air* (1908), the "Zeppelin Menace" was perceived as a constant threat in British skies in the years before 1914.[6] The serial papers of the Harmsworth Press were particularly fond of tales in which Britain was invaded by German, French, Russian, even Japanese armies, spearheaded by a fleet of airships and aeroplanes bent upon destroying British defences.[7] Such fictions helped to persuade readers that a future war was inevitable and that the flying machine would play a significant part in that war. The ideas mooted in popular fiction were constantly reinforced by the persuasive claims of press barons, scientists, and military commentators like Alfred Harmsworth, proprietor of the *Daily Mail*, the aeronautical engineer F. W. Lanchester, and Lieutenant J. W. Dunne, the first army officer to learn to fly and an untiring advocate for a military air service.[8] They fuelled the public's apprehension about attack from the air.

Aviation developed rapidly, particularly after 1908, when successful airships and aeroplanes were developed in France and Germany, including Count von Zeppelin's giant airships. In 1909, for example, the French pilot Louis Bleriot succeeded in crossing the English Channel in an aeroplane of his own design, and by the summer of 1914 the air speed record stood at 126 mph. Aeroplanes had reached heights in excess of 20,000 feet and could remain airborne for many hours.[9] Once the flying machine had become a practical proposition, European armies began to experiment with both airships and aeroplanes, while concerned individuals in Britain began to demand that the government take steps to create a military air service and seriously consider the problem of defending British skies. Considerable pressure was brought to bear on the authorities by Alfred Harmsworth, the air-minded proprietor of the *Daily Mail;* by the Aerial League of the British Empire, a pressure group formed to persuade the government to create a military air service; and by the authors of popular fiction, who used their imaginative stories to alert the public to the danger of ignoring the air weapon.[10]

Equally there was a groundswell of enthusiasm for aviation within the army itself. Many officers, particularly the young and adventurous, had come to believe that the aeroplane would play a significant part in future warfare. In 1911 the Balloon Section of the Royal Engineers, which had existed since the late nineteenth century, was re-organised and renamed the Air Battalion. In addition to its captive balloons and small airships, it also acquired several aeroplanes for "experimental" purposes. But the pressure groups and even some within the military considered this to be an inadequate response considering the military potential of the air weapon. In late 1911, during the Italo-Turkish War in North Africa, the Italian army successfully employed a small air detachment of both aeroplanes and airships against the Turks. These machines proved useful for both reconnaissance and the photographic mapping of the region. Italian pilots even carried out offensive operations against the enemy—dropping small bombs which caused little physical damage but had a terrifying effect when dropped on Turkish troops or their Arab levies.[11] Faced with such evidence of the potential of the air weapon and under increasing public pressure, the British government set up an inquiry into air matters and, in February 1912, the committee recommended that a Flying Corps should be created. It would consist of two wings, one to serve the needs of the military, the other for the Royal Navy (which soon became the Royal Naval Air Service), with a central flying school to train personnel. The Royal Flying Corps came into existence in April 1912 with a total strength of 20 aeroplanes, although it was intended that the RFC should eventually have seven squadrons—about 100 machines.[12]

The invention of the aeroplane had created a revolutionary method of rapid communication and added a new and potentially devastating weapon to the arsenals of the nations, but it also resulted in a new heroic icon—the airman! The aeroplane was exciting, modern, and romantic—the agent through which humankind could master the skyways. But in the early days flying was a hazardous business and required skill and a great deal of courage from those who attempted to master the art of aerial navigation. Thus, Louis Bleriot, Claude Grahame-White, Glenn Curtiss, and even those most unprepossessing figures Wilbur and Orville Wright, were elevated to heroic status, the ultimate explorers of the modern age. A 1911 illustration from *The Sphere* perfectly encapsulated the public attitude to these new heroes: "With the Death or Glory Boys" reads the caption for George Scott's painting of a daring aviator as he strives to set yet another record. At his shoulder rides Death—a constant reminder of the dangers of flying.[13] Airmen quickly became national heroes, celebrities who were hailed in the streets and feted in restaurants, and who attracted enormous crowds to their flying exhibitions and races. By 1910, the popular serial paper *Boys' Realm* claimed that Britain was becoming "air mad" and that "John Bull was awakening to the challenge of the air."[14] Issue 422 of the paper was dedicated as a special Aviation Issue and came with a free model glider for every reader. The paper also began a series of articles, "Heroes of the Air," which valorised the air pioneers. By 1914, then, the airman had joined the pantheon of contemporary heroes. Attracted by the sheer excitement of flying as much as by the military potential of the aeroplane, many young army officers learned to fly at their own expense and transferred to the Royal Flying Corps when it was created, believing that when war came, the air would offer the most exciting arena of combat. In popular fiction, flying machines bombed cities and terrified the inhabitants into submission, fought great battles in the sky and destroyed the most powerful navies in the world; but in reality, when the British Expeditionary Force went to war in August 1914, accompanied by its small air detachment, there was little understanding about what exactly the airmen were expected to do, beyond providing reconnaissance for the army as a new and untried form of cavalry.

GHQ in France saw the primary role of the RFC as information gathering, to act as the "eyes of the army." However, in the "Air Section" of the War Office's *Field Service Regulations* (1914), published just before the war, aircraft had been assigned a far more aggressive role, and particularly offensive action to prevent enemy scouting. To this end, it explained that "aircraft are usually provided with some form of armament for the attack of hostile aircraft in the air." It was clearly understood that the most effective way of dealing with enemy aircraft was to "attack them with armed aeroplanes."[15] Thus pilots were to expect some form of aerial combat. On air-to-ground attack, the *FSR* noted "aircraft are also capable of offensive action against troops on the ground by means of machine guns and bombs," while machines "equipped with explosives or incendiary bombs may accomplish the destruction of magazines, oil tanks, concealed guns, etc."[16] The RFC *Training Manual* added that bombing attacks against enemy troops at night would be particularly demoralising.[17] Clearly then, fighting in the air, bombing military targets and enemy troops were to be considered legitimate activity for the Flying Corps. However, the problem was that while the theory of air warfare was largely in place, the technology to achieve such goals had yet to be developed. Thus when the four squadrons of the RFC flew to France with the BEF, pilots had little more than their service revolvers, assorted rifles, and several antiquated machine guns with which to carry out offensive operations. GHQ in France expected little from the Corps beyond reconnaissance and supplying information to the BEF, and even the information gathered by pilots was often dismissed. During the opening moves of the war, before the trench deadlock set in, the RFC did perform valuable scouting operations at Mons and on the Marne, but many fliers, frustrated by their passive role, were also developing ways to hit out at the enemy. At first this was limited to pilots dropping a few small, hastily improvised bombs on enemy positions or taking pot shots at enemy aircraft with their revolvers or rifles, but RFC aircraft were slow and unwieldy, adequate for slow reconnaissance patrols, but unsuited for manoevering for combat against other aircraft. Consequently, few enemy machines were brought down. Lieutenant Louis Strange of 5 Squadron later recalled fixing a Lewis gun onto his Avro and attacking enemy troops and trains.[18] Later his squadron took to carrying a supply of small Hales bombs or improvised petrol bombs and dropping them on targets of opportunity, such as enemy troops or supply columns. But in the sweeping movements of mass armies during the opening phase of the war, the doings of the RFC attracted little public attention. One of the few authors who did note the presence of the RFC in France was V. Wheeler-Holohan, but in an article in the *Boy's Own Paper*, he felt it necessary to point out that, "the aeroplane plays a small part in actual fighting. The day of the bomb dropping machine which devastates cities and annihilates fleets . . . has yet to come."[19]

During the first months of war, the contribution the RFC was making in France was largely ignored by the Press Bureau at the War Office, for there were few exciting or dramatic episodes in the air war that could be exploited. Routine reconnaissance or artillery observation was important, and sometimes deadly for the airmen that flew such missions, but was hardly the stuff of adventure. All attention was firmly focused on the army and the dramatic events at Mons, on the Marne, and at the first Battle of Ypres. The only novel to refer to military aviation, and then only tangentially, during the opening phase of the war was, as we have seen, Herbert Strang's *A Hero of Liege*, published in late 1914. Considering that the Germans had taken the last Belgian fortress at Liege on 7 August, Strang and his publisher must have worked remarkably fast to have the book on sale before the end of the year. The novel is more a tribute to the Belgian army's gallant stand at Liege than a story about the war in the air, but one of the heroes, Remi Pariset, is a Belgian airman. Pariset and the young Englishman, Kenneth Amory, help delay the German advance and render assistance to the hard-pressed defenders of the fortress at Liege. Using Remi's aeroplane, they finally escape the invaders, and Amory heads home to England intending to join the RFC.

Many of the leading authors of juvenile fiction had written air adventures before 1914, but these had dealt in exotic adventure and fantastic machines. Compared to these exciting prewar fictions, the realities of the war in the air in 1914 and 1915—scouting, the occasional pot shot at enemy machines, and so on—were dull. Consequently, in order to produce enthralling propaganda stories, writers reverted to the sort of flying adventures they had produced

"Fighting in the Air," *Young England*, 1915.

before 1914, complete with amazing flying machines, superweapons and extraordinary pilots. In Guy Thorne's *The Secret Sea-Plane*, published in early 1915, for example, not only does the Royal Naval Air Service develop a giant flying boat which can operate in all weathers, it also develops the "Vortex Gun"—a superweapon that fires powerful blasts of compressed air. The gun proves highly effective against enemy aircraft when mounted on the new seaplane. Yet despite its potential, the new craft is only used for home defence, and even when finally sent to attack a Zeppelin base, it simply transports a raiding party who land and then destroy the enemy airships with explosives.[20] Clearly, the author had little understanding of how the air weapon might be used in warfare. Nevertheless, it is a fearsome invention and one that, in fiction, quickly establishes British supremacy in the air. A Claude Grahame-White and Harry Harper novel, *The Invisible War Plane*, imagined a machine covered with a paint-like substance which neither "reflects, deflects or absorbs light, and is at almost all angles of vision . . . quite unseen by the human eye."[21] To complement this "invisible" aircraft, there is a new bombsight which ensures almost total accuracy. Used by the RNAS, the machine sinks submarines, destroys enemy aeroplanes, and is generally unbeatable. Interestingly, Grahame-White, Britain's most celebrated air hero before the war, had joined the RNAS in 1914 and had taken part in the raid on the Cuxhaven Zeppelin base in December, yet his novel lacks virtually any degree of realism.

Even as late as 1916, fantastic machines were still appearing in popular fiction, most notably Percy Westerman's *The Secret Battleplane* and *The Red Kite* by W. A. Henry. *The Secret Battleplane* (1916) is a curious mix of fantasy, adventure, and criticism of the conduct of the war, a quality rare in juvenile fiction at this time. But again we have the invention of a revolutionary flying machine. The novel is set in 1915, at the time when the new German Fokker monoplanes with synchronised machine guns had come to dominate the skies over the Western Front (see discussion that follows). In the novel, the inventor Desmond Blake has perfected a giant battleplane—the answer to the German Fokkers that have "outclassed" RFC machines. Blake offers his machine to the War Office but, as he later explains to his young assistants,

[T]he authorities . . . [were] decidedly frigid. They were awfully polite, but somehow they failed to come to any practical decision. Wanted a scale model, as if it would serve the same purpose as the actual machine I proposed to submit. I offered to have a battleplane complete, including engines, for inspection and test within fifteen days, but I was informed that this was unnecessary until the plans had been inspected by a sub-committee. Altogether half a dozen sub-committees tried their hands with my plans. . . . Afterwards I discovered that hardly a single member knew anything about practical flying.[22]

Despite its obvious advantages, the War Office are reluctant to take the machine because of its unusual design—it has flapping wings which provide for vertical takeoff and landing and exceptional speed and range. Faced with this conservatism and excessive bureaucracy, the inventor decides to wage his own personal war against the Huns. The prototype goes into action, destroying Zeppelins and aeroplanes, and is even used to bomb Berlin. Before the wonder machine is destroyed, it has aided ground forces to advance on the Western Front, sunk German shipping, and, most usefully, enabled the inventor to convince the War Office to mass-produce the battleplane which will soon bring about Germany's defeat. *The Secret Battleplane* was one of the few novels for young readers published during the war to criticise the military authorities for negligence in air matters.

The "Red Kite" is of a more conventional design, a powerful monoplane, but possessed of great range and speed and several innovative weapons. Flown by its inventor, who bears a personal grudge against the Germans, it destroys Zeppelins with its steel beak and chews up enemy aircraft with its metal propeller. The pilot even conducts a vendetta against the German High Command, bombing their headquarters whenever and wherever they can be located. With its vertical takeoff facility and its ability to hover over its target, the Kite is a highly advanced and dangerous weapon. Before it finally disappears "somewhere over Germany," the machine has struck terror into the heart of the Fatherland.[23] It might be assumed that these stories of brilliant inventors and their fantastical machines were simply exciting fiction which enthralled readers but which ultimately betrayed the ignorance of some authors about aviation matters; but they did serve an important propaganda purpose. In 1915 and 1916 the public, already demoralised by the stalemate of the trenches, were now faced with Zeppelin raids on their cities and the failure of the RFC to deal with the new armed German monoplanes on the Western Front.[24] Thus when things were going badly for the Allies in the air, authors of propagandist adventure stories invented these fantastic war machines, all-powerful superweapons that would, in fiction at least, turn the tide, restore British air supremacy, and perhaps boost the confidence of readers in Britain's military air service. But for most Britons it was the German airship raids (usually referred to by the public as "Zeppelins" regardless of which company built them) on Britain in 1915 that more than any other event, dramatically brought the war in the air to their attention.

Both the German army and navy operated airships, and by late 1914 both services were keen to attack the British homeland. They argued that such attacks, particularly if directed at London, would "demoralise the enemy's determination to prosecute the war." The Kaiser, however, was reluctant to sanction the destruction of British cities; when he did eventually agree, he still prohibited attacks on London. Thus the first air raids were carried out in early 1915 against coastal towns. However, the services finally persuaded the Kaiser that attacking the capital would have a far greater effect, and the first raid on London took place on 31 May 1915.[25] Zeppelin attacks continued until 1917, but the airship was a haphazard weapon at best and unsuited to the stress of war: dependent upon good weather conditions and extremely vulnerable to incendiary ammunition. Yet, the Zeppelin's enormous size, its ability to hover silently over its target, and the lack of any real system of air defence over Britain meant that such attacks had tremendous impact on the British people. For the first time in the modern age, British towns and villages were liable to direct attack from the enemy. The raids caused relatively little material damage or loss of life but spread considerable alarm and an almost hysterical demand for retaliation. As Henry Newbolt suggested, "it is in the main frightfulness rather than destruction which they [the Germans] have demanded from their Zeppelins."[26] Thus when Sub-lieutenant R. Warneford of the RNAS succeeded in destroying a Zeppelin near Ghent on 6 June 1915, he was awarded the Victoria Cross and his achievement was hailed as a triumph of British skill and heroism in popular histories and serial papers.[27] For propagandists, the bombing of England clearly revealed the utter ruthlessness of the Hun, and they exploited it unmercifully. After describing the first air raid on Yarmouth, Sir Edward Parrott noted:

People stood aghast at this new form of German "frightfulness." It was directed, not against fortresses or places of military importance, but against peaceful civilians in open, unprotected towns. It was sheer murder, and was intended to terrorise the British people and bring them to their knees.[28]

Newbolt even went so far as to cite the German press which, he claimed, demanded that "more women and children must be killed in order to subdue Britain."[29]

Before 1914, the British attitude towards the aerial bombardment of enemy cities was unambiguous. The commander of the RFC, Sir David Henderson, stated the official position when he suggested that such attacks were "uncivilised"; that "no nation would risk the odium that such attacks would bring."[30] Such behaviour, it was argued, would be an infringement of the existing "rules of war"—the generally accepted conventions which were intended to make war less barbaric. Yet this gentlemanly attitude was quickly abandoned under the pressure of war. As we have seen, British pilots were attacking German troops from the air during the first few weeks of the conflict, and more formal bombing raids on enemy airship bases and factories had been conducted before the end of the year. But in the aftermath of the Zeppelin raids on Britain, public opinion demanded far more aggressive action. Particularly influential were a number of articles in the press demanding retaliation against German cities. Typical of these was a lead article in the *Daily Express* in June 1915, written by the novelist H. G. Wells. Wells pointed out that the only way to end the war was "to go through the air to the German rear and smash up their munitions factories."

We want aeroplanes going to and coming from Germany like ants about an anthill, like bees between hive and clover, but going each with its two or three hundred pounds of high explosive, and coming back empty, from now until the war ends. A daily service of destruction to Germany.

He went on to argue that aeroplanes were as easy to build as motor cars and that there were many young men eagerly waiting to be trained as aviators. Moreover, the rigid, methodical, obedient German was unsuited to war flying, whereas the individualistic English or French aviator, "hungry for adventure," and with better "bodies, nerves and hearts" would always have the edge. Therefore, he claimed, all that was needed to achieve victory was 10,000 aeroplanes.[31] As we have seen, propaganda denigrated the German soldier as dull and unimaginative, and now the same approach was used to describe German pilots. Yet it should be noted that German airmen like Oswald Boelcke and Max Immelmann virtually pioneered the techniques of aerial combat (see discussion that follows), and that almost every significant technical or tactical innovation in aerial warfare—from synchronised machine guns and parachutes, to purpose-built ground attack aircraft, was developed by the German air service.[32]

By late 1915, with the British air service facing public criticism for its failure to protect the homeland and achieve air superiority over the Western Front, propagandists went onto the offensive. Parrott was anxious to assure his readers that it was not only the Germans who were waging aggressive war in the air, and he went on to detail the bombing raids made by British airmen on "fortified" places in Germany—the Zeppelin base at Cuxhaven, the German seaplane base at Zeebrugge, and on military targets behind the front lines during the battle of Neuve Chapelle.[33] The use of the word "fortified," of course, highlighted the difference between British airmen and their German counterparts. German airmen, "baby killers," bombed indiscriminately, killing innocent noncombatants, while the British attacked only legitimate military targets. Bombing, then, became an important propaganda theme in many of the novels of the air war.

Despite the fact that both sides began bombing attacks at about the same time, when the Germans attacked British cities their behaviour was considered "uncivilized," "Hunnish," and "barbaric." Consequently German airmen became prime targets for the propagandists. The destruction of at least one Zeppelin became almost mandatory for the hero of any self-respecting novel of air warfare, and German airshipmen were heaped with abuse. A chapter describing an RFC raid on a Zeppelin base in Roland Walker's *Dastral of the Flying Corps* is entitled "Strafing the Baby-Killers." In another chapter, the eponymous hero witnesses a Zeppelin attack while on leave in London. Incensed by such barbarity, he rushes to the nearest airfield, borrows a spare aeroplane, and takes off after the airship. A trail of "wanton destruction" leads him to the raider.

A number of bombs had already been dropped, and away to the northward several fires could be seen where the night raiders had left their victims behind, in the shape of burning homesteads, where the victims were women and children, old men and invalids.[34]

Needless to say, Dastral finds and destroys the Zeppelin. But later in the novel, the author describes an RFC bombing raid on the main Krupps factory outside Essen, and this provides an opportunity to contrast British and German bombing policy. While the Germans use bombing as an indiscriminate weapon to terrorise the innocent, the British are concerned only to hit military targets. On their way to the Krupps factory, Dastral's squadron pass over the city of Cologne. His observer spots the town hall and exclaims "What a target!" To which the pilot replies, "Yes, but there are women and children down there, Jock, and I am not a pirate." At Krupps, the squadron even endangers itself by flying at minimum height in order to ensure that all their bombs hit the target and not the homes of innocent civilians.[35] Percy Westerman seems to have been the only author untroubled by moral considerations when it came to bombing the enemy. In *The Secret Battleplane*, Blake the inventor decides to attack Berlin. The British authorities, he claims, have wanted to do this for some time but have been held back by fear of reprisals. "Sickly sentimentality," he scoffs; "the Germans were the first to use poison gas, the first to torpedo merchant ships and gloat over the Zeppelin raids on British towns." Now, he explains, it is time to employ "Mosiac Law," "An eye for an eye; a tooth for a tooth. By Jove! Three British shells for every German one, and a ton of high explosive for every kilogramme of T.N.T."[36] Blake then takes matters into his own hands and attacks the German capital.

The bombing of their cities, however, profoundly shocked the British people, and many believed that the government had failed to create an air service of sufficient strength to protect them against such raids. In response to these attacks, Parrott and other propagandists felt it necessary to demonstrate that during the years before 1914 the British government had been at pains to ensure that the nation had indeed been well prepared to wage war in the air.

We British were the last of the great European nations to apply themselves to the air, but by the outbreak of war we were well equipped. The British Royal Flying Corps consisted of a military wing and a naval wing. Each wing was divided into squadrons, consisting of twenty-four aeroplanes. . . . Our airmen, if they were not so skilful as the French, were competent and very daring.[37]

Herbert Strang, in his 1916 explanation of the war for children, completely ignores the moral dilemma over bombing but is at pains to show how well Britain was prepared for war in the air. Exaggerating the actual figures, he informed his readers that in 1914 the government had arranged that "eight [squadrons] should accompany the Expeditionary army, thus making a total of ninety-six aeroplanes in active service."[38]

Strang was clearly following the propagandist line here, for in his prewar novels like *The Air Scout* and *The Air Patrol*, published shortly before the war, he had taken the government to task for their tardiness in creating and equipping a military air service and for ignoring the danger of attack from the air.[39] In reality, when the RFC was ordered to France with the British Expeditionary Force in August 1914, it could muster just four understrength squadrons and less than 100 flying officers. The situation was so desperate that even privately owned aircraft were conscripted for military use. It was a source of constant amusement for the infantry that one RFC machine flew reconnaissance missions over the Front throughout early August bearing on its fuselage the legend, *The Daily Mail*.[40] In their fictions, however, authors supported the notion that the authorities were well prepared for war in the air. Rowland Walker's 1917 novel, *Dastral of the Flying Corps*, was typical, telling readers that when England realised that war was inevitable,

many great men were beginning to say that the side which gained the mastery of the air, would also gain the mastery of Europe and the world. In no country was this recognised more than in England, and at early dawn even remote villages were often stirred, and the inhabitants thrilled by the advent of the whirring 'planes and air-scouts, whose daring pilots were preparing to wrest the mastery of the air from the enemy.[41]

Yet, as we have seen, the government only created the RFC after a long campaign by pressure groups and only after the viability of aircraft in war had been demonstrated by the Italians in North Africa. Even then, little was really done to prepare the Flying Corps for war: it was seriously understrength, its equipment was generally poor, and little thought had been given to how it might carry out offensive operations. Most curiously, however, considering that the army saw the main role of the aeroplane as reconnaissance, there was no training whatever for observers until 1916. Until observer training was introduced, any spare pilot or mechanic was delegated for the job. But the fiction that in 1914 Britain had been well prepared for war in the air was even maintained by the official history of the war published in 1922, although in private its author, Sir Walter Raleigh, was prepared to admit to a friend that "before the war we were far behind other nations in air work."[42] But perhaps the most serious weakness in the air service was in flying training.

In propagandist fiction, learning to fly was always remarkably easy, and the British, as Wells had pointed out, were "racially" suited to war in the air. The common belief was that anyone with "sensitive hands" and a "good seat" could fly an aeroplane. The fallacy that flying was akin to riding—a requisite for all British officers—had orginated in the early days of flying, but even as late as 1917, Brigadier General Sefton Brancker, Deputy Director General of Military Aeronautics, explained that

There are few Englishmen who won't make good pilots as long as they have sufficient experience. Flying is perhaps a little easier than riding a horse because you sit in a comfortable armchair instead of a slippery saddle on a lively horse.[43]

However, as Denis Winter has shown, of 14,166 British pilots killed during the war, no less than 8,000 had been killed in training accidents.[44] But even if a pilot survived his training and actually reached an operational squadron in France, his life expectancy was remarkably short due to a training pro-gramme that had taught him little more than how to take off, fly straight and level and little else. Such basic skills were, of course, a pre-requisite for re-connaissance and artillery spotting, but totally inadequate when complex ma-noeuvres were required to avoid anti-aircraft fire or escape from a more experienced German pilot. Lieutenant (later Air-Vice Marshall) S. F. Vincent was sent to France in May 1916 and later recalled that he had never flown a single-seater or performed a "turn over 45 degrees of bank, never fired a gun in the air nor had any lecture or instruction in air fighting."[45] Compared with the rigorous training programme of the German and French air services, British pilots were ill-served by the authorities. Yet in R. Wherry Anderson's *The Romance of Air-Fighting*, the author, an official of the Royal Aero Club, could inform his readers, "how simple is the task of mere flying."[46] And such beliefs easily transferred into fiction. For example, in Brereton's novel *Under French's Command*, a young officer, anxious to transfer to flying duties, is ac-tually taught to fly by his pilot uncle at a military aerodrome in France and is flying on active service within days.[47]

Positive propaganda, however, could not hide the fact that through the early part of 1915 the RFC was suffering heavy casualties, and by the end of the year the realisation that war flying was actually an extremely dangerous un-dertaking was beginning to take root. Thus recruitment began to suffer. A consequence of this was that some writers of juvenile fiction began to produce more direct recruiting propaganda for the Flying Corps. As we have seen, most authors voluntarily assumed the role of recruiting agents for the military. Initially, however, for the glamorous and exciting air service this had been unnecessary; indeed the Corps had been oversubscribed with eager volun-teers. Concerned to get the right sort of young men, the RFC had become highly selective about who it commissioned, and many young men who lacked the "right background" had been rejected. The romantic fictions of air war, of course, acted as covert recruiting propaganda—suggesting to young men that here was the most romantic and exciting branch of the military. But from 1915, such propaganda became more obvious. With increasing casualty rates, the Corps became desperately short of pilots. Despite the chirpy accounts of war flying that permeated the popular press, it seems likely that young men had begun to realise that fighting in the air was just as dangerous, just as brutal as the fighting in the trenches. Faced with this impending crisis in recruit-ment, some authors assumed a more direct role for recruitment. The popular writer Captain Frank Shaw provides us with an interesting example. In late 1915, Shaw, then serving in the balloon section of the RFC, was chosen by the War Office as a recruiter on the basis of his reputation as an author of boys' fiction. Shaw used his contacts within the publishing world to sell his message, and *Chums* and the other story papers that had published his prewar tales of adventure now printed his recruiting letters for the Corps. Shaw adopted an interesting line that exploited the elitist reputation of the RFC and the sporting instincts of his readers. After pointing out how badly young men were needed and how the Huns ("girl and women killers," as he called them) had to be stopped, he went on to explain that the army's most exciting branch not only offered, ". . . honour and glory in this big game," but also that the pay is "the best to be got." He ended with, "Come on lads, be proper sportsmen, now," and invited them to see him in the Polo Pavilion at Roehampton Golf Club, or whatever venue where he was to attend.[48]

Recruiting propaganda for the RFC/RAF (the RFC was renamed the Royal Air Force on 1 April 1918) in the boys' serial papers became common for the remainder of the war years. Even in the last few months of the war, *Chums* was still running such material, and still focusing on the romance of aviation.

There is a wonderful magnetic attraction about the life of an air pilot. In his machine he sees sights that no one who has never left terra firma can even imagine. Ten or even twenty thousand feet up, with the clouds like a billowy sea stretching above, below, and around him, he watches the glories of sunrise, and the fierce wonder of the storm. Through gaps in the mist he sees wonderful visions of the earth beneath.[49]

"The RAF," the article continued, will attract "the best types of modern British youth, and for those who are fit, keen and real sportsmen, the service offers unparalleled opportunities for promotion, honours and distinction." However, during 1916, such recruitment had been helped along by the development of fighting in the air and the emergence of the "aces"—successful pilots who had shot down several enemy machines.

Reconnaissance, spotting for the artillery, and bombing would remain important functions for the RFC throughout the war, and fighting in the air developed to ensure that these activities could be conducted without interference from the enemy. It was these aerial duels, often between well-known and successful air fighters, to gain "command of the air," that captured the imagination of the young and became an enduring icon in the popular culture of the war.[50] As we have seen, even in August 1914, pilots on both sides were trying to destroy their opponents in order to deny them the opportunity to locate the position and strength of their own ground forces. Arming aircraft with light machine guns became commonplace, but these were usually mounted in the observer's cockpit and had a limited arc of fire. The illustration on page 57 appeared in a late 1915 issue of the serial paper *Young England*, a visual explanation of the fighting functions of aircraft for its readers. In the early years, aerial fighting was a haphazard activity, and air combat did not really progress until the development of faster, more manoeuvrable aircraft and the invention of the synchronised machine gun. This was mounted in front of the pilot and timed to fire through the propeller; in effect synchronisation turned the aeroplane into a flying gun which the pilot simply aimed at his opponent. Anthony Fokker, a Dutch designer and manufacturer supplying the German army, apparently made the real breakthrough in armed aircraft in early 1915.[51] By August, the synchronised machine guns, mounted on Fokker E monoplanes, and flown by German pilots like Max Immelmann and Oswald Boelcke, began to have a devastating effect on Allied pilots, and this led the German government to develop and exploit the ace system—a propaganda ploy to inspire the nation through the exploits of the "young eagles of the Reich," fliers who excelled in aerial combat.

In his novel *With the Allies to the Rhine*, Captain Brereton explained how the system had developed, deliberately ignoring the contribution of the German air service.

The daring, the dash, the indomitable fighting of the British and French and Belgian aeroplanists had taught the Germans a considerable lesson. Man for man, as a general rule, they were not to be compared with the British flyers, and with few exceptions, did not excel. In the case of the French, however, the war rapidly brought to the fore men known as "aces," who excelled beyond their brothers—and that meant much, for the daring and elan of our Gallic friends in the air was something to wonder at. These "aces" were known throughout France and the Allied armies because of the number of their victories, and the numbers marked down to each approximated in many cases almost a hundred.[52]

Despite Brereton's hundreds, in the French and German air services, a pilot became an ace when he had shot down five enemy aircraft, but sooner or later all the combatant nations succumbed to celebrating this elite group of air fighters. More importantly, and again ignored by Brereton, was Boelcke's decision in mid-1915 to organise fast, armed aircraft into aggressive hunting groups to drive the Allies from the skies. By early the following year the Germans had gained the mastery of the air over the Western Front. The RFC, awaiting deliveries of new fighting planes, fought back but were unable to regain command of the air until later in the year.[53] Thereafter, air supremacy over the Western Front depended upon the ebb and flow of technological developments and the output of aero manufacturers. However, for the public, mastery of the skies was reduced to the heroism of the young airmen who fought their lonely "sporting" duels in the sky, and it was this element of the war in the air which offered the most fertile ground for stirring propaganda.

In popular accounts of the war, aerial combat quickly became characterised as a sporting activity for gentlemen. The Flying Corps had always seen itself as an elite and had shown considerable care in selecting its pilots. Senior commanders, like David Henderson and Hugh Trenchard, believed that only public school/university men made good pilots; horsemen and sporting blues were thought to be particularly worthy. A few noncommissioned officers were trained as pilots in the early years, but the experiment was "not favourably reported on, and the opinion [was] often expressed that men chosen from the . . . ranks . . . do not make good pilots."[54] It was not until later in the war that the number of noncommissioned pilots was increased, with no noticeable decrease of skill.[55] Particularly one thinks of James McCudden, who enlisted as a mechanic before winning his wings and a commission and who went on to become the most successful combat pilot in the RFC.[56] But as John Morrow has pointed out, the RFC was essentially a "corps of commissioned officers . . . recruited as much as possible from the ranks of public school sportsmen and drawn to war flying for the adventure."[57] Thus, in 1921, when Walter Briscoe published his biography of the British ace Albert Ball, he called it *Boy Hero of the Air: From Schoolboy to VC*, and described it as "a school story, an adventure tale, and an air story all rolled into one."[58] In popular culture, then, and especially in adventure fiction, it became fashionable to sanitise the brutality of the war in the air by representing it as simply just another exhilarating sporting adventure for ex–public school boys, and by late 1916, air fighting/sport metaphor had become commonplace in popular propaganda.

In R. Wherry Anderson's account of air warfare, commissioned by Wellington House, for example, the author explained that fighting the Prussians in the air was one of the "noblest enterprises permitted to youth."[59] He went on to suggest that lion hunting had hitherto been considered the finest sport in the world, but "the finest sport today is to ascend to the upper atmosphere and assist there in the supreme task of defeating the world's tyrants." Anderson's influential text on the glamorous nature of fighting in the air was intended for young Americans, but it was also readily available in Britain and drew upon many ideas already in circulation. For example, the official booklet *Fighting in the Air* by Major L. W. Rees, issued to trainee pilots of the RFC in 1916, had claimed that "the British pilot always likes the idea of fighting" and "fights for the sport of the affair if for no other reason."[60] But many pilots themselves subscribed to such views. Cecil Lewis later wrote of his time in France, "it was a marvelous life, a sport, a game."[61] Amyas Borton, an RFC pilot serving in the Middle East, wrote to his father in late 1918 bemoaning the approaching end of hostilities, "I am daily expecting the BAD NEWS OF THE TURK DECIDING TO PUT UP HIS HANDS AND END THE BEST WAR I AM EVER LIKELY TO GET MIXED UP IN!!"[62]

Classic air fighting, the one-to-one aerial duels that would became such a common image in the air novels and pulps of the interwar years, only began to appear in popular fiction towards the end of 1917; but even then, authors were just as likely to have their RFC heroes doubling as spies behind enemy lines as in the cockpit. In Escott Lynn's *Knights of the Air*, for example, the hero, a gifted pilot, spends much of his time attempting to discover the date and location of the coming German offensive. This involves night landings behind enemy lines, breaking into German headquarters, and kidnapping enemy officers. It almost appeared as if most authors did not believe that stories of the aerial exploits of the RFC alone would sustain the interest of their readers. An interesting example here was Rowland Walker, who still placed his pilot heroes in the most unlikely situations, but appeared to have a better understanding of the air war than his contemporaries. Walker claimed to have served in the RFC on the Western Front, and indeed he did seem to have a greater familiarity with the machines and tactics being used in France and to understand the technicalities of flying better than most authors at the time. In between their extravagant adventures behind enemy lines, his fictional heroes still manage to carry out many of the more routine duties of an airman—spotting for the artillery, reconnaissance patrols, and so on. And it is in Walker's novels that we first see the romance of the aerial duels that provided the substance for so many later novels.

In his *Dastral of the Flying Corps*, the climax of the novel is the battle between the RFC hero and the German ace, "the arch-fiend of the air," Himmelman (see later discussion). In a later novel, while his hero Deville McKeene, an ace pilot in the RFC, doubles as a secret agent, even gaining access to von Richthofen's aerodrome, the climax of the novel is the aerial dogfights over the Front. In one scene a British squadron, the "Eagles of d'Aubigny" including McKeene, clash with a German squadron led by Richthofen. In the heat of battle, with machines falling all around, the two aces seek each other. Richthofen spots McKeene's machine high above and climbs towards it. The Englishman, with the advantage of height, spurns his advantage "with all the chivalry of the olden days" and waits until his enemy has reached the same height. Then at 18,000 feet above the trenches the "two great stars of the Western Front" meet and, the author tells us, "Never since Immelmann went down before an English youth of eighteen years had the . . . Front witnessed such a fight." As they climb, dive, and wheel through the sky it seems they are equally matched. Then Richthofen makes a fatal error. Going into a spin to avoid the Englishman's guns, he leaves his recovery too late and as he levels out he discovers McKeene has followed him down and is now on his tail. McKeene's gun rakes the German's cockpit. The "gallant" Richthofen, dead in his aircraft, crashes on the British side of the lines. The British, honouring a brave foe, bury Richthofen with full military honours and McKeene, although wounded, is in attendance, "for that is the English way."[63]

The development of air fighting and the media's recognition and promotion of particularly skilful and successful pilots added a new dimension to the manner in which the air war was represented in popular literature. For those at home, fighting in the air seemed to offer an alternative to the grim squalor of the trenches—the last arena of modern warfare in which the courage and skill of the individual warrior could affect the outcome of battle: a battlefield on which the reader could still find romance, adventure, and some semblance of chivalric behaviour. For the public at large, the lengthening casualty lists and the stream of wounded and disabled men returning from the trenches in France suggested that this was a very different kind of war from any that had gone before. This was confirmed by the failure of the British summer offensive on the Somme in 1916 and the extraordinary film about the battle released by the government. It was becoming increasingly obvious, then, that the war in the trenches had been reduced to a form of industrialised mass killing, in which death came anonymously from machine guns, artillery shells, or poison gas. Combatants rarely saw the men who killed them, and bravery and fighting skill counted for little—life or death was reduced to a simple matter of luck. In contrast, the air war was believed to be markedly different. For the propagandist, young airmen fighting their battles in the clean, clear skies over the Western Front, according to accepted rules of conduct based on the medieval chivalric code, retained some vestige of romance in an otherwise squalid war. Air services formed such a small part of the vast armies engaged in France that airmen still appeared to retain their individuality in a way that was impossible for the infantryman. Air combat seemed to hark back to the days when killing was an art and not techno-industrial murder, as the airmen hunted their prey in the clean air and then closed in for the final duel where chivalry and individual skill made the difference between life and death.

The myth of the chivalry of the air war probably originated in 1916, with Henry Newbolt's influential *Tales of the Great War* when, writing of the war in the air, the author noted,

Our airmen are singularly like the knights of the old romances, they go out day after day, singly or in twos and threes, to hold the field against all comers, and to do battle in defence of those who cannot defend themselves. There is something especially chivalrous about these champions of the air; even the Huns, whose military principles are against chivalry, have shown themselves affected by it.[64]

Newbolt had found yet another hero for his adolescent admiration to add to the captains of the first eleven, and martyred soldiers. But in 1916–1917, at a time when the Somme offensive was grinding to a halt and the British public was becoming increasingly war-weary, the idea of the chivalry of the air struck just the right note, and the notion of airmen as chivalric warriors quickly became commonplace. Anderson, for example, told his young readers that fighting in the air is

[the] revival of the honourable curtesies of the duel—nay, more, the revival of the ancient chivalry of the Knight Templars. As he soars aloft, the airman has at the back of his mind, the idea that he is out to meet a champion belonging to the same knightly order as himself. . . . From their respective hangars Ivanhoe and Sir Brian de Bois-Guilbert sally forth to personal combat.[65]

When Auberon, Lord Lucas was killed fighting in the air, his friend, Maurice Baring, Trenchard's ADC, wrote a poem in his memory which suggested that Lancelot and Tristram had welcomed the fallen hero into their exalted company. "The poem," as Peter Parker has noted, is a positive "repository of chivalric imagery."[66]

In *Our Flying Men* by Mrs. Maurice Hewlett, and written for the Propaganda Bureau at Wellington House, the author noted that British pilots were "just the pick and cream of our manhood. They are heroes, who one can compare with those of Greek, Norse and Roman fame, and their deeds are making history."[67] And this chivalric view of the war in the air was officially sanctioned in October 1917, when the Prime Minister paid his extravagant tribute to the RFC.

The heavens are their battlefield; they are the cavalry of the clouds. High above the squalor and the mud . . . [t]hey fight out the eternal issues of right and wrong. Every flight is a romance, every record is an epic. They are the knighthood of this war. . . . They recall the old legends of chivalry, not merely by daring individually, but by the nobility of their spirit.[68]

These ideas quickly became embedded in popular fiction. Rowland Walker, for example, adopted the idea for *Dastral of the Flying Corps*. Set in 1916, the author explains that the German air service had come to dominate the skies over the Western Front because of the skill of their top scoring pilot, Himmelman. Dastral, the young English hero of the novel, sets out to find and destroy the German ace. After a hard-fought duel, Dastral damages the German's machine and watches him plunge to earth. However,

The next moment the daring young pilot gazed almost ruefully down upon the tangled wreckage far below. He was amazed at his own work, riding up there alone, for he was now the Master-Pilot of the Skies. Even so, somehow, his chivalrous young heart was sad, for a brave man never finds pleasure in the death of another brave man, and your true hero has always a gentle soul.

Then, reaching down into his cockpit, he took up the wreath of laurel he had placed there that morning for just such a contingency; and attached was a card that read:

To Himmelman—bravest of the brave—the Pilot of the Western Skies.
A tribute of respect from his conqueror.
Dastral of the Flying Corps.[69]

Dastral, the incredibly confident and extremely well-prepared hero, throws the wreath onto the wreckage below. But what is important here is that Walker has reduced the war in the air to a simplistic tournament between champions.

Germany dominates the air because of Himmelmann, and when he dies, dominance passes to Britain in the guise of Dastral.

Because of the apparently chivalric nature of the air war, even German pilots could be respected: Boelcke, Immelmann, and Richthofen were heroic figures for many British pilots, and were even praised in the Allied press,[70] but this did not usually apply to most Prussians, apparently. In Walker's later novel, *Deville McKeene: The Mystery Airmen*, there is a sequence in which the hero outwits the German ace Manfred von Richthofen. This provides the author with an opportunity to point out that,

[H]ad the gallant Richthofen been a true Prussian, he would have stormed and fumed. More he would probably have had half a dozen men shot, in the hope that therefore he might have killed the spy. But there is something about the airman, and the azure blue, and the mystic world of the above the clouds, that ennobles his character, and redeems it from the baseness of the common soldier. Perhaps it is his association with the skies. At any rate, so it was with this gallant pilot.[71]

It should be noted that Richthofen was indeed a doyen of Prussianism. But in air warfare, there were superficial echoes reminiscent of knightly combat: pilots were carefully selected—young, fit, educated, mostly upper or middle class—and they alone were the cutting edge of the air arm, the fighting elite. The ground crews could be seen as the squires who prepared their officers for battle; substitute a Sopwith Camel for a war-horse and the analogy is complete; and authors were at pains to establish the fact that airmen were indeed an elite. Walker tells us that in 1914, "The most daring of our English youths left the public schools and universities, and strained every nerve . . . to gain the coveted brevet of a pilot's 'wings' in the Royal Flying Corps."[72] And as in the Middle Ages, there were even champions—the aces—who became popular heroes because of their success in battle. But while the French and Germans might make stirring propaganda from the deeds of their most successful airmen, the British were far more ambiguous about such matters. The official policy of the Royal Flying Corps was not to single out individual heroes, claiming it was invidious and that when a hero "fell" it was bad for morale.[73] Nevertheless, newspapers were quick to single out successful individuals like Albert Ball, Edward Bishop, and James McCudden, and heroes of the air were frequently celebrated in books. Claude Grahame-White and Harry Harper's *Heroes of the Flying Corps* recalled a number of stirring aerial adventures of RFC heroes, while Parrott offered chapters on Lieutenant Rhodes-Moorehouse, Captain Lanoe Hawker, and Captain James Mc-Cudden, among others.[74] As we have seen, authors of juvenile romance created their own fictional air heroes and even the RAF ditched its own policy when necessity dictated. In early 1918, the unassuming British ace James McCudden was persuaded to write his autobiography, *Five Years in the Royal Flying Corps*. Heavily ghosted by C. G. Grey, editor of the *Aeroplane*, and bearing Lord

An Aerial Dog-Fight, Escott Lynn, *Knights of the Air*, 1918.

Trenchard's seal of approval, the volume was clearly officially sanctioned RAF propaganda.[75]

Only Westerman's *Winning His Wings* played down the romanticism of the war in the air. The novel, set during the last months of the war, tells the story of Dick Daventry, a young RAF cadet. The author, who served in the Royal Naval Air Service, offers a more realistic picture of flying training and air combat. Daventry witnesses several of his fellow cadets killed in training accidents, and those who fall in battle are "horribly burnt and battered."[76] Refreshingly, Daventry actually finds that victory in the air is difficult against experienced German pilots, and when he is shot down he worries that his wounds will become gangrenous.[77] Finally, no longer fit to fly, Daventry is transferred to the RAF boat section, rescuing airmen who have been forced down over the Channel. *Winning His Wings* is in many ways a tad more realistic novel about the air; nevertheless, Westerman was still constrained by many of the conventions of RAF propaganda. "British and French airmen are sportsmen," he tells us. "ready to rush in whenever an opportunity offers, and scorning to decline a combat against heavy odds." Germans, however, "are almost invariably cold-blooded, scientific men who calculate their chances deliberately before venturing to meet their aerial foes." "Professionals," in other words, as opposed to the enthusiastic amateurism of English pilots.[78] Despite its obvious propaganda, the novel does something to eliminate the most blatant myths of the war in the air, yet equally manages to express something of the magic of flying that captivated so many young men.

The ecstasy of it all! To find himself controlling a swift aerial steed, to handle the responsive joy-stick, and to make the machine turn obediently to a slight pressure on the rudder bar. Anxiety was cast to the winds. The sheer lust of flight in the exhilarating atmosphere gripped the cadet in its entirety.[79]

By the end of the war, the airman had become the ultimate warrior hero for much of the public, and their appetite for tales of the air war continued unabated throughout the interwar years. Partly this was due to myths created by wartime propaganda, and partly to the airmen themselves, who had persuaded the public that they were the only branch of the armed forces which really understood modern warfare. According to this argument, only the air generals had not been discredited by the incompetence, blunders, and unnecessary bloodshed of the war. Moreover, in the heat of battle, they had forged the ultimate weapon that in future would render armies and navies obsolete.[80] We now know that these were hollow claims; that the war in the air was as ruthless and as brutal, and just as much a bloody learning experience, as the war waged in the trenches; while the leaders of the RFC/RAF demonstrated the same lack of imagination and the same stubborn commitment to faulty doctrine, and made the same mistakes as their colleagues on the ground. Yet due to wartime propaganda, aerial warfare alone managed to retain much of its romantic image as a clean and noble form of fighting. The spirit of the chivalric airman was even enshrined in air force history by Sir Walter Raleigh, the first official historian of the RAF. Raleigh, an elderly academic steeped in a lifetime's study of heroic literature, soon became enamoured with the romantic mythology of air warfare. By 1918, when he started work on the official history, he had come to believe that the "Spirit of England," had been embodied in the airmen, the "young gallants who were gay and reckless."[81] Consequently, his history is a story of heroic individual acts, nobility, and outstanding success. The biographies and memoirs of the air fighters that were published after the war in the main supported this romantic view. In the 1930s, Cecil Lewis's elegant memoir, *Sagittarius Rising*, could still powerfully evoke the specialness of air fighting, the essential superiority of the airman over other modern warriors. Fighting in the air was "like the lists of the Middle Ages," he noted, "the only sphere in modern warfare where a man saw his adversary and faced him in mortal combat, the only sphere where there was still chivalry and honour."[82] And it was this romantic representation of war that so appealed to the public. It was almost as if having perfected methods for mass slaughter on an industrial scale, the British had then to find an antidote, an alternative that preserved the fiction that battle still required some element of individual skill and daring. Representing war in the air as individual and heroic and masking the brutality with a chivalric veneer did exactly this.

CHAPTER 4

Sideshows: Gallipoli, Mesopotamia, Palestine, and Africa

It was to defend our empire, as well as to ensure the observance of treaties and to restore peace and liberty in Europe, that we set out to destroy the military domination of Prussia. After three years we saw that power weakened, but we also saw it possessed of wide territory in Belgium, France, Serbia, Rumania and Russia. Nevertheless, the German dream of empire in Africa and Asia had not been realized. Thanks to our armies in the south of Palestine and on the Tigris at Bagdad, there was no overland route for them to Egypt or India.

—Sir Edward Parrott, *The Children's Story of the War*[1]

The deadlock on the Western Front at the end of 1914 persuaded some British politicians, and particularly Winston Churchill and David Lloyd George, to consider other battlefields where the war might be brought to a successful conclusion. Rather than sacrifice more young men in France, they argued for an indirect approach by destroying Germany's allies through Allied offensives at Gallipoli and in the Balkans. Yet, as Beckett points out, the "soldiers regarded these as sideshows and irrelevant to the main effort." The military consistently argued that Germany had to be defeated where she was strongest, on the continent of Europe and specifically on the Western Front.[2] The argument between "Westerners" and "Easterners" was finally settled when the Easterners won over Lord Kitchener to their cause, but the consequence was that the Great War, which had begun as a continental conflict, was quickly transformed into a world war. However, the Allies soon realised that these sideshow campaigns in the Middle East and in Africa offered a unique opportunity to extend their respective empires.

Thus an assassination in Sarajevo led to fighting in Kut-el-Amara, Jerusalem, Tsingtao, Port Stanley and the Marshall Islands. White men from Europe died fighting for miserable bits of territory in Africa. While Africans and Asians drowned in the mud of Flanders.[3]

As Bernard Porter has pointed out, the war had come as no surprise to British imperialists, who had been expecting something like it for years. The time when European nations could expand freely across the globe had come to an end, and further expansion could only be achieved at the expense of the existing imperial powers.[4] Colonial rivalries and particularly the German desire for empire had undoubtedly contributed to the coming of war in the first place. And when Britain declared war, it did so on behalf of its vast empire, and this provided an opportunity for the British (and other combatant nations for that matter) to attempt to improve the security of their colonial possessions in Africa and for Britain, the shadow empire that had been created in the Middle East, and to forge closer links with the peoples of the Dominions and colonies. There were equally exciting possibilities for further expansion if Germany and her allies were defeated. Thus, while the major focus of the British war effort remained the Western Front, the war quickly spread through the Middle East, into Africa and even into the Pacific. The British High Command might consider campaigns outside Europe as little more than inconsequential sideshows, but in the long term they would have considerable significance for Britain's imperial role. For the propagandist, however, these imperial campaigns provided dramatic examples of an empire united in adversity, and they provided exciting stories for sustaining the morale of the British people.

In contrast to the quagmire of the Western Front, the campaigns outside Europe were often fought in exotic and romantic locations against a non-European enemy and, despite the failure at Gallipoli, were generally far more successful than the Allied offensives on the Western Front. These campaigns offered authors, whose work had hitherto been solidly based on the imperial adventure story, an opportunity to write about an older style of warfare. Rather than trenches, stalemate, and all the paraphernalia of modern technological warfare, the fighting in the Middle East or in Africa was a matter of movement, of ambushes, cavalry sweeps, and exciting small-scale engagements, the elements of war with which most writers were more than familiar. Even the cast list for these sideshows was much the same as their pre-1914 fiction—plucky Britons, sturdy, bronzed colonials—including the glamorous Australian Light Horse—stately Indian Lancers, and loyal Africans. The enemy was invariably non-European, apart from a handful of German officers, and with lots of "funny foreigners" to pad out the cast, Greeks, Arabs, Jews, and traders from the Levant. Little wonder, then, that the writers of juvenile fiction found these aspects of the war fascinating. Yet fictional representations of the war outside Europe also served a more serious purpose, for during the years of trench deadlock in Europe, they diverted the attention of young readers from the futile slogging match on the Western Front and the failed Allied offensives, and offered more traditional, more exciting, more hopeful images of war. There were few extra-European campaigns that the writers of juvenile fiction did not tackle, from Gallipoli and Salonika, to Mesopotamia, and from East Africa to the Pacific. Young readers could immerse themselves in the adventures of lithe Aussies in Palestine, patriotic English officers in East Africa, cheeky midshipmen in the South Pacific, or even young English nurses in Salonika. But it was at the Dardanelles, on the very fringe of Asia Minor, that the war outside Europe really began.

On Boxing Day 1914, Colonel (later Lord) Maurice Hankey, Secretary to the War Council, circulated a paper which drew attention to the deadlock that had occurred on the Western Front and which contemplated various new weapons that might be developed to eventually overcome the stalemate. In the meantime, Hankey suggested, it would be feasible to make use of Britain's naval supremacy to open another front in the Balkans or possibly against Turkey.[5] The Ottoman Empire had become involved in the war in October, when German warships attached to the Turkish navy had bombarded Russia's Black Sea ports. The British and French governments declared war on Turkey on 1 November—the culmination of German attempts to bring Turkey into the war on the side of the Central Powers. The Turkish government, led by Enver Pasha's Young Turks party, were determined to modernise their country and, in exchange for German assistance, were willing to allow their foreign policy and military establishment to be dominated by Berlin. The Germans had for many years been trying to extend their influence in the Middle East and had gained considerable influence in Turkey: by late 1914, the chiefs of staff of both the Turkish army and navy were German, while German officers held many other key posts in the services. The Germans believed that Turkey's entry into the war would tie down British troops to safeguard Egypt and divert Russian troops from the East Prussian Front. And if those powers were defeated in Europe, Germany would have a clear hand in the Middle East and the prospect of an open door to India. Immediately after the declaration of war, the Turks launched an offensive against the Suez Canal, but were repulsed by the British garrison. Hankey's suggestion for opening a second front outside Europe found a receptive audience. Winston Churchill, then First Lord of the Admiralty, was captivated by the idea of naval power becoming the lynchpin of victory; he became an enthusiast. Lord Kitchener at the War Office was less enthusiastic but was eventually persuaded. Lord Fisher, Churchill's First Sea Lord, was opposed, but his political master, with the bit of a new crusade against the Turk between his teeth, was in no mood to listen. If the Royal Navy could force their way through the Dardanelles—the sea route from the Mediterranean to the Black Sea—all manner of good things might follow. As Keith Robbins has explained,

The Gallipoli peninsula could be taken and the way would be open to Constantinople. Turkey would be knocked out of the war, Russia supplied with munitions and neutral Balkan states would be so impressed that they would join the Allies at once.[6]

In 1915 the Ottoman Empire included Palestine, Jordan, Syria, and Mesopotamia (modern Iraq); even Egypt, occupied by the British, was still officially a part of the Empire—a huge swathe of territory that stretched from the Mediterranean to the Persian Gulf and which included territories where the British had developed considerable commercial and strategic interests. Thus, taking the longer view, the defeat of Turkey could only be to Britain's advantage. While the latter had traditionally supported Turkish autonomy, that support had been directed at maintaining Ottoman integrity against the other Great Powers, for as Lord Salisbury had pointed out, it was in the British interest that "as little should happen as possible" to Turkey. Now, however, if Turkey suffered military defeat by Britain's hand, the shadow empire of British interest between India and the Mediterranean could be formalised.[7] And by April 1915, as the first Allied troops were preparing to land on Turkish soil, a government committee was already at work, optimistically dividing the booty, the vast possessions of the Ottomans, into zones of influence for the British and French. Juvenile literature about the Anglo-Turkish conflict spent little time on why Turkey became involved in the war, with the exception of Parrott, who provided a detailed account.[8] Most authors, however, were content to assume that non-European nations, client states such as Turkey, would simply follow the advice of whichever Great Power they were tied to. Turkey was clearly linked to Germany, and thus it was the latter that was responsible for dragging the Turks into the conflict. F. S. Brereton's hurried explanation was typical of the manner in which authors dealt with the issue.

Let us say at once that Turkey had no adequate reason for joining in this vast struggle against Great Britain and her allies; but she was cajoled into that action. Perhaps her leaders were heavily bribed by the Germans?[9]

Thus, the decision to force the Dardanelles and knock Turkey out of the war was taken.

At the beginning of the campaign it was difficult to believe that such a naval operation could fail. The Royal Navy constituted the world's most powerful fleet, while the general consensus among the military was that Turkey was of little account—hardly a serious opponent. On 19 February 1915 the first Allied warships attacked the forts on the Gallipoli peninsula that guarded the channel leading to Constantinople. Initially they had some success, but poor planning, delays, bad weather, enemy minefields, and the accuracy of Turkish artillery forced their withdrawal. It was then decided in London that the enemy strongpoints on the Gallipoli peninsula would need to be cleared by land forces. General Sir Ian Hamilton, with a force of mainly Australian and New

Zealand troops backed by a French division, were already in the eastern Mediterranean, a garrison for Constantinople once that city had been forced to
surrender by the threat of bombardment. Now they were to seize the peninsula and open the sea route to the Turkish capital. It seemed entirely appropriate that Hamilton should have been chosen to preside over what would
become a modern Aegean tragedy, for he was a soldier-poet, a classical scholar,
and a man steeped in the chivalric tradition. A fact-finding trip to Japan had
left him with great admiration for the samurai tradition with its emphasis on
duty, loyalty, and the righteousness of dying in an honourable cause. Unfortunately, while Hamilton was to survive the campaign, albeit surrounded by
considerable controversy, it was the soldiers he commanded that were to suffer
and die for that particular noble cause.[10]

The Allied landing force was ill-prepared for such a venture: there were no
plans, no detailed maps, not even the small ships that would be needed to put
such a large force of men and equipment ashore. Hamilton sailed for Egypt
to prepare the invasion, but it was not until 25 April that the first landings
took place. In the meantime, the Turkish army, alerted by the naval bombardment in February that the peninsula was now the focus of Allied interest,
reinforced their strongpoints and prepared new defensive positions. The landings, around Cape Hellas on the southern tip of the peninsula and at Gaba
Tepe, further up the eastern coast, were a nightmare for the troops, and despite their courage and determination the force of 70,000 men suffered over
20,000 casualties from the well-sited Turkish defences. Even with a substantial
force ashore the Allies were to face further disappointment, for the fighting
on Gallipoli soon turned into another deadlock as the Allies were forced to
entrench opposite the Turkish positions. The bold venture to swiftly seize the
peninsula and move on Constantinople had turned into another Western
Front. Several major attacks on the Turkish lines, even subsequent landings
by imperial troops further up the peninsula, failed to break the stalemate.[11]
Realising that their objectives could never be achieved, the Allies eventually
evacuated the peninsula in January 1916. For the British, however, the Dardanelles adventure became an icon of heroism and endurance—a glorious
failure in the best British tradition—notwithstanding that much of the fighting had been borne by Australians and New Zealanders. As Parrott explained
in his *Children's Story of the War*,

How the British and French landed on the narrow beaches in the face of superior
numbers of the enemy; how they fought their way up the cliffs in spite of artillery,
machine guns, and entrenched infantry; how with superb courage and dogged endurance they established themselves on the peninsula; how they sacrificed themselves like
the Spartans of old. . . . is a story which no Briton can read without mingled pride and
pain: pride in the men of his race who nobly fought and died in the hopeless struggle;
pain, that so much bright and gallant life should have been given in vain. Henceforth
the Gallipoli peninsula is sacred ground. . . . In days to come, when wandering Britons

shall sail by its peaceful shores, they will hush their voices and think tenderly of those who sleep . . . amidst its rugged hills and ravines.[12]

For many of the British troops taking part in the campaign, the prospect of such an expedition initially inspired all manner of romantic images that resonated with heroism—what could be more appropriate for a generation of young men brought up on the deeds of Greek heroes and medieval warriors, than a crusade against the Turk within sight of the plains of Illium? "It's too wonderful," exclaimed England's favourite young poet, Rupert Brooke, when he heard that his battalion was to take part in the landings. And he wondered if he too would do battle on the same hallowed ground on which Achilles and Hector fought their epic duel. Off the coast of North Africa, he wrote to Jacques Raverat, "We've been gliding through a sapphire sea . . . and soon we'll be among the Cyclades. There I shall recite Sappho and Homer. And the winds of history will follow me all the way."[13] Brooke was not the only classical scholar with the expedition; there was the commander General Hamilton, and several of Brooke's friends, including Violet Asquith's brother, Arthur. But alas, poor Brooke died of blood poisoning before the first shots were fired and was buried on the island of Skyros, allegedly the burial site of the hero Theseus. In early 1915 as the campaign got under way, it was all terribly romantic and exciting, and the first novels and stories about the campaign emerged in the summer of 1915. Most authors, however, had only a vague idea about what it was like on the peninsula, and they were equally unaware of how quickly the offensive had ground to a halt.

Percy Westerman's *The Fight for Constantinople* was published just five months after the first landings. In the novel, Dick Crosthwaite, a young sub-lieutenant aboard the battleship *Hammerer*, is overjoyed by the news that the ship is to accompany the expedition—"Glorious news! . . . We're off to the Dardanelles. We'll have the time of our lives," he tells his fellow officers, echoing Rupert Brooke.[14] Once in the Dardanelles, Dick has various adventures, including bombarding the Turkish defences and leading a shore party against an enemy gun emplacement. Eventually he is captured by the Turks but manages to escape and return to his ship. The novel was published before the campaign ended, and Westerman finishes on a typically optimistic note. Crosthwaite, wounded after his daring escapade and recovering back aboard *Hammerer*, is desperate to be in at the fall of the Ottoman's capital. He is thus overjoyed when he hears the ship's surgeon tell the Captain, "he'll be up and fit for duty before we force the Dardanelles, you mark my words. He'll be in at the death when we take Constantinople."[15] Presumably inspired by the naval bombardment on the Peninsula and written before much was known about the landings, the novel tells the reader very little about the campaign. And this is equally true of Herbert Strang's novel about Gallipoli, *Frank Forrester: A Story of the Dardanelles*.[16] Here the author uses the familiar plot of the young Englishman trapped behind enemy lines by the outbreak of war and who then has to make his way back to Allied territory—more or less the same formula he had used for the 1914 novel, *A Hero of Liege*, set in Belgium in August 1914.

The eponymous hero of *Frank Forrester* is the son of an English merchant living in Constantinople. When Turkey declares war, young Frank is arrested as a spy but manages to escape. In Egypt he joins the Expeditionary Force as an interpreter attached to the Australian and New Zealand Army Corps (Anzacs) and takes part in the landings at Gaba Tepe, popularly known as Anzac Cove. In reality, the landing of 8,000 troops was largely unopposed. Only later, as the Turks rallied, did the Anzacs suffer heavy casualties, mainly from shrapnel fired from hidden Turkish positions. In the novel, however, Strang has the Australians taking part in wild bayonet charges and other heroic escapades as they storm ashore and dig in. The author tells us little about the appalling conditions under which the Allies fought: the heat, the lack of all kinds of supplies, the difficulty of trying to dig defensive positions in the rocky soil of the peninsula, and the problems of evacuating the wounded under almost constant Turkish fire, but rather focuses on the heroic escapades undertaken by Forrester and his friends. He does refer to the shortage of water, the relentless counterattacks of the Turks, and the heavy casualties suffered at the other landing beaches, and he notes that by May, the Anzacs had ceased to make much progress. But again, the novel was published before the Allied withdrawal, and so Strang ends on a typically upbeat note as Forrester locates and destroys two Turkish artillery batteries. For this exploit he is awarded the Victoria Cross. Clearly, Strang, in common with the British public, knew very little about conditions on the peninsula, but it is unlikely that he would have included them had he known, for it was not an inspiring story.

Only in T. C. Bridges' *On Land and Sea at the Dardanelles* do we gain some insight into the conditions under which the Allies fought. Bridges was a popular Fleet Street journalist who had written a number of books for boys. Thus *On Land and Sea* was somewhat more informed than the work of the other authors we have examined. It is, nevertheless, a curious work; lavishly illustrated with official photographs of the campaign, but highly derivative of earlier novels, particularly *Frank Forrester*. Bridges' hero, the young Ken Carrington, has lived in Turkey with his father. When war comes he makes his way to Egypt and enlists in the Australian army. Unlike most fictional heroes with a public school background, he does not accept a commission but enlists as an ordinary Tommy, claiming that he wants to earn promotion. Bridges reinforces the idea that the Turks have been pushed into the war by the Germans, for on the way to Anzac, Carrington tells his friends,

I know the language and the people. And you can take it from me that the Turks are not as black as they're painted. It's Enver Bey and his crazy crowd who have rushed them into this business. Three quarters of them hate the war, and infinitely prefer the Britisher to a Deutscher.[17]

Later, when a Turkish officer is captured, he tells the Australians, "It is Allah's will . . . And our fate for being driven into an unjust war."[18] However, Bridges is not uncritical of the delays and mismanagement that resulted in the Turks being alerted to the landings. As one character explains,

It's a pity the people at home didn't realise first off that forcing the Dardanelles was almost as important as keeping the Germans out of Calais. If they'd sent us here two months ago instead of fooling around trying to get warships through the straits, the job would have been done by now. As it is, they've given the Turks a chance to fortify all the landing places.[19]

At the Anzac Cove landings, the Australians are desperate to get at the Turks and perform stout work with the bayonet; one Turk is even "spitted like a fowl." The Turks put up a strong defence but are no match for the "long, lean six footers."[20] There are descriptions of the trench system and lots of special missions and dangerous escapes, and the novel ends on the same optimistic note used by other writers when Carrington, recovering from a wound aboard a hospital ship, and depressed that he might miss the end of the campaign, is told, "It will take more than a month to open the Dardanelles. Those who know say it will take three months at least to beat the Turks."[21]

The story of the Anzacs at Gallipoli was the subject for the Australian author Joseph Bowes' novel *The Young Anzacs*, published later in the war. Bowes derived much of his information about the campaign from the war correspondent Ashmead Bartlett, but he wove his tale around the fictional characters Jock Mackenzie, Tim Hogan, and Jack Smith. The trio are working as kangaroo hunters in the outback when they hear that war has been declared in Europe. Enlisting in the Australian Light Horse, they are shipped to Egypt and then take part in the landings at Gaba Tepe, and Bowes dwells lovingly on the sheer exuberance of the young Australians of the Light Horse as they land on the Turkish beaches.

When once the spell of silence had broken, the gallant Anzacs broke into a joyous chorus as they tumbled on shore. They were a parcel of schoolboys. School was over. The holidays had begun. They were breaking out over the school ground in the exhilarating sense of freedom. With jest and quip, with snatch of song and weirdly sounding *cooees* and other antipodean cries, they rushed to the attack of the beach trenches. Not firing a shot, but with the forceful application of cold steel, they drove Abdul and his mates from their barricades.[22]

But Bowes also acknowledges how difficult was the confinement of the trenches for the Australians—men "accustomed to the wide open spaces, and the free and easy life."[23] The author creates the usual extravagant adventures for his young heroes but, despite writing the novel long after the campaign, ends the novel with the Anzacs' bloody attack against Lone Pine. While most authors focused on the campaign at Gallipoli, F. S. Brereton examined an almost unpublicised aspect of the campaign against the Turks in which a British Naval detachment of armoured cars provided support for the Russians in the Caucasus. However, *The Armoured Car Scouts*[24] offers little detail about the Caucasian campaign, but a great deal about the courage and determination of Britain's Russian allies (see chapter 5).

British attitudes towards the Turks were, to say the least, contradictory. The military had expected an easy victory over what they considered a racially inferior enemy, and the strength of Turkish resistance took them by surprise, as did the martial qualities of the individual Turkish soldier. Indeed, that may well be one reason why British propaganda made so much of the German military presence at Gallipoli and elsewhere through the Middle East and which, it suggested, provided a "stiff backbone" for the Turk. One of the frequently used justifications for why Britain was fighting the Ottomans was the claim to be liberating the indigenous people of the region from the tyranny of the Turkish yoke. Yet this was official rhetoric for the consumption of those at home. Many Allied soldiers involved in the Middle East campaigns were voluble in expressing considerable dislike for these indigenous people, particularly Arabs and Levanters, and in contrast great admiration for the Turkish soldier. The writers of propagandist fiction generally followed the official line, maintaining that Turkish politicians had allowed themselves to be dragged into the war by Germany, but their representation of the Turkish soldier was as a brave and honourable foe. A 1916 article in *Young England* was typical in its praise for their bravery, tenacity and chivalric behaviour.

Even when he is fighting a desperate campaign the Englishman is sportsmanlike, and this makes him fond of good, clean honest fighting.

Accordingly, when he finds his opponents breaking the accepted rules of warfare words fail to describe his disgust. . . .

When, therefore, in the Dardanelles he came up against "the unspeakable Turk," Tommy Atkins was quite prepared for savagery worse than that of the Teuton. But to his surprise the Turks that manned the Gallipoli forts and trenches have proved clean fighters, quite after Tommy's own heart.[25]

Australians were even more lavish with their praise for the Turk. When a Turkish soldier helps the wounded Tim in *The Young Anzacs*, the author tells us that Tim's "passionate hate of a moment ago turned into respect. A being who could be moved to this extent while the tide of battle was running furiously, and blood lust was prevailing on both sides, was truly following the example of one greater than Mahomet."[26] The government, clearly concerned at this widespread attitude towards the Turk, whose empire they were bent upon acquiring, even went so far as to get Wellington House to issue a booklet refuting the gentlemanly conduct of "Johnny Turk."[27]

The tenacity of Turkish resistance at Gallipoli eventually persuaded the Allies that a breakthrough to Constantinople was impossible, and at the end of 1915, the decision was made to evacuate the Allied forces from the peninsula. This was done in stages with amazing secrecy between 6 and 8 January 1916, and with minimal casualties. But with such an ignominious ending to such a chivalric endeavour, propagandists quickly lost interest in the campaign. An article published in *Young England* completed the story and reinforced the "glorious failure" explanation of the expedition. The author, Guy Waterford, admitted that the Allied failure to force the Dardanelles was "hugely disappointing," but after briefly describing the campaign, he concentrated on the magnificent gallantry of the troops and the brilliance of their commanders who achieved such a successful evacuation.

So ended the Dardanelles campaign. It closed with a feat of naval and military management which was a veritable miracle. Disaster had been predicted. Even the optimists had feared a heavy toll in men killed and wounded and precious freights sunk. Yet all had been accomplished in orderly and masterly fashion, without the loss of a single man.[28]

If the undertaking had failed, he argued, it nevertheless gave to "the world such a new and astonishing proof of hardihood and audacious bravery on the part of our troops that for the British Empire Gallipoli will go down in history as a name of pride almost as much as sorrow."[29] Writing for an adult audience some months later, the poet John Masefield, who had served throughout the campaign with the Red Cross, referred to the expedition, "not as a tragedy, nor as a mistake, but as a great human effort, which came, more than once, very near to triumph."[30] Masefield dedicated his volume to Hamilton, whom he compared to "Roland at Roncevaux, defending Christendom from Islam." As Parker notes, even disasters as unequivocal as the Gallipoli campaign could be dignified by references to chivalry.[31] But however it was dressed up, Gallipoli was still a humiliating defeat, particularly because it had come at the hands of a non-European foe, and after early 1916 it was ignored by writers seeking tales of glory with which to inspire the young.

Of more direct strategic importance to Britain was the Turkish threat to her oil supplies. Most of the nation's oil came from Persia, via the Anglo-Persian pipeline, to the Abadan refineries on the Persian Gulf. Even before the opening of hostilities with Turkey, the government of India had sent an Anglo-Indian Expeditionary Force, the Sixth Indian Division, to the Gulf to secure the oil refineries and safeguard British supplies. The Force landed on the mainland and advanced towards Turkish-controlled Basra, taking the city on 22 November 1914, and Kurna, at the mouth of the River Tigris, in early December. Thus, by the end of the year, the oil route to the Gulf had been secured, and British forces had established strong defensive positions around Abadan, thus posing a threat to Turkish control of Mesopotamia—the land between the Tigris and Euphrates. "Mesopotamia—a nasty place," claims one of the characters in F. S. Brereton's *On the Road to Bagdad*, "up north of the

Persian Gulf—heat-mosquitoes-Arabs!"[32] And Mesopotamia was indeed a nasty place. According to Jan Morris, much of it was empty desert "inhabited by lawless predatory Arabs who loathed nearly everyone, the rest a wide and fetid fen, inhabited by marshmen who detested everyone else."[33] There were no paved roads or railways, and the great rivers provided the only real means of communication. In summer it was too hot and in winter bitterly cold. During the wet season over 10,000 square miles became swamp. Mesopotamia, Mespot to the British soldier, was a thoroughly unpleasant a place to be. But while the War Cabinet in London believed that with the Gulf secure the Expeditionary Force had achieved its goal, those on the spot, backed by the Indian government, had their eyes on a greater prize—control of the entire region. The commander of the Expeditionary Force, General Sir John Nixon, sent one of his divisions northwards up the Tigris towards Kut and Ctesiphon, as a preliminary move before advancing on distant Baghdad. The division was under the command of Major General Charles Townsend, a banjo-playing eccentric with considerable ambition, but limited ability.

Brereton's novel *On the Road to Bagdad* deals with the opening phase of the campaign. The central character here is a young Indian Army officer, Geoffrey Keith, attached to the Expeditionary Force. Keith's guardian, an Indian political officer, had taken the young man into Mesopotamia on one of his prewar missions, so Keith knows the country and speaks fluent Turkish and Arabic. Sent on a reconnaissance mission with a detachment of Indian Lancers towards Basra, he captures an Arab chieftain, who gives him detailed information about the Turkish defences of the city. The patrol later runs into Turkish cavalry, and Keith's first action occurs. This, however, is nothing like the entrenched warfare of the Western Front or Gallipoli. Here, the glamorous Indian cavalry career wildly across the wide plain, lances lowered, pennants flying, bugles blowing. They smash into the Turks, send them reeling, and chase the remainder off the field; very exciting and the way "real" war should be fought. As one of Keith's fellow officers exclaims, "My word . . . But that was something! If that's war—the sort of war we're likely to have in Mesopotamia—then the more of it we have the better."[34] The Force moves on up the Tigris, but after taking Basra, Keith and his friend Philip are captured. This provides Brereton with the opportunity to compare the racial characteristics of both Turks and Germans. Their Turkish captor is civilised and charming, and deeply regrets that the Sultan has allowed the "hated" Germans to lead the empire into a war—both Englishmen consider him a "most excellent fellow." The German liaison officer, von Hindemaller, though, is very different—bullying and unpleasant, and at one point even tells his prisoners that he wishes he could "screw the neck of every Englishman" and bury them in the sand.[35] The novel ends with Keith's escape from captivity and a settling of the score with Hindemaller, before he rejoins the Allies. Thus, Brereton, like Herbert Strang, reduces the war to a largely personal conflict between Briton and German, against the backdrop of the romantic and colourful East.

While Keith languishes in captivity, the author provides the reader with a summary of the stirring events the young Englishman has missed. Brereton tells us how General Townsend's division reached the city of Kut-el-Amara and defeated a Turkish army at the Battle of Ctesiphon.

The same dash, the same almost reckless bravery of the British and Indians, the same natural, friendly rivalry between the two races of soldiers, sent them forward against the Turkish trenches like an avalanche.[36]

However, after Ctesiphon, Townsend was forced back on Kut and besieged by a superior enemy force in December 1915. For Brereton the siege of Kut was due simply to a question of numbers, but in reality Townsend was just too reckless, and his ill-considered advance left him isolated from the main Allied force. A relief column failed to break through to Kut, and, short of food, ammunition, and medical supplies, Kut was eventually surrendered to the Turks in late April 1916. A second defeat at the hands of the Turks was a bitter blow for the British, but Brereton, of course, managed to put a positive spin on the disaster.

Yet, one may ask, was the loss of the remains of this gallant division all loss to the British and their allies? And [one] may reply with confidence that it was not so. For that hazardous approach to Bagdad had held a numerous force of Turkish soldiers, while the resistance of our men at Kut had kept the enemy troops from operating in other parts of Asiatic Turkey.

For example, argued Brereton, it had helped the Russian offensive in the Caucasus by drawing Turkish forces away to the south, and assisted the British troops defending Egypt. The Mesopotamian expedition on the whole, he continues, has demonstrated to Turkey that an alliance with Germany will not save them; it has acted as a warning to Persia, where German agents are active, not to become involved in the war at the bidding of the Kaiser; and it has shown that the Allies do not lack the resolve to wage unceasing war against those who threaten the peace of the world.[37] How exactly the destruction of a British division achieved that is not made clear. Brereton, however, had little detailed knowledge of the events that followed Townsend's defeat, and as he admits towards the end of the novel, "At this time [summer 1916] actual news of our troops in Mesopotamia . . . is meagre."[38]

But the disaster at Kut, coming so soon after the failure at Gallipoli, forced the War Office to take direct control of the campaign rather than leaving it in the hands of the Indian government. The Expeditionary Force was re-inforced, and a new commander was appointed, General Sir John Maude, a cautious but able soldier. Maude re-organised his forces, recaptured Kut, and led an advance on Baghdad, which he entered on 10 March 1917. However, just months after his triumph, he died of cholera in the city. His untimely death, coming so soon after his greatest triumph, ensured that the deeply religious Maude was elevated into the pantheon of Christian soldier martyrs that included such exemplars as Havelock and Gordon. Within a year of his death he was being hailed as the "most skilful general that the war had developed on the British side." Maude was undoubtedly a skilful general and extremely popular with his men for his genuine concern for their welfare, but his success appeared even greater when viewed against the seemingly endless succession of failures in France and the apparent incompetence of the Western Front generals. It was ironic that just as the war appeared to have finally thrown up a general who knew how to win, he was snatched away. Nevertheless, propaganda made the most of the opportunity, and the tributes were extravagant, "If the world were peopled by Joe Maudes what a charming place it would be," wrote one of his Eton contemporaries on hearing of his death.[39]

The other fictional accounts about the campaign, *Through the Enemy's Lines* (1916) and *Carry On: A Story of the Fight for Bagdad* (1917), were both by the prolific Herbert Strang, and both reveal the authors dependence on press reports. The first novel adopts the standard Strang format: a young Englishman in Mesopotamia searching for his archaeologist father becomes embroiled in the war, runs afoul of a wicked Prussian officer, renders great service to the British military, and is finally recommended for a commission. *Carry On* is more interesting in that it deals with the adventures of a British intelligence officer and his work behind Turkish lines. While it includes the usual ingredients—sinister Prussians, the hero's capture and escape, and the standard Strang diatribe against the Germans—it does take the reader through the capture of Baghdad. The author, an ardent supporter of British imperialism and with a canny eye to the future, was clearly concerned to demonstrate that British actions in Mesopotamia were not simply blatant conquest, but a collaboration between the indigenous peoples of the city and the British.

Without parade or the insolence of victors the British troops marched into the city, between crowds of inhabitants, a mixed population with elements from almost every race known in the East, shouting and dancing and clapping their hands. For the first time in history the city of Haroun al Raschid welcomed a western conqueror.[40]

Writing a more considered version of the story at the end of the year, Parrott reinforced the notion that not only were the British welcomed as liberators but would undoubtedly improve the quality of life of the inhabitants. Before the British took control of Baghdad, he noted,

The decay of the city was due to plague and famine, and to the laziness of its Moslem citizens. The death-rate is very high indeed, for there is no sanitary system of any kind. Every kind of decaying filth is thrown into the rivers, the water of which is brought to the city by canals and aqueducts.[41]

He then goes on to describe the improvements the British army have started to make and concludes with, "It is clear that the people of Bagdad were overjoyed to see the British enter, and to know that the old bad days of Turkish oppression were over."[42]

But for the British, the fall of Baghdad did not mean an end to the fighting in the Middle East, for the war cabinet had now decided on the conquest of the remaining Turkish provinces, Syria and Palestine.

The campaign in Palestine, literally the last Crusade, witnessed not only the final defeat of the Ottoman Empire, but the liberation of Jerusalem by a Christian army, 700 hundred years after it had fallen to Islam, and the creation of a vast new province of the British Empire—a triumph which almost expunged the bitter memory of Gallipoli. The conquest of Palestine hinged on the capture of Gaza, which lay astride the main route from the Suez Canal. The Turks had heavily fortified Gaza, as a Turkish general tells his Australian prisoners in Joseph Bowes's *The Aussie Crusaders*, "Your great Gibralter is not more impregnable than Gaza."[43] Bowes, an Australian vicar, had written several adventure stories for boys before 1914, but in 1916 he embarked on a trilogy of novels based on the exploits of the Australian Light Horse in the Middle East, from Gallipoli to the capture of Jerusalem. Interestingly, and unlike most other authors who were dependent upon the same sources, Bowes admits that his novels are based on popular newspaper reports, and particularly those written by Ashmead Bartlett, army dispatches, and interviews with returned veterans. The adventures of his fictional characters were thus grounded in the official version of events, but supplemented by eyewitness accounts. His description of the fortifications around Gaza, for example, was taken virtually intact from official reports,

[I]t was protected by a perfect labyrinth of deeply-cut trenches, with strongly protected redoubts at frequent intervals, all of which were manned by 10,000 veteran Turks. Heavy batteries were under the control of the Austrians. Every device known to modern warfare was used to defend the position from assault. Large bodies of troops lay within a few miles in readiness to move to its relief if it were in danger.[44]

It was indeed heavily defended, yet in March 1917, the army of Sir Archibald Murray, comprised mostly of imperial troops, actually fought their way into the city before being forced to withdraw. But the conquest of the Holy Land was finally undertaken by General Sir Edmund Allenby, who succeeded Murray in June 1917.

Allenby was one of few really gifted British generals of the war. A classicist, a bibliophile, and a keen naturalist, he inspired confidence among his troops and devotion among his staff. More importantly, he surrounded himself with extremely competent staff officers and proved capable of a degree of subtlety

The Turk Surrenders, F. S. Brereton, *With Allenby in Palestine*, 1919.

singularly lacking in other British generals. Allenby was not afraid to experiment with the new weapons that technology had placed at his disposal—
aircraft, armoured cars, tanks, off-shore torpedo boats, and unorthodox
tactics. He shrewdly made use of T. E. Lawrence's Arab irregulars to create
havoc with Turkish communications and supply routes, and he bombarded
the Turks and their allies with propaganda that undermined their cause. The
exploits of Lawrence of Arabia and his guerrilla army were virtually unknown
to the public during the war itself, but in the postwar years he became one of
the most celebrated and romantic figures of the campaign in the Middle East
and became a model for numerous adventure story writers.[45]

Despite the inherent racism of the British, Allenby never underrated the
Turkish army, and he made elaborate preparations for his advance north, securing his supply lines and taking Turkish strongholds to safeguard the rear.
Brereton expressed something of that determination in his novel *With Allenby
in Palestine—A Story of the Latest Crusade*, "neither desert nor lack of water
nor disease could arrest the advance towards the Promised Land." He also
notes the careful preparations that were made:

General Allenby . . . worked his way forward gradually. He massed vehicles and beasts
at his water-base ready for an advance, and made sure that success or failure would
find his troops thoroughly well provided for.[46]

Allenby made a show of attacking Gaza, but actually sent his main attack
against Beersheba, taking the Turks by surprise. But he did not rely on stealth
alone, and Bowes describes the careful preparations on the eve of battle, "The
story of the capture of Beersheba is the story of a splendidly planned movement in which infantry and cavalry combined." Later he likens the action to
the work of an orchestra,

Each piece of this combination of war units was to contribute to the harmony of the
whole. It is a matter of history that not one instrument in that great movement made
a discordant note or fell below the ideal. The capture of Beersheba was in sober truth
a triumph of staff work.[47]

But the advance still meant hard fighting for the Allies. Bowes gives plenty of
praise to the "splendid men of the Home Counties" and the "gallant Welsh,"
but unsurprisingly he awards first place to General Charles Chauvel's Anzac
cavalry, who swept around Beersheba in a great flanking movement to cut off
the city and attack from the rear.

Gone in a moment were fatigue and thirst. Filled with the joy of battle, the squadrons
raced to the charge through the moonlit night. Using their bayonets as lances, they
literally swept over all opposition. Line after line was taken with breathless haste. The
Turks, fear-stricken, fled at last before the terrific onrush of the dreadful Giaours.[48]

And Beersheba fell to the Empire's arms, as Brereton describes,

and with the ancient place some two thousand prisoners and fifteen guns. Men of England, Scotland, Ireland, and Wales, of Australia and New Zealand, trod the streets of this little place teeming with so many memories, and drank greedily from the famous wells around which Abraham, Isaac and Jacob had pastured their flocks.[49]

Allenby bombarded Gaza with his artillery, and the demoralised Turkish army fell back. On 7 November, the Allies entered Gaza and prepared for the advance on Jerusalem.

In both Brereton's *With Allenby in Palestine* and Bowes's *The Aussie Crusaders*, the fictional heroes enter Jerusalem disguised as Arabs in order to spy out the Turkish defences. In the event, such escapades served little purpose, for as the Allies took the Turkish positions in the surrounding hills, the Turks began to withdraw, and an attack on the city was unnecessary as the "white flag of surrender waved from the gateway of Jerusalem. At eight o'clock on the morning of the 9 December, 1917, the Mayor came out with a flag of truce and made full surrender to General Allenby's representative."[50] Both novels describe Allenby's entry into the city, and the accounts are so similar they betray the fact that both are based on the same official dispatch. Emphasising that the Allies came not as conquerors but as liberators and with full regard for the susceptibilities of the Christian, Jewish, and Islamic inhabitants, "no shot was fired into Jerusalem. No fighting marred its actual fall. General Allenby entered with but a small bodyguard, reverencing the traditions of the place."[51] As we have seen, these novels portrayed the campaign against the Ottoman Empire as a war of liberation, and in the most noble tradition, pointing out that Britain was fighting not for selfish gain but to deliver subject peoples from the terrible Turk! The idea is probably best expressed by Brereton in *With Allenby in Palestine*. After the triumphant delivery of Jerusalem by the new crusaders, we are told,

Christendom discovered itself once more, after long weary years, in possession of Jerusalem, the sacred city, while the down-trodden peoples, in Turkey, in Palestine, and in Mesopotamia, breathed freely after years of subjection. . . . Christians, Armenians, Arabs, Mohammedans, and Jews greet the arrival of the British with acclamation.[52]

But it was also very much an imperial occasion. As Parrott tells us, Allenby entered Jerusalem on foot with a guard of honour composed of imperial and dominion troops, and only as an afterthought were a few French and Italian soldiers included. "There was no doubt," he wrote, "that British prestige in the East had been greatly increased by the capture of Jerusalem."[53]

With Jerusalem lost and their armies in retreat, the Turkish empire was teetering on the brink of total collapse, as Brereton explains. After the fall of the Holy City,

British-Indian troops dashed forward, and, in the course of a few breathless weeks, Damascus, Beirut, Aleppo, and other places were captured, while practically the whole of the force was either killed, wounded or captured. It was the end of Turkish dominion in the Holy Land, it coincided with the downfall of Turkish power in Mesopotamia.[54]

Yet the Turks did rally, and Allenby crushed what remained of their armies at the Battle of Megiddo (Armageddon) on 21 September 1918. Turkey finally capitulated at the end of October, and the Ottoman Empire was divided into various states under the protection of the French and British.

Through the claim to be liberating the east from Ottoman tyranny backed by the right of conquest, Britain could legitimately lay claim to the whole Middle East and bask in the glory of such chivalric enterprise. And many continued to believe it was a chivalric enterprise. The romance and chivalry of the war in the Middle East were probably dismissed by most soldiers who served there as propagandist fantasies,[55] yet there were many who felt the same as Brereton and Parrott—and even held onto those beliefs in the bleak postwar years. In 1923, for example, the actor Vivian Gilbert published his book *The Romance of the Last Crusade*—a curious work, part fantasy, part memoir, and dedicated to Sir Ian Hamilton. On the eve of war, the fictional hero of the introduction, a descendent of a medieval knight crusader, muses upon how wonderful it would have been to take part in that last crusade, "Oh, for the chance to do as one of those knights of old, to accomplish one thing in life really worth while." Then comes the war and what follows are the author's own war experiences in the Middle East. We are introduced to the horrors of modern warfare, but Gilbert, despite the death of his two brothers and a third crippled, concludes that with the fall of Jerusalem to the Allies, "We had finished our crusade, peace and freedom were in the Holy Land for the first time for five hundred years—and it all seemed worth while."[56]

The fighting in the Middle East and the diverse peoples encountered by the Allied armies provided ample opportunities for authors to exercise their views on race. The Turks surprisingly got off lightly, for they fought bravely and observed the accepted rules of warfare. Most animosity, however, was directed at their German "masters," and it is clear that the consensus view was that the Turk had been led astray by the devious agents of the Kaiser. However, the other races with which the Allies came into contact were far less commendable. Strang has villainous Kurds and sly and oily Arabs, while Bowes provides a number of incidents where the straight and manly Aussies are compared with the childlike, superstitious, and untrustworthy Bedouins, and all heap scorn on the Levanters—the mixed-race traders of the area.[57] Nevertheless, writers did need to exercise considerable caution in their comments on race, for given the confused political situation of the Middle East and the Arab Revolt, it was not always clear who one's friends were. This tension is clear in juvenile fiction, for while novelists were writing about oily Arabs and untrustworthy Bedouins, the respectable story papers were emphasising the nobility and high moral code of the "Bedween."[58] An editorial in the *Boy's Own Paper*, for example, even paid tribute to the Arab leader, Chief Mohammed Bib Salim, who was serving on a British gunboat on the Tigris. For one particularly brave act this "brave and sinewy son of the desert" had been awarded the Distinguished Service Medal.[59] Strang, Brereton, and Bowes all covered themselves by providing at least one noble native who becomes a loyal follower of the Allies. This trusted servant is often made to claim that he wants nothing more than to continue to serve the British after the Turks have been defeated[60]—which was perhaps just as well, for that was exactly the relationship that Britain intended for the newly liberated people of the Middle East. But the least reported of all the sideshows—the dismal campaign in Salonika—received little attention from the writers of juvenile fiction.

In early September 1915, Bulgaria had been persuaded to join Germany and Austria in the invasion of Serbia. The collapse of Serbia would give the Central Powers a direct route to Constantinople that would threaten the Allies clinging to the Gallipoli beaches. The French were particularly keen to send assistance to the Serbs and persuaded the British to contribute men to an expeditionary force. However, as Serbia was a landlocked state, the only route by which such aid could be sent was through Salonika. After the Allied force had landed, the Bulgarians were able to drive a wedge between the Expeditionary Force and the Serbians.[61] Given this new situation, the sensible thing to do would have been to withdraw, but the Allies, reluctant to suffer another retreat that would damage their prestige, elected to stay in Salonika. Although reinforced by new divisions, including Italian and Russian troops, they showed little initiative in mounting an offensive until late in the war, thus giving rise to the German claim that Salonika was their "largest internment camp."[62] But the campaign did inspire one of the few war novels to feature a female protagonist and a rare glimpse of the Balkan background—Bessie Marchant's *A VAD in Salonika*.

From 1915, women began to play a far more active role in the war effort on the home front,[63] but nursing was virtually the only way in which women could come close to the battlefield, and a considerable number of nurses were eventually employed in France and on the other fronts. For those who lacked a nursing qualification, service with the Voluntary Aid Detachment (VAD) offered a variety of domestic jobs in hospitals. The VAD was popular with young women during the early years of the war, even though many chaffed at the unnecessary discipline and the menial nature of much of the work, but it did allow women to feel they were part of the fighting front. The central character in Marchant's novel is 16-year-old Joan Haysome, a volunteer in Lady Huntly's VAD Hospital, and the author tells us that Joan was "patriotic to her finger-tips. Indeed, she fairly bristled with patriotism."[64] When Lady

Huntly obtains permission to send a unit to the Salonika Front, Joan's mother surprisingly gives permission for Joan to accompany them. "I think I shall let her go. . . . We are compelled to send our boys into the danger zone, so why should our girls be withheld? We do not love our daughters better than our sons."[65] In Salonika, in a British hospital near the marshes of Lake Betchik, Joan comforts the wounded (none of whom suffer from anything too gruesome, of course), helps capture a spy, and finishes up marrying a gallant British officer. Clearly the author simply uses the Balkans as an exotic location for her tale of the VADs at war. Only Herbert Strang offered more detail about the campaign in a short story in *Burton of the Flying Corps*. Burton, the young British pilot, is attached to the Salonika expedition. Forced down behind enemy lines, he is instrumental in saving a group of Serbian refugees seeking the protection of the Allies. Burton defeats the "marauding Bulgars" and outwits the sinister German officer leading them. Writing in 1916, Strang does admit that the campaign is going badly for the Allies and that the intended aim of saving Serbia has so far failed, but he fulfils several of the aims of British propaganda—Britain as a loyal friend of the Serbs, doing all that is possible to liberate their country, while the Allies are clearly the defenders of the weak and oppressed.[66] The expeditionary force in Salonika achieved little that would make headlines, but the victorious Allied campaigns fought in colonial Africa received only marginally more attention.

By 1914, Germany had acquired a number of colonies in Africa—German East and South West Africa, Togoland, and the Cameroons. As we have seen, the German dream of an African empire had been of considerable concern to the British before 1914, and the war provided the opportunity to foil any such hopes of German expansion in Africa, or elsewhere for that matter. Within months of the outbreak of war, the first German colonies, Togoland and the Cameroons, fell to the British and French.[67] Charles Gilson's 1916 novel *Across the Cameroons* is essentially an imperial adventure wherein a young Englishman, Harry Urquhart, sets out to beat his treacherous German cousin to a lost treasure in the jungles of the Cameroons. The story is set against the British invasion of the colony and provides an opportunity for Gilson to comment on German barbarism and the nature of colonial warfare. At one point, Urquhart witnesses a battle between British and German troops. As the British infantry advance, Gilson describes their calm and determined attack: "sunshine glinting on the steel of their bayonets . . . polished buttons, and the badges on their coats," a very traditional form of battle, in fact, in which British guts and cold steel win the day, and Gilson appears to regret the passing of this style of warfare, noting:

A battle fought under such conditions—which are rare enough in these days when the spade has become an even more important weapon than the rifle—is one of the most magnificent and impressive sights it is possible to see.[68]

A predominantly South African force, led by the Boer general Louis Botha, quickly captured German South West Africa, and in 1915, an allegedly eye-witness account appeared in *Chums* written by an "old reader," Lionel Warren, who had served with the Transvaal Light Horse during the campaign. War-ren's account is a detailed record of a successful campaign without the exces-sive heroic descriptions that the paper was noted for.[69] The editor clearly felt that the conquest of the German colony by troops largely comprised of men who had only recently fought against the British was an inspiring example of how the war had unified the empire. But only one novel dealing with the campaign in South West Africa seems to have been published, Eric Wood's *How We Baffled the Germans*. Here two boys, the sons of English settlers, wage a private war against the enemy by inciting a native rebellion.[70] But while South West Africa was quickly conquered, German East Africa (now Tanza-nia) was a different matter. Britain expected an easy victory, for although the German garrison was large, some 35,000 men, it was mainly comprised of Askaris, native troops. There were actually less than 5,000 German soldiers in the colony. The Germans, under the command of the Prussian general von Wahle, did not wait to be attacked but immediately went onto the offensive, invading British East Africa, intending to take the British port of Mombasa. The garrison there, however, held the German attack, and by July 1915 the Germans were in retreat, and the British conquest of German East Africa had begun. Nevertheless, the campaign took far longer than expected. Finally, in July 1916, the South African Jan Smuts was placed in command of the imperial forces, and by the end of the year, Germany's last colony in Africa was virtually captured. The British, however, had not reckoned with Colonel von Lettow Vorbeck, a gifted and courageous soldier. Although significantly outnum-bered, Vorbeck organised his European and native forces so effectively that he was able to hold out for some considerable time by waging a guerrilla campaign. When Allied superiority proved too much, Vorbeck took his re-maining troops, slipped over the border into Portuguese Mozambique, and was still at large when the war ended in November 1918.[71]

East Africa, of course, was familiar territory for authors of imperial adven-ture stories, so it was hardly surprising, then, that the war in East Africa inspired novels from both Percy Westerman (*Wilmshurst of the Frontier Force*) and Herbert Strang (*Tom Willoughby's Scouts*), and both published at the end of the war—a sort of literary dessert for readers who still remained unsatisfied after devouring the main course of fictions set on the Western Front. The British soldiers of these novels not only wage war against the enemy but equally against the terrain, the climate, poisonous snakes, and unpleasant rep-tiles; and of course they indulge in the traditional occupations of the African adventure story such as hunting. The central characters in both novels per-sonify the archetypal imperial hero, who had been established in popular fic-tions long before the war: not simply soldiers, but empire builders as well. Dudley Wilmshurst and Tom Willoughby are young, bronzed, lithe, clear-eyed, and intensely patriotic. Both are deeply concerned about the welfare of the Africans in their care. Although remarkably young—Willoughby is still in his teens—as Englishmen they instinctively know how to behave in dealing with subject races. Committed to fair play and justice for all, they are bound by a keen sense of duty and honour. Wilmshurst, a second lieutenant in the "Nth" West African Regiment, has the knack of "handling African troops. . . . firmness, strict impartiality, and consideration for the welfare of the men under his orders." Naturally, his men, mostly from the "Haussa" tribe, are devoted to young "Massa Wilmst."[72] Dudley's West African regiment is sent to reinforce the colonial forces already fighting in German East Africa. Herbert Strang's Tom Willoughby isn't a soldier, but in Africa on business—a sort of embryonic imperial entrepreneur. However, finding himself in German East Africa when the war is declared in Europe, he feels he must play his part in the great struggle. Escaping from the Germans to avoid being interned, he becomes the focus for African resistance, attracting a group of dissident warriors who refuse to be pressed into German service. Willoughby, despite his lack of military experience, falls back on the inherent martial instincts of his race and is able to drill his men, teach them to use modern rifles, and create a private army, the Scouts of the title, while his sense of decency and fair play towards his men and their families earns their devotion.[73]

Tom Willoughby's Scouts is little more than a reworking of the author's 1914 story, *Sultan Jim: Empire Builder*. In that novel, as we have seen, the hero, Jim Saltoun, discovers a lost tribe in the unexplored borderlands between German and Portuguese territory and saves them from German aggression. The Africans, grateful at being saved from the tyrannical Germans, elect to become part of the British Empire with young Jim as their commissioner. In the world of fiction, it appeared that Englishmen had an inherent ability to govern native people with wisdom and justice. The Germans, of course, compare badly with these shining paragons of benign imperialism. Although committed to "create for our Kaiser a great empire in Africa," as one German officer explained, they have little sympathy for or understanding of the native population. They are simply there to exploit these territories for the benefit of Germany, while the indigenous population provides the means of doing so: "Ve Germans can make ze niggers work," boasts one particularly bullying German sergeant. The Germans treat Africans with contempt: "Black Schweinhunds" appears to be their favourite expression for describing them. They maintain iron discipline with kicks, punches, and the schambok (a whip made from rhino hide). Consequently, they are despised, even by their own Askaris. Westerman describes how the unpleasant Hauptmann Max von Argerlich is so unpopular with his black soldiers that during one skirmish with the British, a bullet whistled past his ear which could only have been fired by one of his own men. Not knowing who the real culprit was, he has "half-a-dozen executed" hoping that the real perpetrator will be among them.[74] In Strang's novel, the Germans

Fighting in Africa, Percy Westerman, *Wilmshurst of the Frontier Force*, 1918.

seem more alarmed that Willoughby is setting a bad example for Africans by defying German authority than by the damage he causes to their war effort. But because the Germans are so universally disliked by the tribes they exploit, they are haunted by the prospect of a "great rising of blacks" that could result in their losing control.[75] For Westerman, Africans take on the characteristics of their masters, and there are major differences between the Africans who serve the Germans and those in British service. Although all are "children by nature," superstitious and lazy, they can be "developed into smart and efficient soldiers" under the right leadership.[76] Under British officers, they are brave, loyal, and honourable and fight with determination and great courage. By contrast, the German Askaris skulk around, are cowardly and untrustworthy, and often bully the local natives. However, when captured by the British they invariably want to change sides and join the fight against the Germans. Curiously, under British officers, these captives are quickly redeemed and become good and loyal soldiers. A 1916 article in *Young England* claimed that the ability to turn uncivilised tribesmen into useful soldiers was a British talent. "We British may fairly claim to have an aptitude which is next door to genius for transforming the African native into a reliable and (what is more) a self-respecting, well-behaved soldier."[77] Interestingly, in both Strang and Westerman African troops play a not inconsiderable part in the fighting, yet in the children's histories they are rarely mentioned. Parrott, for example, devotes four chapters to the campaign in East Africa but makes no mention of the contribution of African regiments.

In these novels, the liberation of Africans from German tyranny and the obvious advantages of living under British rule justify the British presence in Africa and the conquest of the German colonies, but the novels also offer practical guidance in imperial management. Strang, writing just after the war, was clearly aware that some of the colonies taken from Germany and Turkey would be absorbed into Britain's empire, and thus he justifies such claims with a lecture on the benefits of British imperialism. The Germans have tried to create an empire by brute force and terror, and failed, he argues. "Tigrish greed," claims Major Burnaby, an officer in the British force, "offers no real basis for an empire," and he compares this approach with the British example. Britain has never sought to dominate other countries and people, he explains,

Our Empire is a gradual, almost an accidental growth: much of it has been thrust upon us. . . . We have taken up the burden of rule in barbarous countries . . . or countries like India and Egypt where civilisation has decayed, and which but for us would either be bear's gardens or hotbeds of slavery and oppression. I don't say that our motives have always been of the purest or our ways the best; but I do say that we have never, as a state, set before us the deliberate aim of grabbing what doesn't belong to us, forcing all civilisations into our particular mould, and subjugating all other nations by sheer brutal terrorism.[78]

Thus, in fiction British war aims in Africa, as elsewhere outside Europe, were not simply to protect existing colonies and interests, or to defeat German or Turkish invaders, but to rescue the indigenous people from the harsh rule of German/Turkish terror. Yet clearly, British expansion in the Middle East or Africa at the expense of the Ottomans or Germans was invariably for economic or strategic gain—factors ignored by ardent imperialists such as Strang and Westerman, who chose only to see the beneficial effects of British imperialism for indigenous people. That the natives of German East Africa so eagerly choose to follow Strang's fictional hero suggests that here is another example of empire being "thrust upon the British"; and Britain, that benignly paternalist nation, could in honour hardly refuse. But the fact was that the acquisition of German East Africa was yet another link in Cecil Rhodes's Cape to Cairo plan for the British domination of Africa—an aspect that appears to have escaped Strang's notice. Yet after the war, in the final territorial settlement of Africa, Britain gained considerably. German East became the British protectorate of Tanganyika, the existing colonies of Gold Coast and Nigeria were enlarged at the expense of Togoland and the Cameroons, and South Africa took over the administration of German South West Africa.

In the final analysis, these sideshows were marginal to the outcome of the war. German military power had to be defeated on the Western Front. But campaigns in exotic locations offered inspiration for authors looking for adventurous stories that distracted readers from the squalor of the war in France and offered more traditional, more glamorous images of warfare. They equally provided the opportunity to write in glowing terms about the contribution of the dominions and colonies, and to demonstrate how Britain and her empire were fighting, not as conquerors, but as liberators, champions of freedom whose only mission was to assist those who suffered under the German-Turkish yoke.

CHAPTER 5

Brave Sons of Empire and Loyal Allies

This war is no ordinary war, as the least intelligent will admit, and one of the particular points for which it is notorious is the cosmopolitan character of the men who form the magnificent British force which our Empire has thrown into this battle of nations.

In the ranks there are to be found men from every part of the world where the British flag flies, and indeed from many other quarters. They have come from towns and backwoods and prairies of Canada, from the rugged interior of Newfoundland, from the farms and cities of Australia, and from a hundred different places.

Here, there, everywhere along the line in Flanders and in France, the Allies—Belgian, French, Portuguese, and Russians—strike at the invader, crush his formidable defences with their overpowering gun-fire, and slay his soldiers.

—F. S. Brereton, *Under Haig in Flanders*[1]

In 1914, the British Empire covered almost a quarter of the world's surface and included hundreds of millions of people—an immense racial, religious, ethnic, and linguistic diversity—but "Britain's ability to marshal, however imperfectly, the vast human and material resources of this Empire gave the nation tremendous advantages."[2] Empires, as De Groot has explained, are by definition exploitative, but one cannot fail to be surprised at the willingness with which the "exploited" rushed to stand shoulder to shoulder with their exploiters in 1914. De Groot well captures the bathos of that moment when he quotes a telegram to Prime Minister Asquith just after the ultimatum to

Germany had expired, which read, "Do not worry, England. Barbados is behind you."[3] With the declaration of war, territory after territory, like Barbados,
pledged their allegiance and total commitment to the war. Almost a million
Indian soldiers served overseas, along with 500,000 Canadians, 300,000 Australians, 100,000 New Zealanders, 80,000 white South Africans, and "hundreds of thousands of Indians, Africans, Chinese and West Indians served in
military labour units outside their nations."[4] It was indeed, the Empire's finest
hour, a moment of total unity and cohesion that would never be repeated. At
home, British propagandists accepted this demonstration of loyalty as only
right and proper, for as J. Holland Rose pointed out, the Empire is not "a
close preserve kept for ourselves; it is a free and hospitable community where
all peoples share alike on equal terms."[5] This notion of the Empire as a free
association of nations held together by bonds of kinship, mutual trust, and
affection became a dominant theme in British wartime propaganda. Dominion troops were hailed as distant sons of Empire loyally responding to the
Motherland's hour of need; an idea clearly expressed in Lauchlan Watt's
"Children of the Flag."

> If honour's call must summon all,
> And the blood-kin do not lag,
> Have we no care to claim our share—
> We are children of the flag.
> If from far and wide, across the tide,
> Homewards the grey waves swing,
> We are ready to come to the roll of the drum,
> For Empire and the King.[6]

Canadian frontiersmen, Australian outbackers, and South African hunters
had much to offer. These were courageous, hardy adventurers, men who constantly faced and surmounted the challenge of the unknown, but still loyal to
the homeland—exactly the sort of men Britain needed in her hour of need,
and who, their racial energy renewed by contact with the wilderness, would
re-invigorate the blood of the race. Just such a man was the subject for an
article in *Young England* in 1916. The unnamed hero of the piece had been
educated at a Manchester grammar school, then left for Canada. There he
worked in a circus, served with the Royal Canadian Mounted Police, and
accompanied Steffansson's expedition to the far north in early 1914. Attempting to pacify a drunken Indian, the young emigrant was badly wounded. But
having dispatched the Indian, he bravely stitched up his own wounds. Hearing
about the war, he travelled for two months through the wilderness to Halifax
and on to England, where he enlisted in the BEF. Now serving in France he
has earned high praise from his officers for his sharp-shooting.[7] With men
such as this fighting for the Empire's cause, how could victory be in doubt?

There were, however, some imperial subjects who saw the war as an ideal opportunity to renew their struggle for independence. In late 1914, for instance, some 12,000 Afrikaner rebels opposed involvement in the war and attempted to bring down Louis Botha's government.[8] Equally, in 1916 Irish nationalists saw the war as an opportunity to throw off the English yoke, and French-Canadians were noticeably reluctant to volunteer. But other nationalists believed that supporting Britain now would bring future rewards. Mohandas Gandhi, for example, argued that serving the Empire's cause would bring greater independence for India in the future. "The gateway to our freedom is situated on French soil," he argued.[9] After all, this was a war for freedom and self-determination, ideals from which the colonies could hardly be exempt. Even amongst loyalists there was a belief that in contributing to the victory they were furthering their own goals of greater autonomy. Max Aitken (Lord Beaverbrook), the Canadian press baron and a tireless propagandist for the Allied cause, believed that Canada's claim for greater independence would be furthered by Canadian troops on the battlefields of Flanders.[10] But difficult questions as to where and when principles of independence and self-determination were to be applied were ignored or glossed over in wartime literature, and propagandists clearly believed their task was to produce shining examples of imperial unity in which the loyal sons of the Dominions and colonies flocked to aid the Motherland. Instantly forgotten were the bitterly fought colonial wars that had inspired so many boys' adventure stories before 1914; almost overnight, Brereton and the other writers transformed savage Zulus, unscrupulous Boers, and wily, treacherous Pathans into loyal subjects of the King—an imperial brotherhood in arms. Prewar rebellions and acts of dissidence by subject peoples were easily dismissed as simple family squabbles or were caused by outside agents—particularly the Kaiser's spies. The idea that Germany was bent upon inciting rebellion within the empire became common. Talbot Mundy's popular 1916 story set in India, *King of the Khyber Rifles*, for example, has the novel's hero, the young officer Athelstan King, foil a plot by German agitators to stir up another mutiny. In John Buchan's *Greenmantle*, Richard Hannay undermines the German plan to arouse the "hordes of Islam" against the British.[11] Thus, united by a common bond and shared interests, the Empire went to war. Yet despite the noble rhetoric, colonial troops were often poorly treated and subject to racism and abuse, particularly Africans and West Indians, while in the white Dominions there were frequent complaints that the lives of their soldiers were being needlessly squandered by incompetent British generals. But none of these criticisms were to be voiced during the war, and propaganda focused only on the loyalty and daring of Britannia's distant sons.

While novelists were anxious to sell the imperial idea to the young, and the notion of the family of empire was widely supported, most imperial propaganda actually came in forms other than adventure fiction—posters, garish illustrations of wide-eyed Pathans or Sikhs charging frenziedly into battle in the boy's weeklies, coloured charts of uniforms or flags of the empire, cigarette

"Coloured Troops of the Allies," *Boy's Own Paper*, 1918.

cards, picture postcards and lantern slides, many of which were initiated by Wellington House,[12] and in cinematic propaganda. Herbert Strang's book for young readers, *The Empire at War*, is essentially a brief history of the Empire and deals only briefly with the military participation of the imperial forces in the war.[13] Even in adventure fiction, the sons of empire most commonly appeared in minor roles, part of the supporting cast rather than leading players. The Australian presence was noted in virtually all the novels dealing with the Middle East, South Africans invariably appear in novels set in Africa, but only in a handful of novels and stories are colonials centre-stage, and then they usually turn out to be recent emigrants from Britain. Much the same is true of the popular histories. Parrott, for example, offers short chapters on the Canadians at First Ypres and Vimy Ridge, on the Anzacs at Gallipoli and Beersheba, and on South African and Indian divisions, but his work, like that of most other authors, is firmly centered on the English hero.

Canadians, the "Sons of the Maple Leaf," were the first imperial troops to arrive in Europe—they were in action on the Western Front as early as October 1914—but Canadians were already icons of heroic adventure in juvenile literature. W. H. G. Kingston and R. M. Ballantyne had set a number of adventures in Canada, and F. S. Brereton had later continued the tradition in novels such as *A Boy of the Dominion* and *A Sturdy Young Canadian*. The Canada of fiction was a pioneering nation mainly comprised of the best of young England, where "slackers are deported; but young active fellows, with pluck behind them, and with grit and strength and health . . . make good every time."[14] Thus, the clear-eyed, sturdy British immigrant, toughened by his contact with the wilderness and wise in the ways of hunting and trapping, was already a familiar figure to young readers. Canada was highly praised because it was so like an idealised preindustrial England: industrious, patriotic, conservative, but without the minor irritations of the homeland. Of one far-west pioneer town, Brereton noted, "a railway draws its steel lines through the heart of the settlement, while a school is already building. That is the way with Canada, red tape has scarcely an existence; it is merely a bad memory imported from the old country."[15] Despite the lack of military tradition or a standing army,[16] Canadians were enthusiastic volunteers, and Dominion soldiers served in Europe throughout the war. Their determination and courage earned considerable praise in the British press, and Canadian divisions were often praised for their tenacity and courage on the Western Front: during the Second Battle of Ypres in 1915, on the Somme in 1916, at Vimy Ridge, and as the first Allied troops to enter the bitterly contested village of Passchendaele in 1917.

At Ypres in 1915, it was a Canadian division that held the front after the German gas attack had forced French colonial troops to withdraw from the line. Without gas masks and heavily outnumbered, the Canadians held the German advance, and Parrott was fulsome in his praise.

Every Briton may thank God that the Canadians were where they were when the cloud of poison gas sent the Turcos fleeing in panic to the rear. These sons of the eldest daughter of the Empire, who prior to the war knew little or nothing of the art and discipline of warfare, were now called upon to save the situation when all seemed lost.[17]

Brereton struggled to find the right words to describe the heroic manner in which the Canadians had saved the day—"the superlative 'super' is hardly sufficient," he wrote.[18] Then he goes on to describe their counterattack against a German position,

Men from Winnipeg—those big, raw-boned fellows who have made a name for themselves in Canada; sons of the Empire from so far away as distant Vancouver; men in the uniform of the Canadian Scottish; soldiers from every corner of the great Dominion leapt to obey that order. Raced forward with waving rifles and bayonets . . . and threw themselves impetuously amongst the enemy.

They took the position "exterminating" more than a thousand Germans, "for in that amazing charge nothing could arrest these men of the Dominion." "Reader," he adds, "they speak of that charge still amongst the German armies."[19]

The gallant Canadians at Hooge and Sanctuary Wood were also lavishly praised by Brereton, who claimed that here they showed the same spirit and valour they had first demonstrated in 1915.[20] Parrott relates the story of how the body of a Canadian soldier had been found surrounded by "fifteen of the enemy, whom he had killed with bombs or the bayonet before he himself had been slain." Elsewhere he explains that the young German defenders were unable to face up to the Canadian veterans and many simply surrendered. Quoting from a correspondent's report, he notes, "the Canadians were very kind to these wretched youths. They gave them cigarettes and sips of coffee, and attended to those who were wounded."[21] Ferocious in battle, gentle in victory, the Canadians were indeed the flower of imperial manhood. The Canadian divisions on the Western Front were also the subject for several propaganda films made for British and Dominion audiences, including *Canadian Victory at Courcelette* (1917) and *Our Heroic Canadian Brothers* (1918).[22] Canadian achievements were also praised in the novels of Rev. Charles W. Gordon, writing under the name Ralph O'Connor, a chaplain attached to the 79th Cameron Highlanders of Winnipeg. In novels like *The Major* (1917) and *The Sky Pilot of No Man's Land* (1919), O'Connor makes no attempt to diminish the suffering and cost of victory but does suggest that in such a noble cause victory was more important than the fate of individuals.[23]

The first Australian and New Zealand volunteers also expected to serve in Europe, but they were diverted to Egypt and later to the Dardanelles, and it was that campaign which provided exciting opportunities for propagandists to praise the fighting qualities of the Anzacs (Australian and New Zealand Army Corps). Australians and New Zealanders were the subject for the Australian writer E. C. Buley, who described their achievements in two popular histories for young readers.[24] In Britain Parrott was equally laudatory, relating a number of stories of personal bravery at Gallipoli, and particularly during the battle for Lone Pine.

As soon as the bombardment ceased, the Australians . . . leapt forward with that magnificent dash which has given them a leading place among the finest soldiers of the world, and flung themselves on the deep and roofed-in trenches at Lone Pine. . . . It was a magnificent feat of arms.[25]

But while such tributes were common in the press and popular histories, Australians featured far less in fiction. The hero of Strang's *Frank Forrester* is English, but the author has much to say in favour of the Australian troops in the unit to which he is attached. In one scene a patrol is attacked by a superior Turkish force, but the Aussies, outstanding fighters that they are, stand their ground and return fire, "calmly, methodically, relentlessly, plying their bayonets upon the few [Turks] who came within their reach." Even when the enemy is forced to withdraw, the "Diggers" are anxious to pursue and finish the job, prompting the author to remark, "The Australian in action has only one glorious failing: like the thorough-bred courser, when his blood is up he is hard to hold."[26] Anzacs were invariably described as bronzed, free and easy with their "cobbers," and noted for their strength and physique: T. C. Bridges, for example, describes them as "long-legged athletes from the sheep ranges and cattle runs."[27] But Australians were, as we have seen, the central characters in the fiction of the Australian novelist Reverend Joseph Bowes. In Bowes's trilogy, the central character, Jack Smith, is second generation Australian, son of an English settler and a "half-caste girl." On leaving grammar school, Jack rejects a settled career in favour of a more adventurous life, becoming in turn a jackeroo on a sheep station and a kangaroo hunter. In the outback, he meets Jock Mackenzie and Tim Hogan, both recent immigrants to Australia, and together they enlist in the Australian Light Horse when war is declared, eventually serving at Gallipoli and in Palestine. Jack becomes an officer, but even a commission makes little difference to the close bonds of friendship that exist between the three pals. Bowes, who partly based his fiction on the reminiscences of military friends, captures much of the easy-going informality that characterised the officer–other-ranks relationships among Australians, and their loose attitude to discipline when out of the line. The only British novelist to focus on Dominion soldiers at any length was Percy Westerman, who foregrounded New Zealanders in his novel *A Lively Bit of the Front*.

The novel opens in 1917. Malcolm Carr and Dick Selwyn are both 17 and typical New Zealanders. Malcolm is over six feet tall, supple, with clear-cut features and a chin that "betokened force of character." Dick was of similar

The Chivalric Aussie rescues a wounded Turk, Joseph Bowes, *The Anzac War Trail*, 1919.

height, heavier and more muscular.[28] Both boys are desperate to follow Malcolm's brother Peter, who is already serving in France. A letter from another friend tells them that Peter is missing in action. Anxious to take revenge on the Germans, the boys lie about their age and enlist in the New Zealand Rifles. En route to France, they stop over at Cape Town and are billeted with a Maori battalion. There they discover that South Africans have very different attitudes towards non-white troops; "the Boers for instance were prone to treat the Maoris in a similar manner to the Kaffir 'boys.' They could not understand how a white man could treat a Maori as equal, being ignorant of the high moral and physical standard of the latter."[29] After one particularly nasty incident, the boys arrange a boxing match between their Maori friend Te Paheka and a particularly arrogant Afrikaner. After a difficult fight, Te Paheka emerges as the winner and then, "a vociferous cheer from Afrikanders, Anzacs and Maoris alike greeted the victor. For that brief instant, then, the sporting instincts of the South Africans triumph over racial prejudices."[30] Eventually the New Zealanders arrive on the Western Front just in time to take part in the Battle of Messines, in which they distinguish themselves, alongside their British brothers-in-arms. However, apart from the occasional reference to New Zealand, and the use of common Anzac slang, there is little to distinguish Westerman's New Zealanders from the British troops that he most commonly wrote about.

Australian and Canadian troops made a significant contribution to Britain's war effort, and the press were often fulsome in their tributes:

Never while men speak our tongue, can the blood spent by the Canadians at Ypres and by the Australians and New Zealanders at Anzac be forgotten. That rich tribute of love and loyalty to the highest ideals of our race has not been wasted.[31]

Nevertheless, Canadians and Australians were often critical of British military leadership and had little time for the British class system. Australians particularly were too independent, too free from the restraints of the class system, and most British officers considered them ill-disciplined, bad-mannered, argumentative, and with little respect for rank. Douglas Haig feared they would set a bad example for the more malleable British soldiers. Haig found his colonial generals "ignorant and conceited," once describing a visiting group of Canadian politicians as "well-meaning but second rate sort of people."[32] None denied, though, that Dominion troops were gallant fighters. Thus Australians and Canadians were often used to spearhead attacks as expendable shock troops. Inevitably this created resentment that was clearly reflected in the official war histories of Australia and Canada, and which ensured that in the postwar world Dominion governments would demand greater independence from Britain.[33]

In his novel about the campaign in East Africa, Percy Westerman informed his readers that the Allied Expeditionary Force consisted of men from Canada,

New Zealand, Australia, India, Rhodesia and South Africa, then added, seemingly with some surprise, "even the Boers who, fourteen years previously had fought doggedly and determinedly against England [have] volunteered for service."[34] It was the loyalty of white South Africans to the Old Flag that most authors cited as a particularly wonderful example of loyalty to the imperial idea. In *The Wonder Book of Soldiers*, editor Harry Golding not only emphasised that old enemies were now reconciled and sharing a common cause but that it had been Britain's once implacable foes, the Boer generals Louis Botha and Jan Smuts, who had been most enthusiastic that South Africa should fight by Britain's side. Golding even went so far as to quote Botha's speech to the South African legislature,

Only two paths are open—the path of faithfulness to duty and honour, and the path of disloyalty and dishonour. . . . to forget our loyalty to the Empire in this hour of trial would be scandalous. . . . Our duty and our conscience alike bid us to be faithful and true to the Imperial Government in all respects.[35]

However, neither Golding nor Westerman made any mention of the several thousand Boers that had attempted to overthrow Botha's government in 1914, nor the concessions that Britain made to the South African Defence Forces— that they would serve only under their own commanders or the unofficial understanding that they would serve only in Africa. And, with the exception of Westerman, no author made any reference to the inherent racism of white South Africans. Most authors avoided such unpleasant facts and concentrated on the positive aspects of the contributions of South Africans, their physical strength and stamina, their knowledge of bush fighting, and their commitment to imperial unity.

Acknowledgement of the contribution to Britain's war effort by Indian and African troops was equally underplayed in patriotic fiction but was noted in the popular histories and serial papers. Indian divisions, particularly the cavalry, were frequently the subject for short articles and illustrations, where their often exotic appearance provided a colourful alternative to drab khaki. *Young England*, for example, ran a series of full-page illustrations of imperial soldiers in action, including sepoys and even the machine-gunners of the West African Field Force. Herbert Strang's novel of the war in East Africa has the English hero defeating the Germans only because of the loyalty and bravery of the native Askaris and the men of the Rhodesian Native Police.[36] Equally, in Percy Westerman's *Wilmhurst of the Frontier Force*, victory is dependent upon the King's native troops. But whatever views these authors might have held before 1914 and how often Indians and Africans featured as the "Other" in stories of colonial warfare, it was now imperative that those old hostilities be put aside and to emphasise that in the present struggle against the Central Powers the Empire was one family bound together in common cause. But of Britain's non-white troops it was the Indian Army that received most attention. For as

Harry Golding noted, the "splendid loyalty of the Princes and peoples of India and the magnificent services of Indian troops in France, Mesopotamia and Palestine have led to a much greater knowledge and appreciation of the Army of that Country."[37]

The first Indian divisions were deployed on the Western Front in September 1914, and despite problems with the weather, diet, and the unfamiliarity of the terrain, acquitted themselves well. Parrott refers to a German source in which an anonymous author notes, "To-day for the first time we had to fight against the Indians, and Heaven knows those brown rascals are not to be underrated. At first we spoke with contempt of the Indians. Today we learned to look at them in a different light."[38] Particularly feared were the Gurkhas and the Sikhs. However, the damp and cold of northern Europe, an inadequate diet, and the unfamiliarity of the terrain resulted in low morale and poor health among Indian troops. As Parrott explained, conditions in France proved just too difficult for the Indians. "It was all so strange and new—the awful roar of the great howitzer shells, the fighting from holes in the ground, the endless stream of shrapnel, the bitter cold, and the absence of those fierce, furious charges in which they delight" proved too much, and they were transferred to warmer climates in the winter of 1915.[39] However, many of the problems faced by Indian troops were created by the British High Command itself. Initially, Indian soldiers were issued less than a quarter of the rations provided for white soldiers, and their clothing and equipment was generally inferior to that of the British army.[40] Even in the Middle East, little consideration was given to the fact that the predominantly Muslim Indian troops were expected to fight their co-religionists, the Turks. Little wonder, then, that Indian soldiers were sometimes accused of lacking keenness for the fight, and suffered a high incidence of self-inflicted wounds in order to be returned home.

Only in Brereton's novel *On the Road to Bagdad* do we catch a glimpse of the pre-1914 glamour of Indian troops in action. This occurs when he describes a cavalry charge of the Mahratta horsemen against the Turks.

The pennons at the tops of their lances waved, a sharp order snapped down the ranks, and in a trice the lances were lowered. That trumpet blaring in the distance had set every horse in the troop curving and prancing. . . . The horses were off, the men leaning low down in their saddles, their eyes glued on the enemy, their knees gripping their horse and their lances pointed well out before them.

What a shout those Indian *sowars* gave![41]

But while the novel deals with the campaign in Mesopotamia, in which the Indian Expeditionary Force played a major part, this is the only episode in which the Indians are centre stage. At the end of the war, when Harry Golding paid tribute to the Indian contribution to victory, he was careful to show that whatever Indian soldiers had achieved had been a result of years of training through English example. "The Indian Army of today is an astonishing monument to the power of British rule," he wrote. For here were a people divided by religion and caste who had been welded into an effective fighting machine by a handful of English officers.[42] Adopting the same patronising attitudes as Westerman and Strang, who had argued that Africans could only become efficient soldiers under white leadership, he concluded "Where the Sahib leads the Sepoy follows."

The Sons of Empire paid a high price to secure Britain's victory. Some 62,000 Indians died in the Great War, alongside 60,000 Australians, 56,000 Canadians, 17,000 New Zealanders, and 7,000 white South Africans. There is no record of losses among soldiers from the black African colonies and the West Indies, nor of the Asian and Chinese labourers who endured, suffered, and died on the Western Front and in the other theatres of war.[43] Only in Westerman's *Winning His Wings* do we catch a glimpse of these unnamed and unrecognized labourers for victory. Here Dick Daventry, on his way to a new airfield, witnesses a German bombing raid. The raider hits a collection of huts near a field hospital and, ironically, a prisoner of war camp. But from the damaged huts there is an "excited babel" of voices, as a mass of Chinese labourers rush to take revenge on the German prisoners caged nearby. "The Chinks, as the Chinese labourers are termed" had used their "oriental cunning" to raid an arms store nearby and were now on their way to kill the German prisoners with Mills bombs. Order was finally restored, but an elderly Chinaman explains to Daventry that, "Bochee-man him dropee bomb on English-man . . . English-man he dropee bomb on Bochee-man—can do. Bochee-man dropee bomb on China-man; him dropee bomb on Bochee-man—no can do." When an officer explains that the Germans are prisoners and must be respected, the Chinese point out that as they are also being confined in barbed wire compounds they cannot understand the logic.[44] Other contingents who contributed to Britain's cause were also rarely mentioned. A 1919 issue of the *Boy's Own Paper*, for example, did feature a brief article on "Coloured Troops of the Allies" to accompany a rather splendid colour plate, but this was little more than a check list of the diverse peoples who served with the Allies, suggesting that such support was proof positive of the justice of the Allied cause.[45] It seems clear, then, that while British propaganda for the young did not completely ignore the contribution of the nonwhite peoples of the Empire, the fictional action story was reserved almost exclusively for Britons.

In 1914, for the first time since the Crimean War, Britain found herself waging war as one partner in a European coalition, and this inevitably created problems for authors who had long been convinced that Britons were the chosen people and for whom, as Parker has noted, "abroad was somewhere an English chap went to sort out other nations, either the savage or the treacherous."[46] For most British writers, then, to be foreign was to be both inferior and funny. A common feature of pre-1914 adventure fiction was a cast list in which the minor parts were played by untrustworthy, selfish, or amusing Europeans, and even when these characters were not downright treacherous, they were usually cowardly, hysterical, or idle. From August 1914, however, the war story was suddenly expected to offer far more positive national images and to promote the cause of allied unity. During the early months of the war it was Belgium that received the most attention. The press lavished considerable attention on the suffering of "little Belgium" to justify British involvement in the European war and to encourage recruitment. But if this was, as the politicians claimed, a war to rescue that nation from tyranny and oppression, then Belgians clearly needed to be represented as brave, heroic, and worthy of the British blood that would inevitably be shed to save them. Thus much was made of Belgium's attempts to resist the invader. In O'Neill's first volume, there is a chapter entitled "How Belgium Saved Europe," which is not only a handsome tribute to this "nation of heroes," but which also suggested that the gallant stand of the Belgians, which had after all failed, nevertheless bought enough time for the other Allies to mobilise and bring their own forces to battle.[47] Publishers quickly took advantage of the attention being lavished on Belgium by the press and republished popular histories of that country which reminded readers of the earlier struggles of the Belgian people for independence. T. C. Jack, for example, reissued Mary MacGregor's *The Story of the Netherlands: The Romance of History*, detailing the "great fight for freedom in the Sixteenth Century in which the Belgians of that day showed the same high qualities which they are exhibiting to-day."[48] Other authors scoured the history books to find examples of brave Belgian patriots. In his collection of stories about boy soldiers, *The School of Arms*, Ascott Hope retold the story of young Henri Conscience and his exploits to free Belgium from the Dutch.[49] And popular fiction during the first few months of the war developed similar themes.

In late 1914, Herbert Strang's novel *A Hero of Liege* focused on two young heroes, the English youth Kenneth Amory and Remi Pariset, a young officer in the Belgian Air Service. Together they defy the German invader, capture spies, and take part in the heroic defence of the Belgian forts, eyewitnesses to the bravery of Belgium's army. At the end of the novel, with most of "little Belgium" in enemy hands, the author repeats O'Neill's suggestion that it was the gallant Belgian army that had "saved France by throwing the German war machine out of gear." By sacrificing themselves, Belgians had bought time for the Allies, thus ensuring the inevitable German defeat.[50] In 1914, Strang's praise for Belgium was in marked contrast to his earlier views. In 1907, for example, his novel *Samba: A Story of the Rubber Slaves of the Congo*, had roundly condemned the Belgians for their appalling cruelty to their native subjects in the Congo, a novel which *The Journal of Education* had praised as taking up the cause of the rubber slaves suffering under Belgian tyranny.[51] But in 1914 such incidents had become embarrassing and were hastily forgotten as attention was lavished on the Belgians' stubborn defence of the forts outside Liege, and particularly on Lieutenant-General Leman, commander of the forts—the first real hero of the war. Leman had sworn not to be taken alive but was knocked out by a German shell burst and captured. Parrott quotes the old general's moving letter to King Albert asking forgiveness for having failed in his promise,[52] while Ascott Hope recounts the heroic endeavours of several young Belgians in his collection of stories, *The School of Arms*. However, after 1914, with virtually all Belgium occupied by the Germans, and what was left of her army holding only a small section of the Western Front, writers had by and large lost interest in the Belgians. Thereafter, apart from the odd Flemish peasant helping British airmen or soldiers to escape the Germans or assisting Allied spies, Belgium was largely written out of war fiction. Few Britons knew very much about Belgium, or were aware of the atrocities committed by Belgian imperialists in central Africa, and thus, in view of the obvious injustice of the German invasion, it was relatively easy to create a sympathetic image of poor, suffering Belgium. Nevertheless, some authors, their pre-1914 prejudices reasserting themselves, were qualified in their praise—Escott Lynn, for instance, patronisingly noted that the "Belgians are a plucky little race, but Continental soldiers lack the happy-go-lucky, confident air of our chaps." Westerman, adopted a similar view in *The Dispatch Riders*, where one Briton notes, "the Belgians are not a fighting race. Let me see—didn't they skedaddle at Waterloo, and almost let our fellows down?"[53] But if some authors found difficulty in regarding Belgians as worthy comrades-in-arms, it was even more difficult to forget the long, antagonistic history of British relations with France and now to suddenly have to laud the French army as loyal, brave, and reliable allies.

Throughout the nineteenth century, France had generally been regarded as Britain's most dangerous imperial rival, and this had been widely reflected in popular culture. A number of successful adventure novels had been set against the bitter struggle of the Revolutionary and Napoleonic Wars, and these had established a stereotype of the excitable, gesticulating, and untrustworthy Frenchman, motivated by self-interest, and with an extraordinarily inflated opinion of French culture. Only a few years before 1914, Brereton, for example, had described the French in the most unflattering terms: devious, selfish, and hysterical![54] Around the turn of the century, Alfred Harmsworth directed the editors of his boys' papers to use the French as the enemy in their many tales of the Great War to come. This situation, however, began to change after 1904 with the signing of the *Entente Cordiale* between Britain and France—Harmsworth switched the attention of his editors to the German menace, noting that "we detest the Germans. . . . They make themselves odious to all Europe," adding that he would not wish "anything agreeable" to Germany to be printed in his papers.[55]

But Francophobia still ran deep, and even after the outbreak of war in 1914, many authors, while apparently praising the French, often slipped in comments that perhaps revealed a more ingrained hostility. Strang frequently comments on the slovenly, unsoldierly appearance of the French, while Brereton emphasises their hysterical reaction to almost any crisis.[56] Other writers found more serious problems. When the British were forced to retreat from Mons, Lynn appeared anxious to explain that it was partly due to the failure of the French to support them. In the story *In Khaki for the King*, a British unit, almost completely exhausted, is disappointed to find the French cavalry are not covering their retreat. Oliver, a young British officer, is sent to beg the French general to intervene, but, he was "not at all impressed with the appearance of the general, who was enjoying a very substantial supper." Despite the British predicament, the Frenchman refuses to move his division until the horses are rested. Oliver then points out that Napoleon would have found a way. Thus goaded, the French eventually decide to move.[57] As we have seen, French colonial troops panic when faced with poison gas.[58] Some French generals were treated with a grudging respect by British authors. Joffre was perhaps the most highly praised, for example, perhaps because he was much given to criticising his fellow French generals. However, authors did find heroes among the French. The story of Yves Meval, a 16-year-old French Scout, was widely reported. When Germany invaded France, Meval, too young to join the military, somehow procured an army uniform and rifle and joined the army for the first Argonne campaign. During one skirmish, and despite wounds in the leg, arm, and eye, he fought until he collapsed. Meval, however, survived, and was awarded the Military Cross for his bravery.[59]

But as the war sank into stalemate and casualties mounted, many in Britain began to question exactly what their allies were doing to secure victory. Thus propaganda to convince the British people that the French, Russians, and Italians were pulling their weight became even more important. The work of F. S. Brereton is a useful example here of an author who before 1914 had little time for Europeans, but who became caught up in the need for war propaganda that would enhance positive images of Britain's allies. Brereton's first response was the novel *With Joffre at Verdun*—a story that focused on the valiant defence of the French fortress, told through the experiences of two young French soldiers, Jules and Henri. In the novel, the author overcomes his obvious distaste for the French in truly masterful fashion. Describing Henri, he tells us,

His walk was British, his stride the active, elastic athletic stride of one of our young fellows; and the poise of his head, the erectness of his lithe figure, a symbol of what one is used to in Britons wherever they are met. . . . There was nothing exaggerated about his method of raising his hat to a lady . . . no gesticulations, no active, nervous movements of his hands, and none of that shrugging of the shoulders which, public opinion has it, is so eminently characteristic of our Gallic neighbours.[60]

Jules, our other hero, could also be mistaken for a Briton for, "he too had the distinguished air, that quiet and unassuming demeanor which stamp the

French Veterans, F. S. Brereton, *With Joffre at Verdun*, 1917.

Englishman throughout the world."[61] So what is the explanation; how can these young men be so uncharacteristic of their race? The answer of course is that their fathers, enlightened Frenchmen that they are, fully understood the benefit of an English public school education and thus sent their sons to a "fine old English institution," and on to English universities. There, presumably, under a regime of cold showers, overcooked beef, and organized brutality, all French foolishness had been eradicated from these young Continentals! Now, with these English surrogates as his main focus, Brereton can unfold his tale of high adventure and daring deeds at the defence of Verdun— a battle that was clearly won on the playing fields of a minor English public school!

It was comparatively easy for authors to praise Belgians, and even the French, when suitably Anglicised, might be considered "decent chaps," and for all the lingering Francophobia, France had at least been an official friend since 1904, but Russia was a another matter. The dark, mysterious empire of the Romanovs was neither understood nor trusted. The British public was generally appalled at the almost feudal state in which most Russians were forced to live and condemned the autocratic power of the Tsar. They distrusted Russia's expansionist policies, particularly towards Afghanistan, and were only too aware of the threat posed to India. Antipathy to Russia ran deep, and both Strang and Brereton had produced novels set during the Russo-Japanese War which had come down firmly on the side of the Japanese. In the 1906 novel, *A Soldier of Japan*, for example, Brereton saw the war in terms of the gallant Japanese fighting for liberty against the cruel and barbaric Russians who sought to dominate the Pacific.[62] "Rule Britannia," a 1905 serial in the *Boy's Friend*, had created a scenario in which an Anglo-Russian war breaks out over the Russian fleet destroying British trawlers, which they mistake for Japanese torpedo boats—an incident which did in fact occur as the Baltic Fleet made its way laboriously to the Pacific. And in 1908 one of *Chums'* most popular serials had been Frank Shaw's "Peril's of the Motherland," which told the story of the Tsar's attempted invasion of England.[63] Even under the alliance of war, there was a widespread feeling that Russia was an unworthy ally. A reader's letter published in the *Yorkshire Post* on 3 August 1914 summed up these sentiments, "Russia stands for brute force, any dominance by her in European affairs would be a set back for all the ideals of humanity."[64] However, as George Robb has pointed out, "propaganda glossed over Tsarist tyranny and attributed the shortcomings to a pro-German aristocracy."[65] Thus when war came and Britain and Russia found themselves fighting side-by-side against the common enemy, writers like Strang, Gilson, and Brereton had to overcome their inherent dislike of Russia in order to promote the alliance— an interesting example of the manner in which propaganda attempted to manipulate public opinion to look upon Russia firstly as a reliable friend, then after the Bolshevik revolution as an implacable enemy.

Parrott set the tone, and the other authors of popular histories followed his lead. Russia's problems, he argued, stemmed from the very size of its empire and the diverse races that made up its population. Thus, good and efficient government was difficult. He went on to suggest that her recent defeat by the Japanese was due to poorly trained officers "much given to drink." Now, however, the army has been rearmed and reorganised, and drunken, incapable officers have been replaced by "smart, sober, intelligent men." Although transporting and supplying her vast armies was still proving difficult, he argued that Russia could still field a formidable fighting force.[66] Unfortunately, in the next chapter, Parrott had to deal with the Russian defeats in East Prussia. The author gives little detail about the enormous casualties suffered by the Russian armies, some 80,000 dead and over 130,000 taken prisoner, according to one estimate,[67] but he acknowledges that the Russian invasion of East Prussia was ill-timed; she was not ready for "great adventures." Nevertheless, he leaves his readers on a positive note, pointing out that the invasion "served a good purpose," for it forced the Germans to withdraw troops from the Western Front and thus helped the Allies. So too, the Russian commanders learned lessons that would serve them well in the future.[68] Russian generals actually learned very little from their experiences in East Prussia, but while retaining their enthusiasm for the offensive, suffered continually from lack of war material and the inability of the General Staff to bring up reinforcements and reserves. Thus their offensives, however successful initially, were doomed to fail.[69]

British authors found little inspiration in the doings of the Russian army, and almost until the end of the war, the only Russians to appear in popular fiction were incidental characters. Brereton's 1916 novel, *The Armoured Car Scouts*, is set during the Russian campaign in the Caucasus and is essentially the story of a British armoured car detachment supporting the Russian army. The central character, the young Englishman Guy Grammond, however, has grown up in St. Petersburg, speaks fluent Russian, and has many Russian chums, some of whom are introduced to the reader in the course of the adventure. Guy's best friend, Nicholas, for example, is a westernised and sophisticated cavalry officer and in every respect almost a perfect English gentleman. His men, all peasants of course, are loyal and brave and endure their hardships with fortitude and an almost mystical belief in the cause of Holy Russia; "splendid troops," Nicholas claims.[70] Brereton, of course, found it necessary to minimise Russian disasters in order to boost his readers' confidence in their ally, and here, he falls back on what had become conventional wisdom: Russia was "only partially prepared for war, her transport system unfinished," yet eager to pursue the struggle for "liberty and freedom against the arrogant Kaiser."[71] The Tsar's armies "beat back the Austrians, captured her Galician province [and advanced] to the very doors of Cracow," and wellnigh pour over the German frontier, while the great defeats at Grunwald and Tannenberg are dismissed as setbacks, for "Russia is going the pace."[72] But Russia, as we know, found it increasingly difficult to "go the pace," and propagandists, failing to find anything positive to say about Russia's part in the war, wisely said very little. Incompetent generals, a serious failure to supply the troops in the front line, and rising discontent at home created a revolutionary situation which climaxed in March 1917 when the Tsar was forced to abdicate and a provisional government under Alexander Kerensky took power. Kerensky, dependent upon loans from his Allies, was virtually forced to continue the war. And it was at this point that Charles Gilson's *In Arms for Russia* was published in book form.

Originally published in 1915, as a *Boy's Own Paper* serial, "At the Call of the Tsar," the story focused on a young Englishman fighting with the Russians, and like Brereton's novel *The Armoured Car Scouts*, told the reader very little about Russia or the Russians. Republished in Britain at the time of Russia's crisis, the intention was clearly to inspire the belief that whatever government took power, Russia would fight on with her Allies. The central characters here are the enigmatic Grand Duke Paul Nicholas of Irben and his English chum Bill Rashleigh. We first meet the pair while they are seniors at an English public school in the summer of 1914. Irben is courageous and honourable, but the other boys dislike his intellectual ability and his obsession with international politics—interest in politics was clearly not an attribute English public schoolboys admired. Irben has come to England to learn about English social methods so that he can introduce them at home for the benefit of his people. Thus, Irben is an enlightened aristocrat, who clearly acknowledges the advantages of the English way. Rashleigh, however, finds much to admire in the solemn Russian; they become chums, and when Irben is recalled to Russia because of the July crisis, Bill accompanies him. War is declared as the boys embark, and off the coast of East Prussia, a German cruiser damages their ship. They manage to get ashore on the German-Russian frontier, and Irben decides to visit the German fortress at Konigsberg, in order to learn what he can of the German war plan. The story then follows the usual pattern: the companions are unmasked by a German superspy, escape, and disguised as German soldiers fetch up at Hindenberg's headquarters. Catching sight of the great man, the author tells us that "there was something in the expression of his face which was both sullen and brutal. . . . He looked at once savage, despondent and determined."[73] Unmasked again, they find themselves before a firing squad, only to be rescued at the last moment by a regiment of Cossacks, the spearhead of a Russian offensive. An unremarkable story by the conventions of the time. But what is interesting is the author's attempt to explain Russian reverses and boost his readers' confidence in their Russian ally.

Gilson acknowledges that Russia is perceived as different by most Europeans. "Among the countries of Europe, Russia has stood apart for centuries. Her civilization was never touched by that of the Roman Empire,"[74] and misunderstandings occur mainly because the British know so little about Russia. The strikes and discontent that have plagued her is the work of German agents, but all Russians are committed to the present cause. Even the peasants are ardent patriots, and "man for man . . . superior to the browbeaten conscripts who form the nucleus of the German army. They were men to whom danger was nothing new . . . they are prepared to sacrifice all they possess . . . even their lives—for the cause of Holy Russia."[75] Explaining the early Russian failures, Gilson falls back on the standard explanation, that the country had not fully recovered from the war against Japan, and the modernisation of her army had not been completed. Even so, the Russian invasion of East Prussia had been a strategic success "since it contributed materially to the saving of Paris, but which—it must be confessed—ended in colossal tactical failure."[76] Yet Russia will learn from the experience and will go forward with confidence, united in a single cause. The author goes on to stress the unity of all classes of Russian society, a unity forged by war and the new democratic spirit that now pervades Russia. On one occasion the companions hear the story of Osnas, a Jewish doctor serving with the Russian army. For his bravery under fire, Osnas has been awarded the Military Cross of St. George, and received it from the Tsar himself, an auspicious event because

For centuries the Jews had been persecuted and hated throughout the length and breadth of Russia, and the heroism of Osnas will stand in history for more than an incident of Russian bravery; it was an event which in itself signified the emancipation of the Jews in Russia.[77]

Not only has the war brought about national unity, it is also breaking down the rigid class distinctions that have plagued Russia in the past. While trying to evade capture, Irben, Rashleigh, and the Russian soldier Stakoff prepare a rough meal in a deserted house, and the grand duke insists that Stakoff eat with him: "this is war," he tells the soldier. "The officer and the private can eat from the same dish, warm themselves at the same bivouac fire, just as they can die on the same battlefield, for the same righteous cause."[78] At the end of the novel, having regained the safety of the Russian lines, the Grand Duke and his loyal English companion plan a new campaign against the Germans. "There is much to do," says the grand duke. F. S. Brereton adopted much the same approach and message in his novel *With Our Russian Allies*. But the social changes that appeared to be taking place in Russia and which these authors applauded were mostly window-dressing; empty propaganda intended to inspire British support for a dubious ally. In fact, conditions in Russia worsened under the pressure of war, and by the beginning of 1917, the nation was on the brink of revolution. Strikes and food riots became common in St. Petersburg until finally,

The Volynsky regiment mutinied and others followed suit. The whole edifice of the old regime, undermined by war, weakened by ramshackle organisation, sapped by rampant inflation and riddled with injustice, fell to the ground. On the 2nd. March,

A Russian Bayonet Charge, Sir Edward Parrott, *The Children's Story of the War,*
1916.

after inept attempts to quell the uprising, Tsar Nicholas II abdicated. So the 300-year-old Romanov dynasty came to an end.[79]

A new provisional government under Alexander Kerensky took control, and
desperate for British and French aid, they pledged to continue the war. However, only one novel reflected these truly dramatic changes, Bessie Marchant's
curious story, *A Dangerous Mission: A Tale of Russia in Revolution*, published in
1918.

Set during the last days of the Tsar's reign, the novel's heroine is a young St. Petersburg teacher, Tatna Sobieski. Tatna accidentally becomes involved in a food riot and, believing that she has fallen foul of the secret police, flees to the Caucasus. Here, under the patronage of the benign and liberal aristocrat Baroness Veratz, she sets up a school for peasant children near Tiflis. Yet change is in the air; as a peasant explains to Tatna, "there is freedom coming to Russia now, and the first use she will make of it is to put down the aristocrats who have so long ground the country under their heel."[80] The peasants are generally uncouth, ignorant, superstitious, and violent, prey to any revolutionary firebrand, while government officials are appallingly corrupt and the police simply vicious. Yet there are a handful of young people like Tatna who teach the peasants how to use their freedom so that they will be able to transform Russia. Tatna becomes a "Little Mother" to the people of the region and creates a school and clinic for their children. Finally they learn the "wonderful news," the Tsar has abdicated and that a "bloodless revolution" will transform Russia into the most wonderful country in the world.[81] While Tatna hates the waste of war, she believes that it must be won, otherwise "it will be bad for Russia."[82] What is meant by bad for Russia is not explained, but in fact Kerensky's decision to continue the war led inevitably to a second revolution in October when the Bolsheviks seized power.

Most Britons had applauded the transformation from autocracy to democracy, particularly after May 1917 when the Minister of War confirmed that Russia would fight on with the Allies until victory was secured. Parrott, writing in the summer of 1917, was typical when he noted that the old system of government in Russia had really belonged to the Middle Ages, that the people had no voice in their own affairs, and that the whole system was riddled with corrupt officials. Now, having thrown off her ancient bondage, Russia could go forward to a bright future; indeed, he hoped that the example of Russia would inspire the German people to break free of their own enslavement to the Kaiser.[83] But as the author later points out, before the second revolution was a month old, the Bolsheviks were talking of making peace with Germany.[84] The Germans played along but outwitted the Bolshevik leaders and were finally able to force them to accept a harsh peace signed on 4 March 1918. Parrott seems to suggest that ending the war against Germany was a policy forced upon the Russian people by Lenin and Trotsky, but it seems clear that most Russians had long ago lost any enthusiasm they may have had for the European conflict.[85] Parrott makes little comment about conditions in Soviet Russia, but other authors could not resist dwelling upon the "Red Terror." Brereton, for example, notes that after the October Revolution, Russia was a seething cauldron of revolution, with Bolshevism gaining power and influence.

The better classes there—the officer and the bourgeois classes—were being exterminated, and already a terror worse than that which had existed in France in the great

Revolution of 1789 was sweeping the country. . . . German propaganda had led to an upheaval in Russia, to the downfall and murder of the Tsar, and finally to Bolshevism, a species of super-socialism, influencing the lower orders, or rather the ignorant, the unruly, and the discontented, to attack all others and to aim at the destruction of every institution making for law, order and true liberty. This chaos rendered Russia useless to the Allied cause.[86]

But the problems raised by the Bolshevik Revolution went far beyond the simple loss of an ally, for Bolshevism ultimately aimed at world revolution—and it was widely believed that communism could easily infect the ignorant and the malcontented in any country—even Britain. Thus the Red Peril was considered to be almost as dangerous as the German Menace, and towards the end of the war anti-Bolshevik propaganda was beginning to make its mark in juvenile fiction. Some of the earliest stories focused on the potential dangers of Communist agitators persuading British workers to seek an immediate peace with Germany or even sabotaging the war effort. Typical of this type of material was Radcliffe Martin's "His Bit," a story published in the imperialistic *Chums*, in December 1918. In the story, Jim Bates, a veteran of the trenches but now working in an aircraft factory, prevents a Bolshevik-inspired strike that will damage war production.[87] From that point on, anti-Soviet propaganda became increasingly common in popular literature and endured until the brief alliance with the USSR during the Second World War. The representation of Russia in juvenile fiction before, during, and after the Great War is a powerful example of the manner in which authors reflected the current political climate. But in early 1918, the problem for Britain and France was not that Russia had fallen into the hands of the Bolsheviks, but rather that the armistice between Germany and Russia meant that the experienced troops of the German armies in the east could now be transferred to the Western Front. The United States of America had entered the war on the Allied side in April 1917, and the best hope was to fight a holding action until the American army was ready for combat. However, America relied on the voluntary principle, and in April 1917 their army numbered less than 10,000 men. Its most recent experience had been a limited war against Mexico; thus it would clearly take time to recruit, train, equip, and transport a substantial army to Europe.[88]

Although a great deal of British propaganda had been aimed at enlisting American sympathy for the Allied cause, the United States was rarely mentioned in war fiction until the last year of the war, by which time American troops were in combat in France. However, their position on the sidelines had not prevented American authors from making use of the war as an exciting background for adventure fiction from as early as 1915. The New York publisher A. L. Burt, for instance, ran several series of adventure stories set in the European war, including "The Boy Spies," "Boy Allies with the Army," and "Our Young Aeroplane Scouts"—all of which focused on young American volunteers serving with the British or French armies. By the time American troops were in fighting in Europe, the prolific Horace Porter, author of the latter series, had already produced some dozen novels about Billy Barry and Henri Trouville, two young Americans who serve successively with the British, French and Italian air services. With titles like *Twin Stars in the London Sky Patrol*, *With the War Eagles of the Alps*, and *Lost on the Frozen Steppes*, these novels painted a heroic picture of the war in Europe for young Americans. But Americans, even volunteers, were rare in British literature until late 1917. Parrott was the first to consider America's contribution to the war and was clearly delighted that one of the most powerful nations in the world was now in the Allied camp. In his first volume of 1918, he noted that despite its racially mixed population and the Americans' "peace-loving nature," they were "heart and soul with the President" over the declaration of war; "never did a nation go to war for such unselfish and lofty ends."[89] Having devoted considerable space in explaining America's economic might, he then praised the speed with which American troops had entered the fray. And indeed the first soldiers of the American Expeditionary Force under General "Black Jack" Pershing had reached France in June 1917. Nevertheless, many among the Allies greeted America's late declaration of war with cynicism, believing that the United States had only entered the war at the last minute in order to have a voice in the settlement of a new Europe—a criticism which Escott Lynn clearly felt he needed to address in his 1918 novel, *Knights of the Air*.

While the novel deals with the adventures of young British airmen, a recurring character is the American Nat Brownrigge. Although set during the last year of the war, Lynn is careful to point out that Brownrigge volunteered to serve in the Royal Flying Corps in 1914, thus establishing that some Americans at least had been fighting the Hun since the beginning of the war. Nat, like most fictional Americans, is hugely confident, has an "appealing personality," and is much given to curious expressions like "gotcha" and "you bet." Nat has little respect for authority and is never reluctant to lecture the British on where they have gone wrong. As far as Nat is concerned, the Allies have been rescued from defeat by America: "Fritz would have had your old country bottled if it hadn't been for us coming in."[90] When America is criticised by one of the Englishmen for leaving this rescue until the last moment, Nat explains to his friends that,

We ain't goin' to be hustled. Old Daddy Wilson knows his game. He didn't speak till he was ready, and he ain't goin' to hit till he is ready. But when he does hit, it'll be good and hard, right in old Kaiser Bill's neck—and don't you forget it.

"Do let us know when you're ready," mocks Nat's English friend. But such comments are lost on the thick-skinned American.[91] Lynn does imply that America had always intended to come into the war, for later in the novel, when one of the friends suggests that sinking the *Lusitania* was the Germans' worst mistake because it helped bring America into the war, Nat claims that Americans would have come into the war anyway, mysteriously adding, "I can't say all I know now, but some day the world may know all."[92] Nevertheless, Nat's confidence and his belief that he knows everything sometimes annoys his friends. Doug McCleod, one of the young Britons, confesses to his chum that he finds the American "more than a little irritating," but eventually gives up trying to argue with such a "self-satisfied subject of the United States."[93] Brownrigge, however, is a loyal friend to the young Britons, saving their lives on more than one occasion, but it is possible to detect in Lynn's writing both a sense of relief that America has now joined the Allies, and equally resentment at the Americans' belief that they alone can win the war.

Although American volunteers occasionally appeared in British war stories, only one novel focused specifically on their contribution to the war, F. S. Brereton's *Under Foch's Command: A Tale of the Americans in France*, published at the end of the war. As we have seen, Brereton sometimes found it difficult to praise Britain's allies, but compared with French or Russians, writing about the Americans presented few problems. Americans, after all, shared the same proud, "freedom-loving Anglo-Saxon heritage" as their English cousins. The novel opens in the Rocky Mountains in 1917, where the central characters— Dan Holman and Jim Carpenter—have been working on the railroad. Now, however, they are excited by the prospect of war, with defending American honour, and in dealing with the Kaiser, the "bully-boy" of Europe. Brereton rehearses a string of arguments as to why America has stayed out of the war until 1917. Americans had not been unmoved by the tragedy of Belgium, he explains, but had tried to look upon the war as "dispassionately as was possible."

"No! Not yet—not yet," they had told themselves. "America loves peace: we are a democratic nation, all men, from the president downwards, are equal—as good as one another; we wish no harm to anyone in the world; we desire only to work, to thrive, to live surrounded by freedom and justice."[94]

But in April 1917, even the President lost his patience with German demands that America must cease her seaborne trade. When the news reached Salt Lake City, men sat around discussing what they would do—"Spaniards, who had come to America to delve a way to a fortune; Poles, and Greeks, and Russians . . . Austrians, Turks, and Germans also come here to seek a short road to prosperity." And the verdict is "war at last and not too soon either. Down with Germans and all that's German."[95] Dan and Jim, who, the author tells us, strongly resemble young Englishmen, apart from their skill with a six-gun—"lithe, tall, sinewy young fellows" and "magnificent specimens of American manhood"—help the local sheriff track down a German spy, and then with their friend English Bill, set off for Europe and the war.

After quite amazing adventures involving spies and being torpedoed in the

Atlantic, then taken prisoner aboard a German trawler (they eventually over-power the crew and take the ship to England), they finally get to the Continent at the end of the year. Finding that their exploits are already well known, they are recruited into a "Franco-American transport company" and then to an American unit on the Somme, in time to take part in defeating the German spring offensive. In the chaos of battle, Dan, Jim, and some other Americans team up with the remnants of a British unit, and together they hold a village against almost overwhelming odds. The Germans call off the attack, and Dan and Jim manage to rejoin the American Expeditionary Force. Brereton ends his novel with a handsome tribute to the men who had held the German offensive. "Thus was the fifth year of this awful contest inaugurated. It brought success to the allies, it found their numbers increasing daily by the influx of American troops, and, significant, too, it discovered those American troops to be staunch and sturdy fighters."[96] Of Jim and Dan and English Bill, Brereton tells us that "they are in France as we write. Shoulder to shoulder with their comrades . . . they are opposing the most ruthless enemy that has ever threatened the liberty of mankind."[97] Thus Pershing's Crusaders took their place alongside the other gallant Allies in the Great War for civilization and for democracy. Brereton has little criticism to make of Americans—at worst they are prone to excessive individualism and a belief that they alone can save democracy. But in reality many British (and French) soldiers often resented their better-equipped, better-paid American comrades and envied their supreme self-assurance. Writing in praise of Allies, then, created prob-lems for English authors, and revealed their inherent sense of racial superi-ority and dislike of foreigners, even if they were on the same side. F. S. Brereton is, perhaps, an extreme example of such attitudes. For him, foreign-ers can only be acceptable of they look and behave like Englishmen—only by adopting English attitudes, values, and customs (preferably learned at an En-glish public school) can the foreigner be awarded a measure of equality.

CHAPTER 6

The Last of War, 1917–1918

> So ended the Great War, in brilliant fashion for the Allies. Yet consider at what cost, with what misery, and suffering and hardship this victory was achieved. More than a million sons of Britain had died for it; two million more had suffered wounds; the young men of this era had almost disappeared—but they had died for their Country.
>
> For us the World War ends in Germany, with France and Belgium freed for ever from the invader, with Jim and all his friends, war-worn and weary, yet still on duty with the Allies on the Rhine.
> —F. S. Brereton, *With the Allies to the Rhine*[1]

While the problems faced by civilians on the home front could hardly be compared to the appalling conditions endured by the troops at the battlefront, the war did create unprecedented difficulties and suffering for many civilians. Rationing, shortages, longer working days, concern about family members or friends serving in the armed forces and, after 1915, the possibilities of air raids, all combined to produce a climate of hardship and anxiety. While popular fiction tended to minimise these problems by transforming the home front into a site of excitement and adventure for civilians, particularly boys too young to enlist and young women, it is possible to glean some understanding of the dramatic social changes that were wrought by the war in popular literature. Spies, saboteurs, raiding Zeppelins and bombers, the dangers of working in munitions or heavy industry; or even caring for the wounded and so sharing at least part of their suffering, offered writers a source for inspirational fiction which they quickly exploited. Thus war stories became a significant element not only in fiction for young men but also for young women who, for the first time, became active participants in war in a manner that would have been unthinkable in earlier conflicts.

Many girls and young women found the outbreak of war intensely exciting and hoped to play some part in the war effort. But as Vera Brittain noted in her diary on 6 August, sewing was the "only work it seems possible for women to do—the making of garments for soldiers."[2] The offer to serve in some more positive capacity was initially not appreciated by the government, who expected a short war and who were not prepared to consider women as part of the official war effort. *The Girls' Own Paper*, following the official line of business as usual, suggested that girls (and their mothers) should "avoid comic-opera like efforts that involved horses, tents or pseudo-military uniforms," nor should they use the war as an excuse to "advance the cause of feminism."[3] As Cate Haste points out, women were expected to stay at home and send their men to the trenches, and this many women fervently did. Baroness Orczy, the creator of *The Scarlet Pimpernel* and other popular adventure stories, orchestrated the Active Service League to persuade men to enlist, while, as we have seen, the Order of the White Feather was formed to present apparently fit men not in uniform with a white feather—a symbol of cowardice.[4] Many women, like the poet Jessie Pope, wrote stirring recruiting jingles, such as

Who's for the trench—
Are you my laddie?
Who'll follow French—
Will you, my laddie?
Who's fretting to begin,
Who's going out to win?
And who wants to save his skin—
Do you, my laddie?[5]

Even government posters encouraged women to become active recruiters: "Is your 'Best Boy' wearing khaki? If not don't YOU THINK he should be?" asked one particularly unsavoury example. This dubious form of recruiting for the armed forces created considerable bitterness among many young men who, probably unreasonably, later came to believe that they had been forced into uniform by underhand methods; and this distorted view of women as recruiting agents later resulted in particularly vicious comments by poets like Siegfried Sassoon, Wilfred Owen, and Richard Aldington.[6] However, this transference of blame may well have been due to their need to find a scapegoat for the experience which they, and many others, believed had robbed them of their youth, their comrades, and the world they had grown up in. Yet from their memoirs it becomes increasingly clear that their decision to enlist for the great adventure was more a result of their own romantic view of war than any malignant female influence. But writing verse, persuading young men to don khaki, or knitting mufflers seemed but a marginal contribution to the great struggle for many women who yearned to play a more active part in the war. But as the realisation that the war would not be over by Christmas sank in, increasing opportunities opened for women to serve as nurses, industrial workers, and eventually as auxiliaries in the armed forces.[7] These experiences formed the basis for popular fictions intended to entertain and encourage young female readers.

Nursing had, since the Crimean War, been an acceptable way in which women could play some part in the nation's wars, and for those who lacked a nursing qualification, service with the Voluntary Aid Detachment (VAD) offered a variety of domestic jobs in hospitals. Being a VAD was a popular form of participation for young women during the early years of the war and, as we have seen, provided the basis for Bessie Marchant's novel *A VAD in Salonika*. Significantly, none of these novels, not even those written towards the end of the war, informed the reader about the realities of nursing badly injured men in military hospitals. For that, readers had to wait until the postwar memoirs of Enid Bagnold, Vera Brittain, and other military nurses.[8] The VAD was, by and large, for educated middle-class girls, but the shortage of male industrial workers also created increasing opportunities for young working-class women. While women performed a variety of roles, the most dangerous was undoubtedly in the munitions industry. Brenda Girvin's *Munition Mary* and Marchant's *A Girl Munition Worker* both focus on how young women perform a number of unpleasant and dangerous jobs with skill and tenacity while at the same time coping with the not inconsiderable resentment of their male co-workers. In the first novel, the factory owner is totally opposed to women workers in his factory, and Mary not only has to do her job even more effectively than a man but unmasks saboteurs and spies as well before the chauvinistic factory owner Sir William finally accepts female labour. Marchant's heroine, Deborah Lynch, doesn't encounter prejudice, but she does help trap a German agent helping Zeppelins to target munitions factories, and the author acknowledges that munitions work was dangerous. Deborah is not initially working with explosives, but she is soon transferred to the dangerous task of fusing shells, "the hardest part of that first day was the consciousness of being in such danger. Her nerves were strained to the extremist tension the whole day through. By night she was a wreck."[9] When she mentions this to the forewoman, she is told,

The only way to bear the strain is to lose sight of one's self in the doing of one's duty. Better still, try to feel that you are giving yourself to your country, and it no longer matters to you in what sense the gift is to be used. If you are to be blown to pieces tomorrow, it will not really matter to you, your gift is being used just the same.[10]

Surprisingly, this not only makes Deborah feel much better, but also increases her enthusiasm for her dangerous work. After 1917 the women's services auxiliary were created, and novels like Marchant's *A Transport Girl in France* and *Jenny Wren* by Brenda Girvin dealt with the Womens' Auxiliary Army Corps and the Womens' Royal Naval Service, respectively.[11] Again the girl heroines of these fictions have to face male prejudice and the Hun before proving that they can also make a positive contribution to the war effort.

Not everyone took the efforts of women seriously, though, as the appallingly patronising collection of rhymes and pictures by Hampden Gordon and Joyce Dennys reveal. In *Our Girls in Wartime*, the Womens' Land Army are dismissed with the following:

> Lizzie labours on the land.
> What she does I understand,
> Is to make the cattle dizzy
> Running round . . . admiring Lizzie.

This is followed by similar rhymes disparaging virtually every role performed by women. The authors followed this collection with *Our Hospital ABC*—an equally patronising collection of verses.[12] But the contribution that women made was more sensibly summed up by Angela Brazil in her 1918 novel *A Patriotic School Girl*. At morning assembly at Brackenfield College, the headmistress reminds the assembled school that

> We used to be told that the battle of Waterloo was won on the playing fields of our great public schools. Well, I believe that many future struggles are being decided by the life in our girls' schools of today. Though we mayn't realize it, we're all playing our part in history, and though our names may never go down to posterity, our influence will. The watchwords of all patriotic women at present are 'Service and Sacrifice'. In the few years that we are here at school let us prepare ourselves to be an asset to the nation afterwards.[13]

This is followed by a roll call of old girls and the part they are playing in the war, including nurses, teachers, transport girls, and, significantly, those who are bringing up their children alone having been widowed by the war.[14] And here, Brazil seems to be suggesting that the positive part women have played in national life will continue after the war. But not all girls' fiction was as positive, stressing that the important contribution women were making during the war years was for the duration only, assuming that when peace came gender roles would revert to a pre-1914 model. As Mary Cadogan and Patricia Craig have pointed out, tradition was also served by the many magazine stories for girls which simply used the war as an exciting background for romance which invariably ended with the heroine marrying her plucky Tommy.[15] Nevertheless, the disruption, danger, and anxiety of the home front, combined with a mounting sense that so many lives were being exchanged for so little gain, had created a widespread mood of disillusionment, made worse by anxiety about attack from the air and the seemingly ceaseless activities of spies and saboteurs who were undermining the war effort.

Spies and attack from the air were brought together in Charles Gilson's novel, *On Secret Service*. Although published in 1919, the story is set in the middle years of the war at the height of the Zeppelin menace. The central character here, Daniel Wansborough, is an ex-police inspector now working for S Division, a government department responsible for internal security. Gilson repeats many common wartime myths, one being that long before the war started, the German government had planted thousands of spies and saboteurs in Britain. "Even in those days," he recalls, "England teemed with German spies."[16] In the novel, these agents are controlled by the German intelligence officer, Felix von Arnheim. Von Arnheim's master plan, however, is to develop a system using three agents to triangulate important targets for the Zeppelin raiders. This is a novel twist on what, as we have seen, was a common belief, but Gilson gives the myth substance by explaining the fiendish scheme in detail. Wansborough stumbles upon the plan almost by accident, but once he has the first clue his dogged determination carries him through and results in smashing the German spy ring and von Arnheim's death. German intelligence are naturally disappointed with the master spy's failure, but as the head of German intelligence tells his assistant, the English are "lucky fools," and the greatest German coup is yet to come, for "in a few days rebellion will break out in Ireland."[17] As we know, rebellion did indeed break out in Ireland at Easter in 1916, but it was swiftly dealt with by the British authorities and brought little real comfort to the Germans.

Spy novels were widely read during the war years, reflecting and reinforcing the belief that the country was beset by agents of the Kaiser. Many stories were specially written for younger readers, while some authors like William Le Queux and John Buchan were read by both adults and adolescents. Le Queux's *The German Spy* (1914) and Buchan's *Greenmantle* (1915) were both extremely successful. Influenced by the mood of the times, Arthur Conan Doyle even resurrected the great detective Sherlock Holmes to deal with enemy spies in "His Last Bow" (1917), while in the story papers, ace detectives Nelson Lee and Sexton Blake were often to be found working for military intelligence. As George Robb has noted, it was commonly believed that Germans had infiltrated even the highest levels of British society, and popular fiction, like Dorota Flatau's novel *Yellow English* (1918), for example, reflected this belief in a tale in which wealthy Germans who had married into the British peerage well before 1914 were finally revealed as enemy agents.[18] At the enormously popular fictional "Greyfriar's School," the boys spent much of their time in hunting spies. A likely suspect was the school's German master Herr Gans. But Charles Hamilton was one author who, while still intensely patriotic, disapproved of hysterical anti-Germanism, and Gans turns out to be a good Saxon rather than a bad Prussian. As Harry Wharton pointed out in a 1916 issue of the *Magnet*, "there are some decent Germans—Handel and

Beethoven were Germans, you know, and it would be idiotic to call them 'Huns.'"[19] Presumably, though, in the short catalogue of good Germans, it was clearly an advantage to be dead! But while spies were continually being hunted down by Boy Scouts, school prefects, and girls "of the right sort" in juvenile fiction, that other target of righteous indignation, the slacker—those who have wangled safe jobs at home and left the fighting to others, are rarely encountered. Only in Westerman's novel *Winning His Wings* are they mentioned when two airmen suggest that once the war is over and the troops come home, the slackers will be ashamed of their conduct.[20]

By the last year of the war, then, and despite the upbeat tone of propaganda fictions set on the home front, war weariness was widespread, compounded by disappointment at the failure of military offensives of 1916 and early 1917, and particularly after the Battle of the Somme, which had promised an early end to the war. Nor were Britain's allies doing very much better. During the course of 1917, revolution swept through Russia and, although the provisional government promised to continue the war, the Russian army was in disarray and subject to increasing Bolshevik propaganda that urged an end to the war. The United States of America had finally entered the war on the Allied side, but had only a small professional army, and it would be some time before American armies could make a significant contribution to the war effort in Europe. More worrying, perhaps, were the mutinies in the French army. These were due more to disappointment with the failed grandiose offensives of successive generals and the slapdash manner of supplying French troops in the trenches, together with lack of leave and poor medical care. But these were not mutinies in the strictest sense, for the men involved only refused to take part in another offensive. General Philippe Petain mastered the mutinies by June 1917,[21] but for the British High Command, such events merely reconfirmed the unreliability of the French. However, while these difficulties were never reported in the British press, rumours that all was not well with the French army circulated widely. Looking back at 1917, Parrott acknowledged that a nation that grew tired of the struggle before it had accomplished its purpose was facing ruin and thus, "no pains must be spared to reinvigorate their flagging energies." However, he was careful to point out that it should not be supposed that "at the close of three years of stress and anxiety the British people were war-weary, or that their determination had slackened," rather the government thought it wise to reinvigorate the people by reminding them why they had "drawn the sword," through public meetings. Parrott equally felt duty bound to remind his readers of the need to liberate Belgium and France, defend the Empire, and put an end to tyranny.[22] But he also introduced a new factor, explaining that the British and their allies were now fighting "to put an end to war, the greatest tragedy of human life."[23] And by and large, most Britons probably did cling desperately to the idea that the war was a justified crusade against aggression, tyranny, and war itself, believing that the fighting must be continued: that the sacrifice and loss they had endured "must be redeemed by a victorious peace."[24] The problem was, how was victory to be achieved?

By 1916, the German defences along the Western Front were almost impregnable—strongly fortified positions comprising complex trench systems, barbed wire, deep dugouts, and concrete pillboxes; and despite the optimistic declarations of the generals, a successful breakthrough appeared almost impossible. As early as 1915, some authors of propaganda fiction, as we have seen, had become disheartened and had turned away from the Western Front in order to focus on the sideshows—the campaigns outside Europe which, with the exception of the Gallipoli campaign, more closely resembled traditional warfare. But the military were convinced that Germany had to be defeated on the Western Front for, as Douglas Haig argued, the war could not be won without "engaging the main body of the enemy in a continental war."[25] The problem was, how could this engagement be transformed into victory—how could a breakthrough be accomplished? Certainly ever-larger armies might attempt to swamp the enemy, but there was a limit to the number of men that even conscription could deliver, and as many pointed out, these were not the physically fit, well-educated, and highly motivated volunteers of the early days of the war. As Siegfried Sassoon later noted, replacement drafts coming in to his battalion in 1917 were mostly "undersized, dull-witted, and barely capable of carrying the heavy weight of their equipment." What they lacked physically was mirrored by their lack of commitment and enthusiasm.[26] And this, of course, made encouraging and persuasive propaganda more necessary than ever. But if victory could not be achieved by numerical superiority, perhaps revolutionary new weapons might ensure a breakthrough and restore a war of movement leading to a German defeat.

Chemical weapons were, as we have seen, an early example of this line of thought, but once both sides possessed such weapons any advantage was cancelled out. Besides, poison gas was a morally dubious weapon and difficult to use with any precision. An alternative weapon was some kind of machine that could protect troops from the shattering firepower of modern weapons as they advanced across No Man's Land towards the enemy and by which defences might be overcome. Curiously, in Herbert Strang's 1915 novel, *Fighting with French*, just such a device had been improvised by his young fictional warriors. The British are defending a captured village and expecting a German counterattack at any moment. Knowing that the enemy will be in superior numbers, Kenneth Amory decides on a surprise attack on the enemy rather than simply wait for an overwhelming onslaught on his position. He imaginatively decides to use a lorry, bullet-proofed with sheets of zinc and sandbags, to make the attack. The soldiers take cover behind the lorry, and thus protected from machine gun fire, follow it closely as it crashes through the German barbed wire and into the trenches beyond. The defenders, taken by surprise, are quickly dispatched with hand grenades. Kenneth's colonel is pleased with the young man's capital idea and congratulating the young soldiers, tells them that "there's a fortune awaiting the man who invents a bullet-proof protection for infantry in the field."[27] What Strang had done, of course, was to predict the coming of the tank, which was even then being developed by the Admiralty. But Strang was not the first to predict an armoured fighting vehicle, for the tank had first appeared in popular fiction in a short story by H. G. Wells, "The Land Ironclads," published in 1903 in the aftermath of the Boer War.

In Wells' story, a war between unnamed countries has reached deadlock; the armies of both sides have become entrenched and seem incapable of breaking through their opponents' defences. Then, after a month of stalemate, the "Land Ironclads" developed by the more technologically inclined nation make their appearance. Between 80 and 100 feet long, built from steel and driven by powerful steam engines, these iron monsters move on multiple pedrail wheels. Packed with machine guns and riflemen, the machines smash through the enemy defences, clear the frontline trenches, and open the way for their own infantry to advance.[28] Between the publication of "The Land Ironclads" and 1914, several inventors created designs for primitive armoured vehicles, but the military leaders of Europe showed little interest. This military conservatism and the lack of enthusiasm to consider new ways of war had also been predicted by Wells, for at the end of his story a cavalry colonel who has spent years training his men and horses to perfection is devastated when he realises that against land ironclads, his proud cavalrymen are powerless.[29] Nevertheless, the opening phase of war in 1914 did see the rapid development of the armoured car, ironically sponsored by the Admiralty.[30] While the exploits of armoured car units during the early months of the war provided inspiration for adventure writers,[31] once the war became entrenched, their value diminished. They were easily immobilised in mud and soft terrain and lacked the power to overcome enemy defences, and thus they were relegated to battlefields where mobility was still possible.

However, as J. P. Harris notes, "the technology for an armoured cross-country vehicle already existed."[32] Caterpillar track was already in use, as were internal combustion engines of sufficient power. In early 1915, Winston Churchill, then still at the Admiralty, became interested in developing a vehicle capable of helping infantry to cross the churned up terrain of No Man's Land. A Landships Committee was established to examine various possibilities and a design chosen, but not until January 1916 was a prototype ready. Code-named Tank, the machine was successfully tested and put into production. In early 1916 Douglas Haig planned to use 100 tanks to spearhead his forthcoming attack on the Somme, but production delays ensured that the first tanks did not reach France until August, and then it was less than half the number ordered. Nevertheless they were ordered into battle on 15 September 1916. Their dramatic appearance, however, was limited because they were used singly as infantry support rather than *en masse*, and many suffered mechanical failure. Yet Haig was convinced of their potential, and a further thousand were ordered. At the Battle of Cambrai the following year, 378 tanks, assisted by massed aircraft, did achieve a successful breakthrough in the German line.

The tanks crunched over the wire and trenches and advanced in a single day as far as the British army had in months on the Somme and at Ypres, reaching the German rear zone some three or four miles behind the front line.[33]

But many tanks were lost or broke down, and a German counterattack soon won back the ground that had been lost. Nevertheless, for propagandists, the tank appeared to be the weapon of victory, and they wrote about it with enthusiasm. The use of tanks on the Somme was announced to the British public under headlines like "A TANK IS WALKING UP THE HIGH STREET OF FLERS WITH THE BRITISH ARMY CHEERING BEHIND."[34] Glowing reports of the tanks' success were recorded by war correspondents anxious to boost the morale of readers at home. *The Daily Express* report, by Percival Phillips, was typical of the hyperbole employed.

Sinister, formidable, and industrious, these novel machines pushed boldly into "No Man's Land," astonishing our soldiers no less than they frightened the enemy. Presently I shall relate some of the strange incidents of their first grand tour of Picardy: of Bavarians bolting before them like rabbits, and others surrendering in picturesque attitudes of terror, and the delightful story of the Bavarian Colonel who was carted about for hours in the belly of one of them, like Jonah in the whale, while his captors slew the men of his broken divisions.[35]

But no mention was made of the frequent mechanical failures or the lack of tactical imagination by the High Command that had largely squandered the element of surprise that such novel machines created.

Parrott saw the development of the tank as a clear symbol of British technical superiority. The Germans have always been regarded as inventive, he argued, but "We were the first to invent the 'land ships' known as Tanks." He then goes on to catalogue the effect their appearance had on the enemy: "The Germans were taken completely by surprise, and as the monsters advanced, crawling over the shell holes and trenches, and spitting fire from loopholes, many of them held up their hands in surrender or fled to the rear terror-stricken."[36] The author likened the tanks to caterpillars, a simile later adopted by many writers, including Lincoln Hayward in the *Boy's Own Paper*;[37] and he told his readers that they had been developed by the Director of Naval Construction. After an account of their use on the Somme, Parrott noted that while the appearance of the tanks had raised "wild hopes" among the Allies, those hopes had been disappointed by year's end because while tanks could make the breakthrough possible, the infantry had been unable to secure their hold on the German line. Nevertheless, he concluded by claiming that the tanks had "come to stay," and that if they could be utilized in large numbers, "trench warfare would be a thing of the past, and machine gun redoubts would lose their terror."[38] His account of the use of tanks at the Battle of Cambrai in a subsequent volume was more fulsome, but even he had to admit that by the end of 1917, little had really been achieved.[39] However, writers of adventure fiction, who had retreated from tales of the Western Front in favour of more glamorous adventures in the Middle East or Africa, now began to relocate their war stories back to France where the tank offered not only new opportunities for exciting tales of war adventure, but perhaps the means of ending the war.

In fiction, the tank made its first appearance in F. S. Brereton's novel of the 1916 offensives, *Under Haig in Flanders*, published in early 1917. Roger Norman, the novel's hero, still a sergeant, is wounded in the opening phase of the Battle of the Somme. After recovering he is commissioned for his leadership skills and transferred to the Tank Corps. In France, he meets Bill, an old friend from his battalion. When the latter asks "What's a tank"? Roger replies,

A huge armoured fort, made to grovel its way over the ground and across trenches. Something that's still somewhat of an experiment, though successful already. A new weapon devised to attack the German and force him backward, particularly his machine gunners.[40]

Roger manages to get Bill transferred to the Tank Corps as well, and together they begin to train their tank crew. In September, the tanks go into battle. Brereton notes that the tanks tended to be used piecemeal, and at one point Roger believes he has gone into the attack "almost single-handed." He does, however, reach the German front line, where bewildered German soldiers stumble from their dugouts and surrender to the steel monster. Roger's machine continues to advance, until it becomes wedged in the remains of a dugout system. Unable to free the machine, Roger's crew abandon the tank and fight on foot. Nevertheless, at the end of the novel, Roger is convinced that the tank has proved itself and will eventually pave the way for victory. Brereton had clearly drawn his information on tanks from newspaper reports, but the exploits of the Tank Corps are dealt with only briefly in the novel. Tanks reappear in his final novel of the Western Front, *With the Allies to the Rhine* (1919), when during the Allied offensive of August 1918, it is the tanks that unleash the final blow in the assault, "to right and to left; everywhere tanks beating down the opposition."[41] But 1917 saw the publication of Percy Westerman's novel *To the Fore with the Tanks!* which publicised the new weapon far more prominently.

In the novel, three young soldiers are sent as replacements to their battalion during the Somme offensive. Their unit advances behind the tanks, and when one becomes bogged down in the mud, they help free it. The leader of the trio, Ralph Setley, is fascinated by the machine, and after he wins a battlefield

A Tank in Action, *The Wonder Book of Soldiers*, 1919.

commission he is sent to the Tank Corps. Westerman, however, treats the potential of the tank with more caution than some writers. While Setley is training as a tank commander, his instructor tells him that landships are not invulnerable. "However useful tanks have been and are . . . they have their limitations." He then goes on to explain that a tank is simply a means to an end.

As an adjunct to an infantry attack it is most efficient. When first brought into action landships scored heavily, owing to their novel characteristics. The Huns have now found certain means to counter their offensive. . . . So in the attack exercise discretion until you are astride the enemy trenches.[42]

And when Setley finally takes his tank into action, it does indeed suffer mechanical failures before taking part in a successful massed attack on a German-held village. Like Brereton, Westerman's tale relies heavily on press reports of the tanks in action. At one point in the novel, he even repeats Percival Phillips' report in the *Daily Express* about the captured Bavarian colonel carted around the battlefield in the belly of a tank. Westerman, of course, adds to the original story and has the colonel "trembling violently" after his nerve-racking experience of being under fire inside a tank.[43] However, neither of these novels could attempt to offer a description of what it was like to be part of a tank crew in action. For that, readers had to wait for the spate of tank adventures published after the war when more detail had been made available.

In *Winning his Wings*, Westerman has one episode in which the young airman Derek Daventry is taking part in a combined tank and air force offensive. He is shot down and crash-lands near a British tank. To avoid the German bombardment he seeks refuge inside the tank.

There was very little room to move about. Most of the interior was occupied by the powerful motors and fuel-tanks, six-pounder guns mounted *en barbette*, and machine guns, to say nothing of fifteen men of the original crew. The tank was in reality a moving magazine, for in addition to the large quantity of petrol and ammunition, she carried a stock of phosphorous-bombs, smoke-bombs, and gun-cotton. The latter explosive was for use in the event of the tank becoming disabled and in danger of falling into the hands of the enemy, and it was the duty of the last surviving member of the crew to blow the land-ship to bits should there be a danger of capture.[44]

As the tank goes into action, Derek takes over a machine gun, but finds that fighting inside a tank is an unpleasant affair. The constant lurching over broken ground throws the crew about in a most dangerous way, German antitank bullets penetrate the armour, and even bullets bouncing off the tank's skin cause splinters of metal to shear off the inside walls and these frequently cause injury to the crew. When an enemy shell sets fire to the motor, the "noxious fumes" from the fire make the interior untenable, and Derek and crew are forced to abandon the machine.[45]

In this novel, written at the end of the war, Westerman offers useful guidance on the future of warfare in which artillery, tanks, and aircraft are carefully integrated, a version of *Blitzkreig*, that would become such a crucial factor in the German successes of 1939–1940, which reminds us that by the end of the war Allied commanders had begun to learn how to use tanks and aircraft to spearhead an attack on the enemy trenches. Having chosen the sector to attack, the High Command realise that an infantry attack would be too costly and as the author explains, a prolonged heavy artillery bombardment would give the enemy prior warning of an attack.

So the assault was to be delivered by tanks, supported by relatively small detachments of infantry, while the R.A.F. were ordered to co-operate to their utmost capacity. Every available machine fit for offensive work was to be employed in the operation, the idea being not only to paralyse the Huns in the firing-line, but to prevent reinforcements and supplies reaching them.[46]

It was Westerman who made the only reference to the fact that the Germans had also developed tanks. In the short story, "When Tank Meets Tank," also published in the last year of the war, the author deals with a battle between British and German tanks. The Germans made little real attempt to develop tanks, although they did build the unwieldy A7V. But the first tank battle in April 1917 at Villers-Bretonneux convinced the Germans that the A7V was unsuitable for combat, and thereafter they tended to use captured British tanks.[47] However, in Westerman's story the struggle is reduced to a one-to-one battle in which grit and inventiveness and the technical superiority of the British machine are the deciding factors.[48] However, as Ian Beckett has suggested, because of the tank's limitations, "there was little real agreement within the British Expeditionary Force on whether mechanical warfare truly offered a substitute for manpower."[49] In juvenile literature, it was only after the war that a realistic assessment of the tank appeared. In an article in the 1919 edition of *The Wonder Book of Soldiers* the author acknowledged that initially soldiers were full of admiration for these "wonderful fighting machines," but they soon realised that while invulnerable to bullets, "even a tank . . . can be put out of action by a shell, and that the Germans were not slow to produce an anti-tank gun which did a considerable amount of execution." In getting over rough ground, these "monsters" frequently met with "accidents" and had to be abandoned.[50] Yet, the article concludes, tanks had proved of considerable value, and not least in Britain where many boys and girls contributed to war bonds simply because they bore the emblem of a tank.[51]

By the last year of the war, then, the tank had become a popular icon in war adventure, and around the time of the Armistice a number of articles, stories, and novels about landship warfare were being published.[52] But why did this primitive fighting machine, so prone to mechanical failure, become such a powerful symbol of modern warfare in war fiction? In the early nineteenth century, the irrationality of battle had been disguised by the emphasis on individual fighting skill and the advantage of belonging to a warlike race. Put more crudely, it was suggested that the more heroic and ferocious, the better the individual's chance of survival, at least in fiction. But what the war story celebrated as inherent "martial prowess" was invariably due to the superiority of British tactics, weapons, and discipline. However, the massive employment of modern weaponry in the Great War, which was equally available to both sides, sorely tested this view. As Omer Bartov has suggested, the new technological weaponry employed in 1914—machine guns, high explosive shells, gas, and bombs—made individual talent for war useless, and made the descendents of the chivalric warrior redundant by "putting an end to all individual heroism and character, transforming the battlefield into a factory of death, where victory would be decided by the quality and quantity not of men, but of machines."[53] Life or death in battle was reduced to simple chance—it mattered not how cunning or skilful a warrior was but where he was when the shell landed, or the gas came. Nevertheless, as the chivalric knight of the Middle Ages had been a construct of the medieval chronicler, so by the middle years of the Great War, contemporary propagandists were beginning to create new fighting elites: warriors who had learned to dominate the machines of war.

[T]he new knights of war were the tankmen and pilots, the submarine crews and the highly trained, well-equipped troops of the assault battalions. . . . the impersonality of [modern] war consequently appeared to have been done away with; or at least, men could once more be persuaded that war would give them the opportunity to demonstrate personal heroism.[54]

Thus, the new heroes of the war story were the men who controlled the machines and who, by their technical ability, courage, and tenacity, once again made success in battle a matter of individual skill.

Yet despite the introduction of new weapons, by the end of 1917 the war was still in stalemate. Parrott's summary of the year concluded that while Cambrai and the use of the new tanks had resulted in a successful breakthrough, the advantage could not be held, noting that,

So with the story of a victory and a reverse our record of 1917 comes to an end. Though the year had closed with a set-back, no Briton had lost one shred of faith in the gallant men who were upholding the cause of their country on the battlefield. . . . The nation still stood firm, relying upon the undoubted justice of its cause, the steadfast endurance of its people, and the superb courage of its fighting men.[55]

However, in the spring of 1918, that endurance and courage would be tested to the hilt as the German army unleashed a last throw offensive that cut through the Allied line, took the enemy deep into France, and resulted in considerable panic among the Allies.

By late 1917, the German people were equally suffering from war weariness. The Allied naval blockade was creating serious shortages, and despite virtual victory on the Eastern Front, the human cost of the war had drained the nation; even the military were alarmed at the prospect of facing another Allied offensive in the west. At Mons, in November 1917, the German High Command met to consider their strategy for the New Year, and decided on an offensive in the spring that they hoped would end the war. Codenamed Michael, but often referred to as "the Kaiser's Battle," the offensive was intended to smash through the line between Arras and St. Quentin, divide the British and French armies, and open the road to Paris and the Channel coast. It was, as Correlli Barnett notes, "a grandiose military gamble."[56] Troops no longer needed on the Eastern Front were transferred to the west and together with veterans from France were schooled in new tactics that made use of surprise and infiltration rather than the suicidal mass assaults that in the past had achieved only enormous casualties. This time there would be no long softening-up barrage but rather a brief but deadly bombardment after which the storm troops would infiltrate the Allied positions. Strong points were to be bypassed in order to move quickly into open country behind the Allied lines. The Germans took every precaution to keep their preparations secret, but the British and French were well aware of the coming attack. But lacking a unified Allied command, few precautions were taken, and in the early hours of 11 April 1918, 47 German divisions prepared to attack. At 9:00 A.M., after a five-hour bombardment of the front line, the guns began a creeping barrage and the storm troops began their advance. The bombardment had destroyed Allied communications and headquarters, and gas attacks had immobilised many Allied troops. Shocked by the ferocity of the offensive, the British and French put up little resistance, and by nightfall the attackers had cleared the British lines and reached the open country beyond. The following day, the disorganised British Fifth and Third Armies began to fall back—the beginning of the March retreat that caused such alarm in London, Paris, and Washington.

Parrott, writing several months after the battle, carefully pointed out to his readers that the great onslaught was a sign, not of German strength but of German weakness—the last gasp of a desperate enemy. He also noted the dangers the enemy had faced in attacking so early in the year when, if the dry spell broke, their armies would become bogged down, and then after asking why Germany had been "prepared to stake everything upon this great gamble," offers his answer,

The best observers told us that the condition of Germany and Austria was so bad that he dared not delay. Unless he struck quickly and successfully he would never be able to do so, because the German and Austrian peoples would be unable to bear their hard conditions much longer, and would demand peace at any price.[57]

In fiction, Brereton repeated the message, "it was Germany's last opportunity to snatch victory." But the author does offer some insight into the panic that the breakthrough caused when he adds that during the weeks of crisis every Briton up to the age of 48 and fit to bear arms had been called to the colours, while America hastened her troops across the Atlantic as quickly as possible.[58] Westerman gives us some sense of this panic in *Winning His Wings*. Daventry, his fictional RAF officer, arrives in France just after the beginning of the offensive: "with hundreds of other airmen he had been sent across to assist in stemming the tide of Huns." Landing at his new airfield, a mechanic tells him the Germans are less than 12 miles away and the squadron is falling back—"Apparently we're doing a sort of fox-trot backwards," a fellow officer tells him. Later the squadron is ordered to put every machine into the air in order to slow the enemy advance, and the pilots are told to expect "considerable losses."[59]

In *Knights of the Air*, published in the autumn of 1918, Escott Lynn paints a highly dramatic picture of the opening of the offensive through the experiences of his RAF pilots, Billy Granville and Douglas McLeod, flying above the enemy lines.

The sight was appalling! For eighty miles the German front was literally ablaze; every conceivable sort of shell was being fired upon the British from every conceivable kind of gun. Earth, bricks, pieces of timber, houses, dug-outs were flying in the air; it seemed as if nothing could live through such an experience. Thousands upon thousands of infantry were seen massing for the attack; the ground was literally black with them, and every bomb that Douglas dropped found its mark.[60]

But Billy and Douglas get a much closer view of the German attack, for their aircraft is damaged and they are forced down just behind the British front line. Stumbling into the trenches to avoid the barrage, they witness the onslaught first hand.

wave after wave of gray-clad Germans were seen advancing, and the British front-line trenches blazed with rifle and machine-gun fire. The Germans went down in swathes, but others pressed on, and gradually drew nearer and nearer to the trenches.[61]

The British take a tremendous toll of the enemy, but wave after wave of fresh German troops replace the fallen and force the British to withdraw, back to their own artillery positions, and still the Germans advance. Billy and Douglas take over machine guns, firing until they become too hot to touch, but "still the Germans advanced, sullenly, doggedly, determined to conquer or die—and they died." Towards evening the attack eased, but it was "such day of slaughter not a man of them had ever seen before, or hoped ever to see again." The utterly exhausted Billy and Douglas watch a British battalion counter-attack and take back some of the frontline trenches they had earlier lost. The airmen are full of admiration for these tenacious, daring infantry-men: "'Good heavens!" cried Billy, "such men are more than human." "Yes," said Douglas; "They're British."[62]

In Lynn's novel, a part of the British line is held for a while, but eventually the enemy break through and begin their advance, although every effort is made to stem the German tide. In Westerman's story, Derek Daventry's RAF squadron is thrown into the battle.

A [German] battalion in mass formation moving by the side of a straight stretch of canal afforded fair sport. Derek dived almost perpendicularly, with engines all out until within two hundred feet of the ground, then, flattening out, made straight for the field-greys.
. . . the Boche were instantly thrown into a panic. They broke ranks and fled . . . impeding each other, literally falling over one another, the wretched Boches were at the mercy of the swift battleplane. Machine-guns and bombs both took a heavy toll.[63]

As the author reminds us, Daventry was but one of hundreds of pilots flying several missions every day in a desperate attempt to stem the German advance. Westerman's pilot is wounded before the battle ends, but while the RAF as-sault on the Germans may have slowed their advance, the British were still forced to retreat, and by 5 April, the Germans had advanced 28 miles and taken over 70,000 prisoners. Their armies threatened Amiens and by the end of the month were only 37 miles from Paris. British reinforcements, fresh American divisions, and a determined effort by the battle-weary French ar-mies combined with the physical exhaustion of the Germans to finally halt the enemy, and this allowed for a series of Allied counter-offensives which regained much lost ground. Luddendorff's grandiose gamble had failed.

Once the German advance had been halted, Allied commanders soon real-ised that the effort had exhausted the enemy, and they began to consider their own major offensive, an attack that might finally push the disheartened and weary enemy out of France and Belgium—a belief that inspired many Allied soldiers with a new determination to fight on to victory. As Westerman wrote,

The British and French troops, although "fed-up" with fighting, were loathe to let their foes escape from the noose. After more than four years of strenuous warfare, enduring unheard-of discomfort and privations, they were reluctant to allow the Hun to temporise. They wanted a fight to the finish and to deliver the knock-out blow.[64]

In mid-July, General Ferdinand Foch, the Allied Commander in Chief, attacked the Marne supported by the Americans. In early August, Douglas Haig launched a British offensive on the Somme—an attack with limited ob-jectives that made maximum use of subterfuge to mislead the Germans.[65]

However, as Brereton explained, the second Somme offensive was very much an international affair.

French, American, British troops gripped their rifles; tanks were already snorting close behind the Australian Corps; while the Canadian Corps, hidden in the forest country not so far from the line, was itching for the encounter.[66]

After the massive bombardment, which marked the "opening moment of the greatest battle of the war," the tanks advanced, beating down opposition,

and then the hour for the infantrymen—the men of battle—arrives, that hour for which thousand of gallant souls have been waiting. A roar of voices—shouts and cheers— and then, almost as one man, Canadians, Australians, and their brothers of the British army, Americans, and French, leap from their trenches . . . bound upon some particular mission . . . hidden machine-gun posts bar their progress here and there, rifles rattle, men fall. . . . But others go on without a pause, for they still have work to do.[67]

The failure of their own offensive and the success of the Allied attacks forced Luddendorff and his generals to confront the fact that the German army was cracking under the strain of unceasing battle, and further Allied offensives confirmed that belief. In September, the much-vaunted German defensive system, the Hindenburg line, was breached; the "shattering of the Kaiser's armies and the break-up of his dreams," noted Brereton,[68] and by early October the German leaders were negotiating a ceasefire which finally took effect at 11:00 A.M. on 11 November. Few novels have much to say about the Armistice. Only Westerman's *Winning His Wings* makes any reference to it, and that simply to tell his readers that for the British, Armistice night was a "topping rag," as young servicemen flocked into the nearest towns to celebrate with "crowds of wildly excited people," but

No one yet knew the terms of the Armistice. They were perfectly convinced in their own minds that the war was virtually over and that the Allies were top dog. It was an occasion for jollification and the opportunity was seized.[69]

The war was indeed over; there would be no resumption of the fighting. But in the terms of the Treaty of Versailles, signed the following year, lay the seeds of another, even more destructive world war. In November 1918, relief that the war was finally over and the belief that there would never be another great war was all that mattered. As P. J. Campbell of the Royal Artillery noted, "there would never be another war like this one. The Last War in History! Well, even if I achieved nothing else in life I had done something, I need not feel that my life had been altogether wasted, I had played my part."[70] But although the nation had held on for over four years until victory had been achieved, those involved in the fighting had quickly realised once they got to the Front that the war they were fighting bore little resemblance to the romantic and exciting images of battle created by pre-1914 authors and artists.

Those excited young men so eager for battle in the early months of the war had soon found that in reality there was little nobility or romance in trench warfare. Roland Leighton, for example, the son of the popular writer of boys' historical fiction, Robert Leighton, who had so lovingly described the virtues to be found in chivalric combat in novels like *The Thirsty Sword* and *Olaf the Glorious*, went to war believing it to be "something, if often horrible, yet very ennobling and very beautiful, something whose elemental reality raises it above the reach of all cold theorising."[71] Yet in a later letter to his fiancée Vera Brittain, written after he had experienced a spell in the trenches, he wrote of war with a very different perspective.

Let him who thinks that War is a glorious golden thing, who loves to roll forth stirring words of exhortation, invoking Honour and Praise and Valour and Love of Country . . . look at a little pile of sodden grey rags that cover half a skull and a shin bone and what might have been Its ribs . . . and let him realise how grand and glorious a thing it is to have distilled all Youth and Joy and Life into a foetid heap of hideous putrescence. Who is there who has known and seen who can say that victory is worth the death of even one of these?[72]

Did he, one wonders, number his father among those who rolled forth "stirring words of exhortation," who thought war a "glorious golden thing," and whose stories had helped persuade young Britons that the war would be an exciting adventure?

Among those who experienced the contradiction between the heroic and exciting image of war portrayed in the pre-1914 pleasure culture of war and the brutal realities of modern war, some were determined that future generations should not be exposed to this "old lie." In 1916, for example, the ex-schoolmaster turned soldier, Theodore Cameron Wilson, wrote to a friend pointing out the dangers of romanticising war and accusing writers who had done so of "war-mongering."

Do teach your dear kids the horror of responsibility which rests on the war-monger. I want so much to get at the children about it. We've been wrong in the past. We have taught schoolboys 'War' as a romantic subject. We've made them learn the story of Waterloo as a sort of exciting story in fiction. And everybody has grown up soaked in the poetry of war. . . . All those picturesque phrases of war writers—such as "he flung the remains of his Guard against the enemy," "a magnificent charge won the day," are dangerous because they show nothing of the individual horror, nothing of the fine personalities smashed suddenly into red beastliness.[73]

Such sentiments were also to be found in the bitter poems of Wilfred Owen and Siegfried Sassoon among others, but while many had realised just how terrible war was, it was tempered by the conviction that the suffering and sacrifice must be vindicated by victory. Thus continuing propaganda was still needed to sustain the belief that an Allied victory was inevitable and to encourage the fainthearted, particularly those young men who would soon be called upon to take up arms. But in the fictions published towards the end of the war we can detect some change in war stories as authors, no longer able to ignore the appalling conditions at the Front nor the growing casualty lists, began to introduce a more realistic note into their representations of the war in the trenches.

During the last year of the war, even the intensely patriotic Escott Lynn was beginning to reflect the hard edge of the real war. In his 1918 novel, *Knights of the Air*, German airmen are burnt alive in their machines or "smashed into unrecognisable heaps," while fighting in the trenches was not described in quite the same glamorous terms as it had once been imagined. After a German attack, Lynn tells us that the British survivors were "exhausted . . . blood-stained, capless, grimed with sweat and dust . . . parched with thirst, faint with hunger, and aching with fatigue." And combat is a much less sporting affair. Billy, one of Lynn's young heroes, finds that in bayonet fighting, kicking a Hun in the stomach and then stabbing him in the chest as he falls to the ground is the most effective method of dispatching the enemy.[74] But it was Percy F. Westerman who, after 1917, offered his readers the most realistic view of trench warfare. In *To the Fore with the Tanks* (1917), he details the experience of young soldiers going into the front line for the first time. As they enter the communications trench, a foul smell is noticeable—a mule, long dead, lies half-buried in the mud. One of the replacements slips from the duck-boards and almost drowns in the mud, while another who has failed to keep his head down, is hit by a sniper's bullet—only his steel helmet saves his life. A group of wounded men coming out of the line pass the replacements: one has had his hand blown off, and others "groan and writhe" in pain as they are carried past. Once in the line they take over the dugouts; rough, slimy excavations in the side of the trench, not high enough to stand up in and reeking of the fumes from the braziers. In places, half-buried bodies, "hideously mangled," lay here and there—victims of enemy shelling, which their comrades have not had time to carry out of the line.[75] That night in the dugout one of the new men tries to sleep on a bundle of straw. "His feet and hands were numbed with the cold. His saturated clothes throw off wisps of muggy vapour." But he is so tired that "even a huge rat pattering on the muddy floor . . . hardly troubled him."[76] Here Westerman offers a dismal, but more realistic view of the trenches than the snug, cosy image of trench life described in the earlier war stories of Strang, Newbolt, and Brereton.

The following year Westerman published his novel *A Lively Bit of the Front*, the story of two young New Zealanders. Dick and Malcolm, both 17 years old, find themselves on the Western Front in 1917, just before the Battle of Messines Ridge, and here the author offers a far more graphic representation of the trenches—rats gnaw at the soldiers' puttees while

The atmosphere reeked of numerous and distinct odours. Traces of poisonous gas lurked in the traverses, pungent fumes from bursting shells wafted over parapet and parados, while the report, passed on from various successive occupants of this section of the line, that a dozen dead Huns had been buried under the floor of the support trench . . . seemed to find definite confirmation.[77]

But even these wretched conditions fail to dampen the enthusiasm of Westerman's fictional Anzacs. Just before going into action, both lads admit to being frightened (a major breakthrough here, plucky colonials admitting to fear!), but as soon as the action begins those fears are "thrown to the wind." Nevertheless the fighting is savage.

The air was heavy with suffocating smoke; fragments of shells were flying. . . . shouts, oaths and curses punctuated the crash of steel and the rattle of musketry, as men in their blind ferocity clutched each others' throats and rolled in mortal combat on the ground.[78]

Yet Westerman's novel was still the work of an intensely patriotic writer, a man driven by the need to inspire his readers to "do their bit" for a cause which he believed was morally justified. Thus after the battle, which is of course a minor victory, Dick and Malcolm discuss their experiences, their many comrades who have "copped it," and the immediate future. And here, despite the shocking conditions in which they live and the brutality of the fighting, Malcolm sums up the overriding attitude of the young Anzacs warriors: "[I]t'll be worse before the final battle," he tells them, "but I wouldn't miss it for the world!" This nod to realism in the stories by Lynn, Westerman, and others was tempered by the established conventions of the war story which writers found difficult to escape.

The working-class regular or volunteer had always been a presence in the war story. Mostly they appeared as figures of fun, often speaking in what authors assumed was a cockney or regional accent, and they were inevitably in awe of their young public-school officers. Now, however, they were joined by far more seriously drawn working-class soldiers. In an Escott Lynn novel, for example, we find Sergeant Harry Norman, a regular and a decorated veteran of the South African War. Norman appears throughout the novel, but almost as if to justify this focus on a working-class hero, Lynn has him recommended for a commission at the end of the novel.[79] And this appeared to be a necessary strategy for most authors—the best men from the lower orders exhibited upper-class values and were thus elevated to the status of temporary gentlemen. But promotion from the ranks for non–public school men was uncommon. Far more usual was the situation that occurs in Westerman's *To the Fore with the Tanks!* Almost the entire first half of the novel is centered on three apparently working-class volunteers. However, one of the trio, Ralph Setley, distinguishes himself in action and is interviewed by his commanding officer. After reviewing his brief army record, the CO asks Ralph the all-important question, "'Where were you educated?' Setley told him, mentioning a well-known West Country school. The CO nodded approval," and then tells Ralph that he is being recommended for a commission.[80] Ralph's companions, who have equally distinguished themselves, apparently lack the necessary educational background and are simply promoted to corporal and sergeant, respectively.

By the end of the war, a war that, according to official propaganda, had resulted in unprecedented social levelling as officers and men had fought shoulder to shoulder in the trenches, it was the ex–public school hero who still occupied centre stage in juvenile fiction. At the end of the war, for example, and despite over a million casualties, the overwhelming majority from the lower-middle and working classes, *The Boy's Own Paper* still chose to place the emphasis solely on the sacrifice of public school men. An editorial noted that it was sad to peruse the Roll of Honour pages in school magazines and reflect upon the fallen heroes—the "fine young lives . . . the brave young lads who threw themselves so willingly into the 'great game.'" The editor went on to praise the efforts of schools like Eton, Harrow, and Marlborough to create war shrines where the names of those who have made the "great sacrifice" will be forever displayed: a record of the "proud part that public-school men. . . played in the conflict."[81] And in fiction the ordinary soldier's admiration for his public school officer was undiminished even after four years of war. An interesting example of this was W. E. Cossens' story "The Giant's Robe: A Story of Football and Fighting." Bob Middleton, the star of the school eleven, volunteers in 1914 and distinguishes himself in war as he had done on the school games field. When Middleton is killed in action, the sergeant of his company writes to the boy's mother a letter that demonstrates the regard in which the young officer was held by his men, and the essential qualities of the public school man.

> I have been asked by the boys of our platoon to write and tell you how sorry we all are to loose such a good and brave officer. . . . Mr Middleton was a great sport and use to play football with us wen we was out for a spel and he would talk about fiting the Uns as if we was playing a game.

The sergeant goes on to describe how the battalion was assigned to attack a German position and when the British barrage ceased,

> We was over the top in no time and your son was well ahed as always. Lt. Middleton was . . . throwing his bombs like he was just practisin and calling to us to play up Chalkshires, 3 more goals an we'll go in with the bayernet. . . . He sees a poor chap of a Un wot had bin hit in the chest and was calling out pitiful for a drink. Your son bent down to give him his water bottel when another German . . . shot him in the hart. We have

"Victory," postcard, 1918.

put up a wooden cross in lovin memory of Lt. Robert Middleton. . . . A good sport he died playing the game.

Yrs respectfly, John Grogan, Sgt.

P.S. The German wot shot your son didn't shoot no more.[82]

In their emphasis on the leadership and sacrifice of the public school elite, authors had really moved on very little in their representation of the war since 1914, nor had they lost any of the certainty that Britain had fought a just war. Despite the appalling conditions of trench life and the brutality of the fighting which Lynn and Westerman were beginning to acknowledge, writers of war fiction still portrayed the conflict as the Great Adventure, a not-to-be missed experience for the young combatants.

In 1918 the nation emerged triumphant from the most destructive war in history—what greater proof could there be that God continued to smile benevolently upon the British and their Empire? The nation, according to Owen Wheeler, had "throughout and from the very beginning, 'played the game' and played it as well and as wholeheartedly as it could have been played in any circumstances whatever. . . . She gave her best, and gave it ungrudgingly, never stopping to count what the cost in blood or in treasure might be."[83] The British, then, could derive great satisfaction from the fact that the Royal Navy ruled the waves and the RAF ruled the skies, and while acknowledging the human cost, they took pride in what they had achieved. As F. S. Brereton explained, "with France and Belgium freed,"

the Allies had won a magnificent victory on this Western Front after more than four years of terrific contest, and on other fronts had swept the enemy aside, yet the German required further watching. An Allied force occupied the Rhine while the armistice was in force. . . . German militarism had gone then; German ambition had been curbed; the Kaiser and his malevolent son, the Crown Prince, the Emperor of Austria, the treacherous King of Bulgaria had, like the cunning Constantine of Greece, been cast from their thrones. . . . The Young Turk Party, which had brought its country to ruin and misery, was deposed.[84]

The war had also apparently had even more positive consequences; it had bound the Sons of Empire even more closely to the Motherland through common bonds of suffering and the blood sacrifice. The Empire was secure and, thanks to a rather dubious deal with the French which had divided the strategically important Turkish Empire between the two allies, was considerably larger than it had been in 1914.[85] As the *Wonder Book of Empire* noted in 1919, the war had had many unforeseen consequences, but none as significant as the loss by Germany of every one of her overseas colonies, most of which had been mandated to the control of Great Britain. Eight hundred thousand square miles had been added to the Empire. This, the editor explains, was perfectly justified, for

Our Empire has been welded by blood and tears, by the courage and hopes of many generations, toiling and sacrificing for England's glory. And although we have made serious mistakes, we have no cause on the whole to be ashamed of the way in which we have administered our heritage. . . .

We may all be sure that better times are in store for the peoples who have passed under the sway of the British Empire, which, whatever its faults, is founded upon the bed-rock principles of justice, humanity and freedom.[86]

And if those new subjects failed to appreciate the great benefits of living under British control, as they did in Iraq, Palestine, and elsewhere, the bombing of their villages and a constant military presence would at least keep them in order. But above all, Britain had emerged from the war with her integrity unquestioned, had honoured her treaty obligations, had stood against tyranny and oppression, and had smashed German militarism. The hundreds of thousands of war dead, the cripples languishing in military hospitals, the shell-shocked, the mutilated, and the blind who must face what life remained to them on a miserly pension, were simply part of the price that had to be paid to ensure that the nation's honour remained untarnished. As Elizabeth O'Neill had foreseen in 1914, this was simply one more reason why, for propagandist authors at least, the Great War was "so marvellous a thing."

The young veterans, the volunteers and conscripts, wanted little more than to go home and pick up the threads of normal life. But there were some who had no experience of normal life—those who had gone straight from school to war and who knew little else. For them war had become normal, and some had become addicted to the danger and excitement of battle. As we have seen, Amyas "Biffy" Borton and his brother Arthur didn't want the war to end, they enjoyed it too much! Cecil Lewis, another RAF pilot, later noted in his war memoirs that with the Armistice he felt a sense of anticlimax, "even a momentary sense of regret."[87] Lewis was far too intelligent to want the war to continue, but he had been trained for war and accustomed to the excitement it brought, and in the years after 1918 he sought that excitement wherever he could—in civil aviation, as part of a flying circus, and eventually in China, training pilots for the Nationalist air force. P. J. Campbell, who had spent the war in an artillery battalion on the Western Front, had also become accustomed to war. "It was real," he noted, "home was the dream." And it was Campbell who articulated the question that troubled so many young men who dreaded a return to the mundane, nine-to-five routine they were faced with, "What on earth are we going to do with ourselves now?"[88] The writers of adventure fiction unfortunately tell us little about how their young heroes adjusted to peace after the drama of war, and most novels end with the Armistice. Thus we must rely on only a handful of examples. In W. P. Shervill's *Two Daring Young Patriots*, the heroes, who have spent the war as spies in occupied Belgium, stay on in that country repairing the damage wrought by the Germans and eventually building a successful business.[89] But this is an unusual ending, for the few authors that did address the issue of what happened next suggested that their heroes were still seeking adventure. Westerman's young pilot Derek Daventry, for example, decides to make a career in the RAF because of the comradeship and because it is an "exciting existence."[90] And even as late as the mid-1930s, fictional veterans of the war were still looking for an exciting cause. In Jack Lindsay's *Wings over Africa*, the ex-RAF ace Peter Dawes chucks up his small air freight company in order to volunteer to fight against the Italians in Abyssinia. Peter is unwilling to settle for a life without excitement and danger, and he believes that in Africa he can find the "fighting that his soul loved. . . . A life he had thought past and done with on a bleak November day seventeen long years ago."[91] But not all authors were convinced that the quarrel with Germany had really been laid to rest.

Many Germans, as we know, never accepted the verdict of 1918. The German army, it was widely believed, had not been defeated in battle; rather it had been betrayed by civilians, especially the industrialists and politicians who had lost the will to fight on, and thus the fighting men had been stabbed in the back. The bitterness caused by this betrayal was strengthened by the attempts to seize power in several German cities by revolutionary movements during the chaos at the end of the war. Later, the harsh terms of the Treaty of Versailles stunned the German people, who believed that they had fought a war of self-defence. That resentment was the driving force for Rowland Walker's 1920 novel *The Phantom Airman*, and it suggests that some Germans at least wanted to continue the war against the British. The novel is set just after the Armistice, and here the German air ace Rittmeister Heinrich von Spitzer decides that "rather than submit to the peace terms enforced by the Allies," he will continue the fight.[92] Using a marvellous new aeroplane developed by Professor Weissmann, and accompanied by a handful of loyal pilots from his squadron, he destroys British commercial airships and incites rebellion in the Middle East. When the plan fails and von Spitzer's machine is forced back to Germany by the RAF, he conceives a plan to join the "revolutionists" in Ireland. However, he is pursued to his secret base in Germany by two ex-RAF officers, Sharpe and Keene, now working for the British Air Police. They offer the air pirates a fair trial, pointing out that the professor would only be charged with breaking the peace regulations, but the scientist refuses. "Don't speak to me of peace regulations," he screams, "there can be no peace till Germany regains all and more than she has lost."[93] Both Germans are killed in a final battle.

The idea that Germany, once she had regained her strength, would not long tolerate the conditions of Versailles apparently occurred more often to writers of boys' fiction than it did to politicians. In 1922, for example, the Amalgamated Press story paper *Champion* ran "War of Revenge" by Leslie Beresford, a serial in which Germany wages another war against Britain, even if it is somewhat long delayed.

In retaliation for the humiliating Peace Treaty of 1919 which the German Government was forced to sign the hour has come when German honour must be avenged . . . the Imperial Government considers itself fully justified in announcing that on and from the morning of Tuesday, 13 April 1961, a State of War will exist between Germany and Great Britain.[94]

The Germans use radio-controlled aerial torpedoes to bombard London and other cities and then invade with robotic fighting machines, no doubt inspired by the machines featured in *War of the Worlds* by H. G. Wells. But the British have new weapons in their arsenal as well, and a ray that dissolves metal proves to be the undoing of the invaders. Such stories became common through the 1920s and were resurrected after Adolf Hitler embarked upon his rearmament programme. In 1936, for example, the *Rover* ran "Britain Attacked," a serial in which a German revenge attack on Britain is defeated by Commander Silver, Britain's "Number One Secret Service Man."[95] Thus the relief felt at the defeat of Germany in 1918 was for many tempered by the belief that the peace treaty was so unsatisfactory that it could easily provoke another war. But for most authors, the war of 1914–1918 was the "war to end war," a vindication of all that was best in the British character, and a wonderful example of imperial unity. The British Empire was greater than ever, the world a better place, and those who had made the great sacrifice would be remembered for evermore.

Conclusion

> Of the leading events of the War one fact stands out with great distinctness, namely that Britain throughout and from the very beginning, "played the game" and played it as well and whole-heartedly as it could have been played. . . . Great Britain and her glorious Dominions made their mark and left it clearly stamped for all to see. It is a proud record, not compiled by showy achievements, or made to look larger than it really is by vainglorious talk. It will be a lasting record because it is the result of a great Empire's honest and strenuous endeavour to play in the most tremendous war-drama of history a part worthy of itself and of its splendid past.
>
> —Harry Golding, *The Wonder Book of Soldiers*[1]

In propagandist fiction published between 1914 and 1918, the war story had been an epic of adventure, a moral crusade in which Britons took up the sword of justice, dispatched the German tyrant, and freed the occupied lands held in his cruel hand. Many had died for this noble cause, and many others would carry the scars of battle for the remainder of their lives, but such sacrifice had been worthwhile, for the Empire had been saved. Indeed it was now greater than ever, and victory, it was believed, had brought about a new era of freedom, liberty, and an "end to war" itself. But how would such a positive interpretation of the Great War fare after the euphoria of victory had begun to fade—could such a view still be maintained into the peace after a period of considered reflection?

It has now become commonplace to suggest that with the signing of the peace treaties, there emerged a powerful desire on the part of most Britons to close the door of memory on the years of conflict: the hardship, loss, and suffering was simply too painful to recall. This now-common assumption appears to have derived its substance from comments such as those by Robert Graves and Alan Hodge. Writing at the end of the 1930s, they noted almost with surprise that with the publication of Remarque's *All Quiet on the Western Front* in 1929, "war books suddenly came back into fashion," implying that during the first decade of peace no one wanted to be reminded of the war. Such claims have led academics like Samuel Hynes to argue that for "most of the 'twenties the war was not significantly imagined, in any form."[2] This myth of the war's aftermath suggests that after 1918, following the devastating experience of war, there was little public demand for literary or other cultural representations of the war experience because of their painful associations. When the war was re-imagined in the later 1920s it was filtered through the memory of bitter and disillusioned veterans who believed that the conflict had been a "horrible mistake, a debacle in which brave young men (the 'golden youth' of Edwardian England) sacrificed themselves in the mud and blood of the Western Front's No Man's Land."[3] As the truth about the war, which of course had been hidden from the public during the war years through government censorship and a compliant press,[4] reached the people they were filled with horror and remorse and committed themselves to pacifism, international disarmament, and a policy of peace at any price. As with any myth there are elements of truth here, and although it does represent one contemporary response to the war it was by no means the dominant one; rather, it was a response which originated among the social elites, and particularly among the young, socially privileged survivors of the conflict who were perhaps even more bitter that the decade after 1918 had not brought about the "land fit for heroes" promised by the politicians than they were about the manner in which the war had been conducted. But an argument that suggests that the war was largely ignored after 1914 simply cannot be sustained for two reasons. First, there is the well-documented determination of most ordinary people to keep alive the memory of the war, and second, because positive interpretations of the war, including patriotic adventure fiction, remained popular with readers until well into the late 1930s.

For most ordinary Britons there was a determination to celebrate the war as a justified conflict—a triumph of British courage, tenacity, and strength of arms—and to pay tribute to the fallen, as the many war memorials, commemorative plaques, and shrines erected in towns and villages throughout the United Kingdom testify. "They died the death of honour" was a common inscription on such memorials and one that encapsulates not only an attempt to memorialize the dead but to celebrate the justice of the cause. And this was how many, perhaps most, Britons wanted to remember the war. It was a memory that located the sacrifice of the dead squarely in the chivalric tradition—they had died to save King and Empire and in the cause of preserving the empire and creating a new and better world. Such a view gave meaning to the loss of life, the hardship and suffering, not only for the bereaved but also for many of those young survivors of the trenches. As we have seen, P. J. Campbell, like many others, initially saw noble purpose in the war; his comrades had not died in vain because they had fought to put an end to war. Thus they were honoured as heroes who had given their lives that future generations would live in peace. The Eleventh of November, Armistice Day, became the great annual Festival of Remembrance, but local celebrations ensured that the fallen were an ever-present memory.[5] Curiously, and in contradiction to the rhetoric about "the war to end war," there were often implications in the memorial services that the next generation might well have to continue the struggle. The war memorial at Marlow, Buckinghamshire, for example, was unveiled in 1920 by the Marquis of Lincolnshire. According to the local newspaper, the Marquis "impressed upon the boys present not to forget . . . the way in which their fathers, brothers and relatives had fought that they might live in peace." But "if ever they were called upon to do the same," he continued, "they must do their duty like men."[6]

For the bereaved there were organised pilgrimages to the Western Front, to the great and sombre war cemeteries in France and Belgium, to the arches of remembrance and to view the fields of battle. The Young Men's Christian Association undertook the first tours in 1920, and the Red Cross and British Legion quickly followed, while the enterprising travel agent Thomas Cook soon began to offer tours of the battlefields on a commercial basis.[7] The more adventurous could make their own private pilgrimage using a battlefield guide published by Shell Petroleum or the Michelin Tyre Co. (first published in 1919). A less expensive alternative was a visit to the Imperial War Museum, opened in 1920 at the Crystal Palace in South London. The Museum with its impressive display of weapons, uniforms, paintings, and exciting dioramas, proved enormously popular, but such displays, albeit less impressive, could also be seen at numerous local museums which, as Omer Bartov has suggested, "embody the sacralization of violence"—carefully re-ordered displays of killing machines which proved endlessly fascinating for the public, particularly boys and young men.[8] As the memorials commemorated the fallen heroes and the museums displayed the artifacts of the war, so representations of the war in literature, film, theatre, and art acted as reminders of the nation's triumph and loss, and through them the public could come to terms with the conflict.[9] Even the commonly used phrase "before the war" in everyday conversation served as a constant reminder of what the war generation had endured. The war, then, was not brushed aside in some desperate attempt to erase painful experiences, but was courted as a living memory that was constantly recalled and re-enacted through a variety of cultural artifacts. Thus romantic and heroic fictions of battle written for the young remained popular long after the peace treaties had been signed. And many of those fictions published during the war remained in print for the next two decades, as the publishing and readership history of these fictions demonstrates.

Although Brereton wrote only one adventure novel after the war, his war stories remained in print until the Second World War and were remarkably popular as class and Sunday school prizes for boys and young men.[10] In 1931, the London publisher Partridge reissued a whole series of wartime fictions, including Westerman's *The Secret Battleplane* (first published in 1916) and *Tanks to the Fore!* (1917), and Rowland Walker's *Oscar Danby VC*, that intensely patriotic tale of bravery and sacrifice on the Western Front first published in 1916. Oxford University Press reprinted many of Herbert Strang's war stories from 1933 onwards; *Carry On: A Story of the Fight for Bagdad*, and *With Haig on the Somme*, for example, were last republished in 1936. Nor did these volumes sit unwanted on booksellers' shelves; they sold well, particularly as prizes and rewards, as the following examples demonstrate. The London County Council awarded Brereton's *With Allenby in Palestine* (1918) to a secondary schoolboy in 1931, and *Under Haig in Flanders* (1917) was given as a Christmas present in 1933. The Aberdeen Education Committee provided Westerman's *The Dispatch Riders* (1915) as a middle school prize in 1934, while Captain Charles Gilson's *U 93* was awarded as a Sunday school prize as late as 1942.[11] Throughout the interwar period, then, these novels, which represented 1914–1918 as the Great Adventure, remained popular with boys and young men. Often these fictions were presented to the youth of the nation by parents, schoolteachers, and churchmen, many of whom had themselves served in the war and had direct experience of combat. Yet they consciously made the decision to pass on to the next generation a heroic and justified representation of the war, rather than stories that cast doubt on the morality of the war and portrayed it as degrading and futile. Clearly, then, we have a major contradiction here between these heroic representations of the war and the cynical representations written by embittered survivors such as John Aldington, Siegfried Sassoon, and Henry Williamson.[12]

Heroic fictions written during the years of conflict not only continued to be popular throughout the period but were reinforced by other novels and stories about the war written by a new generation of authors who adopted the same positive view. Between 1928 and 1934, for instance, Seeley Service published John Irving's "Dick Valliant RN" novels, a series of heroic naval adventures, as well as reissuing T. W. Corbin's 1919 *The Marvel of War Invention* with its descriptions of marvellous bombing aeroplanes, tanks, and heavy artillery. During the 1920s and 1930s the Aldine Library published a number of adventurous tales of the war such as Wingrove Willson's *Stories of the Great War*, E. L. McKeag's *Chums of the Northern Patrol*, and Michael Poole's *Macklin of the Loyals*—"a thrilling story of the Great War for boys and girls of all ages," claimed the publisher's catalogue.[13] These authors were joined by many others who achieved considerable popularity and whose books remained in print for years like George E. Rochester and Captain W. E. Johns. Rochester published his first story, "The Funk," in the *Boy's Own Paper* in 1925—a stirring tale of heroism in the RFC. His war stories continued with a number of war flying yarns, and in the 1930s he created the popular "Grey Shadow" novels recounting the adventures of Britain's most daring wartime spy.[14] Rochester could not be accused of not having had first-hand experience of combat, for he served in the Royal Flying Corps on the Western Front and ended the war as a prisoner of war in Germany. Equally, if the Aldine catalogue is to be believed, writers such as Michael Poole and Ernest L. McKeag were also veterans. Most enduring, perhaps, were the "Biggles" stories written by W. E. Johns. Johns had served in the army at Gallipoli and then transferred to the RFC. Shot down over the German trenches, he spent the remainder of the war as a prisoner. Johns continued to serve with the RAF into the 1920s and then became an illustrator and author, creating his enduring fictional hero Biggles (Major James Bigglesworth, RFC), who first appeared in the 1932 story "The White Fokker," published in *Modern Boy*.[15] Biggles was a slightly more realistic creation—an air fighter who, as Denis Butts has pointed out, was "highly-strung" and who "comes close to tears . . . when comrades are lost."[16] Yet despite this nod to the psychological damage wrought upon the individual by combat, there is never any suggestion in Johns's writing that the war was futile or unjust. Nor could the author avoid investing his war stories with the chivalric and romantic cliches that had become attached to the war in the air.[17]

These novels were complimented by the serials and stories published by the popular boys' papers such as *Boy's Own Paper, Chums, Modern Boy*, and *Champion*. In the immediate post-1918 period all the boys' papers were full of war-related material—fiction, articles about heroic episodes, and numerous illustrations. However, through the 1920s some change can be detected in the manner in which the war was dealt with in certain papers. By 1930, for example, while the Religious Tract Society's *Boy's Own Paper* had no shortage of blood-and-guts historical romances, tales of the Great War had been virtually eliminated from its pages. A 1929 editorial on why the two minutes' silence on Remembrance Day must be retained argued that it was essential that the rising generation understand exactly what modern warfare really meant.

Its wanton waste of men and materials, its appalling destructiveness, its filth and cruelty and beastliness—to use the word in its most literal sense—and its utter futility. Few, if any, of the present generation . . . who have "passed through the furnace" want, or are likely to want, another war; but, just as soon as the boys of today, the men of tomorrow, slip back into the old error of regarding war as a heroic, chivalrous adventure, so will the danger of war become once more imminent.[18]

Yet in the same issue, there was an article on the heroic "Bowmen of England" which pointed out that in the hands of stout English archers the longbow was the most "potent weapon on the battlefield" in the days before gunpowder, and which included detailed plans for constructing such a bow. An article on training RAF pilots was little more than recruiting propaganda, while the serial was George Rochester's "Despot of the World," in which the heroic British agent—the Black Beetle—fought his lonely war against the evil Zandenberg, whose dream was to master the world. The Beetle uses considerable violence against Zandenberg's forces, killing many, shooting down their aeroplanes, and bringing his revolver butt down on their skulls with "sickening force."[19] For the *BOP*, then, there would seem to have been a curious distinction between the Great War and other wars of the past or future, which could still be imagined as exciting and romantic; though it seems doubtful if schoolboys perceived that difference!

The more secular *Chums*, however, continued to feature war stories and articles throughout the inter-war period. The 1936–37 Annual, for instance, carried two stories of flying on the Western Front: "The Great Spy Capture," where public school boys apprehend a German spy, and another where an unpopular schoolboy later becomes a hero in the trenches, dying gallantly and finally earning the respect of his peers. Alongside these fictions were articles on heroes of the RFC and accounts of the daring deeds of Lawrence of Arabia and of Major Hansen, who had won a Victoria Cross fighting the Turks, and a tribute to the Gurkha Victoria Cross rifleman Kulbir Thapa, who had won his award on the Western Front. Even the 1941 annual ran Peter Tewson's highly appropriate "Wheels of the Great Retreat," "a moving picture of the epic battle of Mons and the subsequent retreat of the British Expeditionary Force." *The Champion Annual* for 1930 not only carried fictional tales of young heroes such as "The Boy Who Did His Bit" and "Chums of the Clouds" but also an illustrated article on "When Britain Was at War," which included an account of trench warfare on the Western Front, complete with pictures of cheery Tommies advancing during the Battle of Arras and descriptions of the "good-humoured heroes of the trenches." In all of these examples the authors appeared to accept that while conditions in the trenches had sometimes been horrible and that many soldiers had suffered greatly, they were equally agreed that the suffering and sacrifice had been necessary. The war was portrayed as righteous, justified, heroic, exciting, and romantic. And these juvenile fictions were mirrored by the adult war stories of Sapper (Herman Cyril McNeile) such as *Sergeant Michael Cassidy, RE* and *No Man's Land*. These had originally been published during the war while the author was serving in the Royal Engineers, but they were constantly reprinted throughout the 1920s. While McNeile acknowledged that the war he had fought was not the kind of conflict that had been expected, it was still bravely fought for a noble purpose. And one might equally cite the stories of Ian Hay and the Canadian author Ralph Connor.[20]

Nor did the war have any appreciable effect on the public fascination for war stories and idealised heroes. Certainly by the end of the 1920s, some authors of adventure fiction had begun to shy away from stories of the Great War and to substitute new fields of battle for those of 1914 through 1918. The struggle against Bolshevism became a popular theme for juvenile adventure, for example, and the Empire, particularly the new mandated territories of the Middle East, inspired countless fictional escapades for characters based on T. E. Lawrence who now sought to defend British interests in the Middle East.[21] Many novels combined these themes, and the story in which adventurous and heroic young Englishmen defeated a Soviet plot to bring about the downfall of the British Empire became commonplace.[22] Tales of future wars, so common before 1914, quickly resurfaced after the Armistice; they dealt with mysterious Asiatic warlords bent upon world domination, ruthless east European dictators, and even wars in space.[23] In these stories it was still the traditional adventure hero who defeated these imaginary enemies and kept the nation safe.

It has sometimes been suggested that the masculine ideal of the patriotic, self-sacrificing ex–public school hero, the repository of all that was best in English character, had been destroyed for ever in the blood and squalor of the Western Front, but despite the democratisation of shared suffering in the trenches, the idealised stereotypical hero did survive. As Sapper explained when he described the hero of his first postwar novel,

He belonged, in fact, to the Breed; the Breed that had always existed in England, and will always exist till the world's end. . . . Just now a generation of them lie around Ypres and La Bassee; Neuve Chapelle and Bapaume. The graves are overgrown and the crosses are marked with indelible pencil. Dead—yes; but not the Breed. The Breed never dies.[24]

This construction of an idealised English masculinity had been sorely tested by the Great War, and it now often carried the scars of cynicism, but it had endured, and adventure fiction throughout the inter-war period and beyond was content to chronicle its heroes' exploits as they battled for honour, justice, and freedom throughout the world, just as it had recorded their struggle, sacrifice, and ultimate victory on the battlefields of the Great War.

Notes

INTRODUCTION

1. Stuart Cloete, *A Victorian Son: An Autobiography* (London: Collins, 1972), 17–18.

2. Stephane Audoin-Rouzeau, "French Children as Target for Propaganda," in *Facing Armageddon: The First World War Experienced*, ed. Hugh Cecil and Peter Liddle (London: Leo Cooper, 1996), 767. See also Stephane Audoin-Rouzeau, *La Guerre des Enfants, 1914–1918* (Paris: Armand Colin, 1993).

3. H. G. Wells, *Mr. Britling Sees It Through* (London: Macmillan, 1916); Rudyard Kipling, *France at War* (London: Macmillan, 1915); John Buchan, *Greenmantle* (London: Nelson, 1916).

4. Correlli Barnet, "A Military Historian's View of the Great War," *Transactions of the Royal Society of Literature* 36 (1970): 1–18; Brian Bond, *The Unquiet Western Front: Britain's Role in Literature and History* (Cambridge: Cambridge University Press, 2002).

5. See most notably Wilfred Owen's poem, "Dulce Et Decorum Est," in *Wilfred Owen: War Poems and Others*, ed. Dominic Hibberd (London: Chatto & Windus, 1976), 79. See also Peter Parker, *The Old Lie: The Great War and the Public School Ethos* (London: Constable, 1987).

6. Kelly Boyd, *Manliness and the Boys' Story Paper in Britain, 1855–1940* (London: Palgrave Macmillan, 2003), 49.

7. Robert A. Huttenback, "G. A. Henty and the Vision of Empire," *Encounter* 35 (1970): 47.

8. Jeffrey Richards, "With Henty to Africa," in *Imperialism and Juvenile Literature*, ed. Jeffrey Richards (Manchester: Manchester University Press, 1989), 75–76.

9. G. A. Henty, *St. George for England*, quoted in Richards, "With Henty to Africa," 89.

10. G. A. Henty, *Through Three Campaigns* (London: Blackie, 1904), 5–6.

11. G. A. Henty, *A Soldier's Daughter* (London: Blackie, 1906), 24.

12. The following section is largely based on Jeffrey Richards, "Popular Imperialism and the Image of the Army in Juvenile Fiction," in *Popular Imperialism and the Military, 1850–1950*, ed. John M. Mackenzie (Manchester: Manchester University Press, 1992), 80–108, and Guy Arnold, *Held Fast for England: G. A. Henty, Imperialist Boys' Writer* (London: Hamish Hamilton, 1980).

13. *With Clive in India, With Buller to Natal, With Kitchener in the Soudan, With Roberts to Pretoria*, for example.

14. On the pleasure culture of war, see Michael Paris, *Warrior Nation: Images of War in Popular British Culture, 1850–2000* (London: Reaktion, 2000); Graham Dawson, *Soldier Heroes: British Adventure, Empire and the Imagining of Masculinities* (London: Routledge, 1994).

15. See Anne Summers, "Militarism in Britain Before 1914," *History Workshop Journal* 2 (1978): 103–23; W. J. Reader, *At Duty's Call: A Study in Obsolete Patriotism* (Manchester: Manchester University Press, 1988); Cecil Eby, *The Road to Armageddon: The Martial Spirit in English Poplar Literature, 1870–1914* (Durham, NC: Duke University Press, 1988).

16. Paris, *Warrior Nation*, 71–82.

17. On the rediscovery of chivalry, see Mark Girouard, *The Return to Camelot: Chivalry and the English Gentleman* (London: Yale University Press, 1981).

18. W. E. Henley, *The Song of the Sword and Other Verses* (London: David Butt, 1892).

19. Brigadier-General R. C. Hart, "A Vindication of War," *Nineteenth Century* 70 (August 1911): 238.

20. The literature on Baden-Powell and the Boy Scouts is exhaustive, much of it defensive and written from the perspective of its more pacific post-1918 phase. But on its founder's early ideas about national defence, see Tim Jeal, *Baden-Powell* (London: Pimlico, 1991), 357–61.

21. See Richard Soloway, "Counting the Degenerates: The Statistics of Race Deterioration in Edwardian England," *Journal of Contemporary History* 17, no. 1 (January 1982): 137–64.

22. Cecil Eby, *The Road to Armageddon*, 3.

23. Quoted in Peter Berrisford Ellis and Piers Williams, *By Jove, Biggles! The Life of Captain W. E. Johns* (London: Comet, 1985), 11.

24. Newbolt, "Vitai Lambada," in *The Collected Poems of Henry Newbolt, 1897–1907*, ed. Henry Newbolt (London: Nelson, 1908), 131–33. On the connections between sport and war, see J. A. Mangan, "Games Field and Battlefield: A Romantic Alliance in Verse and the Creation of Militaristic Masculinity," in *Making Men*, ed. John Nauright and Timothy J. L. Chandler (London: Frank Cass, 1996), 140–57; J. A. Mangan, *Athleticism in the Victorian and Edwardian Public School* (Cambridge: Cambridge University Press, 1981); Colin Veitch, "Play Up! Play Up! And Win the War: Football, the Nation and the First World War, 1914–1918," *Journal of Contemporary History* 20, no. 3 (1985): 363–78.

25. Fictions that predicted future wars have been most thoroughly discussed by I. F. Clarke in *Voices Prophesying War: Future Wars, 1763–3749* (Oxford: Oxford University Press, 1992).

26. Niall Ferguson, *The Pity of War* (London: Allen Lane, 1998), 15.

27. Ibid., 189, 199.

28. Joseph Bristow, *Empire Boys: Adventures in a Man's World* (London: Harper Collins, 1991); Richards, "Popular Imperialism and the Image of the Army in Juvenile Fiction"; Dennis Butts, "Imperialists of the Air: Flying Stories 1900–1950" in Richards, *Imperialism and Juvenile Literature*, 126–43; J. S. Bratton, "Of England, Home and Duty: The Image of England in Victorian and Edwardian Juvenile Fiction," in *Imperialism and Popular Culture*, ed. John Mackenzie (Manchester: Manchester University Press, 1986); Boyd, *Manliness and the Boys' Story Paper in Britain, 1855–1940*.

29. Mary Cadogan and Patricia Craig, *Women and Children First: The Fiction of Two World Wars* (London: Gollancz, 1978).

30. Two studies that do attempt at least some coverage of juvenile fictions are Samuel Hynes, *A War Imagined: The First World War and English Culture* (London: Pimlico, 1992), and, more substantially, George Robb, *British Culture and the First World War* (London: Palgrave, 2002).

31. Rose Maria Bracco, *Merchants of Hope: British Middlebrow Writers and the First World War* (Oxford: Berg, 1993), 1.

CHAPTER 1: SELLING THE WAR

1. Sir James Yoxall, *Why Britain Went to War*, quoted in Christopher Martin, *English Life in the First World War* (London: Wayland, 1974), 97.

2. Hamilton Edwards, "Britain in Arms," *Pluck* 263 (1895).

3. Sir George Chesney, "The Battle of Dorking," *Blackwoods Edinburgh Magazine* (Poole, UK, 1871): May 539–72.

4. On the fictions of future war, see I. F. Clarke, *Voices Prophesying War: Future Wars, 1763–3749* (Oxford: Oxford University Press, 1992); Joseph Meisel, "The Germans Are Coming! British Fiction of a German Invasion, 1871–1913," *War, Literature, and the Arts* 2 (fall 1990): 41–77.

5. On Harmsworth's paranoia, see Reginald Pound and Geoffrey Harmsworth, *Northcliffe* (London: Cassell, 1959).

6. See David French, "Spy Fever in Britain, 1900–1915," *Historical Journal* 21 (1978): 355–70; James Hampshire, "Spy Fever in Britain, 1900–1914," *The Historian* 72 (winter 2001): 22–27.

7. Robert Roberts, *The Classic Slum: Salford Life in the First Quarter of the Century* (London: Penguin, 1978), 181.

8. Quoted in Eric Quayle, *The Collector's Book of Boys' Stories* (London: Studio Vista, 1973), 143.

9. See for example Herbert Strang, *The Air Scout* (London: Henry Frowde and Hodder & Stoughton, 1912) or *The Air Patrol* (London: Henry Frowde, 1913) and Percy F. Westerman, *The Flying Submarine* (London: Blackie, 1912). On Westerman, see Dennis Butts, "Percy F. Westerman," *Book Collecting and Library Monthly*, October 1968, 186–88.

10. Herbert Strang, *Sultan Jim: Empire Builder* (London: Henry Frowde and Hodder & Stoughton, 1913).

11. Percy F. Westerman, *The Sea-Girt Fortress: A Tale of Heligoland* (London: Blackie, 1914); Erskine Childers, *The Riddle of the Sands: A Record of Secret Service* (London: Nelson, 1903).

12. See Paul Kennedy, *The Rise of the Anglo-German Antagonism, 1860–1914* (London: George Allen & Unwin, 1980).

13. Quoted in Gerard De Groot, *Blighty: British Society in the Era of the Great War* (London: Longman, 1996), 7.

14. On the Anglo-French Staff Talks, see Zara Steiner, *Britain and the Origins of the First World War* (London: Macmillan, 1979), 197–202.

15. Gerard J. De Groot, *Blighty: British Society in the Era of the Great War* (London: Longman, 1996), 7.

16. Ibid.

17. Ibid., 8.

18. J. M. Bourne, *Britain and the Great War, 1914–1918* (London: Arnold, 1989), 7.

19. Ibid., 11–31.

20. Brian Bond, *The Unquiet Western Front: Britain's Role in Literature and History* (Cambridge: Cambridge University Press, 2002), 1.

21. Philip M. Taylor, *British Propaganda in the Twentieth Century: Selling Democracy* (Edinburgh: Edinburgh University Press, 1999), 1.

22. Ibid., 8.

23. G. S. Messinger, *British Propaganda and the State in the First World War* (Manchester: Manchester University Press, 1992), 11–12.

24. On the propaganda of imperialism, see John M. MacKenzie, *Propaganda and Empire: The Manipulation of British Public Opinion, 1880–1960* (Manchester: Manchester University Press, 1984) and John M. MacKenzie, ed., *Imperialism and Popular Culture* (Manchester: Manchester University Press, 1986).

25. Niall Ferguson, *The Pity of War* (London: Allen Lane, 1998), 205.

26. The Order of the White Feather employed squads of women who presented any seemingly fit young man not in uniform with a white feather—the badge for a coward. The Women of England's Active Service League, a seemingly short-lived organisation headed by the popular novelist Baroness Orczy, employed the same methods. See Cate Haste, *Keep the Home Fires Burning: Propaganda in the First World War* (London: Allen Lane, 1977), 56–59; Nicoletta F. Gullace, *The Blood of Our Sons: Men, Women, and the Renegotiation of British Citizenship During the Great War* (London: Palgrave, 2002), 73–97.

27. M. L. Sanders and Philip M. Taylor, *British Propaganda During the First World War* (London: Macmillan, 1982), 38–43; Samuel Hynes, *A War Imagined: The First World War and English Culture* (London: Pimlico, 1992), 25–28; Messinger, *British Propaganda*, 24–52. See also Peter Buitenhuis, *The Great War of Words: Literature as Propaganda, 1914–1918 and After* (London: Batsford, 1989), 37–53.

28. J. D. Squires, *British Propaganda at Home and in the United States from 1914 to 1917* (Cambridge, Mass.: Harvard University Press, 1935).

29. Sanders and Taylor, *British Propaganda*, 40.

30. Ibid., vii.

31. *Schedule of Wellington House Literature* (IWM).

32. Buitenhuis, *The Great War of Words*, 102.

33. Agnes A. C. Blackie, *Blackie and Son: A Short History of the Firm* (London: Blackie, 1959), 53.

34. Hynes, *A War Imagined*, 43.

35. Harold Orel, *Popular Fiction in England, 1914–1918* (Lexington: University Press of Kentucky, 1992), 157.

36. Huntly Gordon, *The Unreturning Army* (London: Dent, 1967), 11.

37. Barry Johnson, "In the Trenches with Brereton and Westerman," *Gunfire* 18 (nd): 15.

38. Herbert Strang, *A Hero of Liege* (London: Henry Frowde and Hodder & Stoughton, 1915); Captain F. S. Brereton, *At Grips with the Turk* (London: Blackie, 1915); Percy F. Westerman, *The Fight for Constantinople* (London: Blackie, 1915); D. H. Parry, *With Haig on the Somme* (London: Cassell, 1916).

39. Elizabeth O'Neill, *The War, 1914: A History and an Explanation for Boys and Girls* (London: T.C. & E.C. Jack, 1914), 15.

40. See Haste, *Keep the Home Fires Burning*, 82–107.

41. O'Neill, *The War, 1914*, 35–36.

42. Ibid., 14.

43. Michael Adams, *The Great Adventure: Male Desire and the Coming of World War 1* (Bloomington: Indiana University Press, 1990), 51.

44. Quoted in Hynes, *A War Imagined*, 12.

45. Robert Graves, *Goodbye to All That* (London: Penguin, 1977), 60, 62.

46. Gordon, *Unreturning Army*, 11.

47. Quoted in Adams, *The Great Adventure*, 100.

48. George Coppard, *With a Machine Gun to Cambrai* (London: Imperial War Museum, 1969), 1; A. Stuart Dolden, *Cannon Fodder* (Poole: Blandford, 1980), 11.

49. On recruiting for the New Armies, see Peter Simkins, *Kitchener's Army: The Raising of the New Armies, 1914–1916* (Manchester: Manchester University Press, 1988).

50. Captain F. S. Brereton, *On the Road to Bagdad* (London: Blackie, 1916), 24.

51. *The Athenaeum*, Supplement, December 1917: 689.

52. Sir Edward Parrott, *The Children's Story of the War,* 10 vols. (London: Nelson, 1915–1919), 1:154.

53. Ibid., 257.

54. Herbert Strang, *England and the War* (London: Henry Frowde and Hodder & Stoughton, 1916), 11.

55. Ibid., 1–2.

56. Ibid., 16.

57. Ibid., 26.

58. Herbert Strang, *The War on Land* (London: Henry Frowde and Hodder & Stoughton, 1916), no pagination.

59. Parrott, *The Children's Story of the War,* 1:134.

60. Ibid., 135.

61. Ibid., 172.

62. Ibid., 135.

63. Escott Lynn, *Knights of the Air* (London: W. & R. Chambers, 1918), 153, 285, 293.

64. Escott Lynn, *Tommy of the Tanks* (London: W. & R. Chambers, 1919), 82, 86.

65. Ferguson, *The Pity of War,* 189, 198.

66. Editorial, *Boy's Friend* 609 (29 August 1914): 135.

67. "The Editors Page," *Boy's Own Paper Annual* 37 (1914–1915): 41.

68. *The Union Jack,* 24 October 1914, quoted in Mary Cadogan and Patricia Craig, *Women and Children First: The Fiction of Two World Wars* (London: Gollancz, 1978), 73.

69. See Cadogan & Craig, *Women and Children First*, 73, 81–84.

70. In 1914, Gilson resumed his military career and served as transport officer for the naval brigade that served at Antwerp. See "Boy's Own Paper Gallery," *Boy's Own Paper Annual* 39 (1916–1917): 236, and his autobiography, *Chances and Mischances: An Autobiography* (London: Nelson, 1932).

71. Escott Lynn, *In Khaki for the King: A Tale of the Great War* (London: W. & R. Chambers, 1915), iii, v.

72. Herbert Strang, *Kobo: A Story of the Russo-Japanese War* (London: Blackie, 1905), and *Brown of Moukden* (London: Blackie, 1906); Percy F. Westerman, *Captured in Tripoli* (London: Blackie, 1912); Captain F. S. Brereton, *The Great Airship* (London: Blackie, 1913).

73. Percy F. Westerman, *The Dispatch Riders: The Adventures of Two Motor-Cyclists in the Great War* (London: Blackie, 1915).

74. Captain Frederick S. Brereton, *With French at the Front* (London: Blackie, 1915), 10–11.

75. Ibid., 2.

76. Ibid., 125.

77. Lynn, *In Khaki for the King*, 124–25.

78. See for example A. L. Haydon, "For England and the Right: A Tale of the War in Belgium," *Boy's Own Paper* (1914–1915); W. P. Shervill, *Two Daring Young Patriots, or Outwitting the Huns* (London: Blackie, 1919).

79. Brereton, *With French at the Front*, 130.

80. Richard Phillips, *Mapping Men and Empire: A Geography of Empire* (London: Routledge, 1997), 93.

81. See the discussion in Cadogan and Craig, *Women and Children First*, 59–70.

82. On Bessie Marchant, see A. Major, "Bessie Marchant, The Maid of Kent Whose Exciting Stories Thrilled Thousands of English Children," *This England* (winter 1991): 30–34.

83. See *A Princess of Servia* (London: Blackie,1915), *A VAD in Salonika*, *A Girl Munitions Worker* (London: Blackie, 1916), *Dangerous Mission* (London: Blackie, 1917), and *A Transport Girl in France* (London: Blackie, 1918).

84. See Gullace, *The Blood of Our Sons*.

85. Bessie Marchant, *Molly Angel's Adventures: A Tale of the German Occupation of Belgium* (London: Blackie, 1915), 114.

86. See for example Alice Massie, *Freda's Great Adventure: A Story of Paris in Wartime* (London: Blackie, 1917); May Baldwin, *Irene to the Rescue* (London: Cassell, 1916); May Wynn, *An English Girl in Serbia* (London: Blackie, 1916).

87. Ethel Turner, *The Cub* (London: Ward Lock, 1915). *The Times Literary Supplement*, 9 December 1915.

CHAPTER 2: AT THE FRONT

1. Jesse Pope, "Cricket—1915" quoted in Peter Parker, *The Old Lie: The Great War and the Public School Ethos* (London: Constable, 1987), 211.

2. Kelly Boyd, *Manliness and the Boys' Story Paper in Britain, 1855–1940* (London: Palgrave Macmillan, 2003), 70–71.

3. See for example, Captain Frank Shaw, "The Boys of the "Marion," a serial that

ran through the 1908 volume of *Chums* (1908), or the anonymous story "The Charge to Glory" in the same volume: 809–10. See also William Johnston, *Tom Graham VC* (London: Nelson, 1906) for a rare example of an adventure novel which dealt with the exploits of an ordinary soldier on the North West Frontier.

4. Jonathan Rutherford, *Forever England: Reflections on Masculinity and Empire* (London: Lawrence and Wishart: 1997), 12.

5. Quoted in Rutherford, *Forever England*, 14.

6. J. E. Minchin, *Our Public Schools* (London: Sonnenschein, 1901), 44.

7. Robert Roberts, *The Classic Slum: Salford Life in the First Quarter of the Century* (London: Penguin, 1978), 160–61.

8. See Geoffrey Best, "Militarism in the Victorian Public School," in *The Victorian Public School*, ed. B. Simon and I. Bradley (Dublin: Gill & Macmillan, 1979), 137.

9. Henry Newbolt, *The Book of the Happy Warrior* (London: Longmans Green, 1917).

10. Parker, *The Old Lie*, 34.

11. Captain F. S. Brereton, *Under Haig in Flanders* (London: Blackie, 1916), 41.

12. Ibid., 45.

13. Quoted in Mary Cadogan and Patricia Craig, *Women and Children First: The Fiction of Two World Wars* (London: Gollancz, 1978), 70–71.

14. Herbert Strang, *Fighting with French* (London: Humphrey Milford, 1915), 31.

15. Ibid., 166.

16. Captain F. S. Brereton, *Under French's Command* (London: Blackie, 1916), 261–62.

17. Rowland Walker, *Oscar Danby VC* (London: Partridge, 1916), 120. Novels that put Boy Scouts into the front line were popular during the first year of the war. In fiction at least, Baden-Powell's concern to prepare British boys for the coming conflict was fully justified. See for example D. H. Parry, *The Scarlet Scouts* (London: Cassell, 1915); Ascott R. Hope, *The School of Arms: Boy Soldiers and Sailors* (London: Routledge, 1915); Frank Fortune, *Stubbs and I* (London: W. & R. Chambers, 1915); J. Finnemore, *A Boy Scout with the Russians* (London: W. & R. Chambers, 1915); Albert Lee, *At His Country's Call* (London: Morgan & Scott, 1916).

18. Henry Newbolt, *Tales of the Great War* (London: Longmans Green & Co, 1916), 4.

19. Strang, *Fighting with French*, 46.

20. Ibid., 59.

21. Quoted in Denis Winter, *Death's Men: Soldiers and the Great War* (London: Allen Lane, 1978), 82–83. On trench warfare, see John Ellis, *Eye-Deep in Hell* (Beckenham, Kent: Croom Helm, 1979); Malcolm Brown, *Tommy Goes to War* (London: Dent, 1980); Tony Ashworth, *Trench Warfare, 1914–1918: The Live and Let Live System* (London: Macmillan, 1980).

22. Cadogan and Craig, *Women and Children First*, 77.

23. Strang, *Fighting with French*, vi.

24. Newbolt, *Tales of the Great War*, v.

25. *Illustrated London News* 3958 (10 October 1914): 500–501.

26. Rutherford, *Forever England*, 23–24.

27. Newbolt, *Tales of the Great War*, 14.

28. Ibid., 15.

29. Ibid., 16.

30. Ibid., 17.

31. Strang, *Fighting with French*, 76–78.

32. Brereton, *Under Haig in Flanders*, 58.

33. See Parker, *The Old Lie*, 166; T. W. Wilkinson, "In the Trenches," *Boy's Own Paper Annual* 37 (1914–1915): 261–63.

34. J. A. Mangan, "Games Field and Battlefield: A Romantic Alliance in Verse and the Creation of Militaristic Masculinity," in *Making Men*, ed. John Nauright and Timothy J. L. Chandler (London: Frank Cass, 1996), 140.

35. Quoted in Colin Veitch, "Play Up! Play Up! And Win the War: Football, the Nation and the First World War, 1914–1918," *Journal of Contemporary History* 20, no. 3 (1985): 372.

36. Percy F. Westerman, *The Dispatch Riders* (London: Blacie, 1915), 50.

37. See Parker, *The Old Lie*, 213–15.

38. Brereton, *Under Haig in Flanders*, 83.

39. D. H. Parry, *With Haig on the Somme* (London: Cassell, 1917), 216, 217.

40. See Dennis Giffard, *Comics of the Great War* (London: Peter Way, 1972).

41. "Puck's Model Toy Series," *Puck* (13 May 1916), 3.

42. "Gay Gus," *The Big Comic* 2, no. 50 (26 December 1914), 7.

43. Brereton's Western Front novels dealing with the British are *With French at the Front, Under French's Command, Under Haig in Flanders, With the Allies to the Rhine.*

44. F. S. Brereton, *With French at the Front* (London: Blackie, 1915), 145.

45. George Robb, *British Culture and the First World War* (London: Palgrave, 2002), 139.

46. Brereton, *Under French's Command*, 41–42.

47. Ibid., 64.

48. Ibid., 109.

49. Escott Lynn, *In Khaki for the King: A Tale of the Great War* (London: W. & R. Chambers, 1915), 181.

50. Brereton, *Under French's Command*, 329.

51. Ibid., 331.

52. Ibid., 332.

53. Ian F. W. Beckett, *The Great War, 1914–1918* (London: Longman, 2001), 126.

54. Basil Liddell Hart, *History of the First World War* (London: Pan, 1970), 203.

55. Brereton, *Under French's Command*, 332.

56. Barry Johnson, "In the Trenches with Brereton and Westerman," *Gunfire*, 18.

57. Ibid., 15.

58. See Mike Finn, "The Realities of War," *History Today* 52 (August 2002): 26–31.

59. Philip Gibbs, *Realities of War* (London: Hutchinson, 1938).

60. Quoted in Ted Bogacz, "A Tyranny of Words: Language, Poetry and Anti-Modernism in England in the First World War," *Journal of Modern History* 58 (1986): 651.

61. Lynn, *In Khaki for the King*, 223.

62. Ibid., 355.

63. Ibid., 343.

64. Brereton, *Under French's Command*, 65.

65. Lynn, *In Khaki for the King*, 361.

66. See Peter Buitenhuis, *The Great War of Words: Literature as Propaganda, 1914–1918 and After* (London: Batsford, 1989), 87–90.

67. Brereton, *With French at the Front*, 164.

68. Ibid., 131.

69. Quoted in Ferguson, *The Pity of War*, 360. See also Joanna Bourke, *An Intimate History of Killing* (London: Granta, 1999).

70. Quoted in Parker, *The Old Lie*, 202–3.

71. Quoted in Ferguson, *The Pity of War*, 208–9.

72. Lynn, *In Khaki for the King*, 167.

73. Strang, *Fighting with French*, 161–62.

74. Brereton, *Under French's Command*, 274.

75. Parker, *The Old Lie*, 226–27; Rev. W. E. Sellers, *With Our Fighting Men: Their Faith, Courage and Endurance in the Great War* (London: Religious Tract Society, 1915).

76. See Arthur Machen, *The Bowmen and Other Legends of the War* (London: Simkin, Marshall, Hamilton, Kent & Co, 1915); Buitenhuis, *The Great War of Words*, 102–5.

77. "The Vigil" was published in *The Times* on 5 August 1914, the morning after the ultimatum to Germany had expired.

78. Newbolt, *Book of the Happy Warrior*, 283.

79. Rutherford, *Forever England*, 72.

80. Sir Edward Parrott, *The Children's Story of the War*, 10 vols. (London: Nelson, 1915–1919), 4:191.

81. Ibid., 192.

82. "The Offensive," *Daily Chronicle*, 24 April 1915.

83. Parrott, *The Children's Story of the War*, 4:192.

84. Beckett, *The Great War*, 176.

85. "Gay Gus," *Comic Life* 893, 31 July 1915, 3–5.

86. Gerard De Groot, *The First World War* (London: Palgrave, 2001), 38.

87. Quoted in Martin J. Farrar, *News from the Front: War Correspondents on the Western Front, 1914–1918* (Stroud, UK: Sutton, 1998), 85.

88. Parrott, *The Children's Story of the War*, 4:356.

89. J. M. Bourne, *Britain and the Great War, 1914–1918* (London: Arnold, 1989), 51–52.

90. Parrott, *The Children's Story of the War*, 6:16.

91. Ibid., 27–28.

92. Brereton, *Under Haig in Flanders*, 81.

93. Herbert Strang, *With Haig on the Somme* (London: Humphrey Milford OUP, 1917), 61–64. Strang had been pipped at the post regarding the title *With Haig on the Somme*, for Parry's novel of the same title had already appeared. A peevish note from the publisher informed readers that, when they became aware of the "appropriation of the . . . title," the preparations for the present volume were already too far advanced to make changes.

94. Brereton, *Under Haig in Flanders*, 81.

95. Parry, *With Haig on the Somme*, 71.

96. Ibid., 299.

97. Bourne, *Britain and the Great War*, 59–60.

98. See also Martin Middlebrook, *The First Day on the Somme* (London: Fontana, 1975); Lynn MacDonald, *The Somme* (London: Penguin, 1983).

99. Bourne, *Britain and the Great War,* 67.

100. Brereton, *Under Haig in Flanders,* 182.

101. Ibid., 184.

102. Captain A. J. Dawson, *Somme Battle Stories* (London: Hodder & Stoughton, 1916), 46.

103. Parry, *With Haig on the Somme,* 2.

104. Strang, *With Haig on the Somme,* 282–83.

105. Dawson, *Somme Battle Stories,* 221–23.

106. Nicholas Reeves, "Through the Eye of the Camera: Contemporary Cinema Audiences and their 'Experience' of War in the Film *The Battle of the Somme,*" in *Facing Armageddon, The First World War Experienced,* ed. Hugh Cecil and Peter Liddle (London: Leo Cooper, 1996), 780–98; Nicholas Reeves, "Official British Film Propaganda," in *The First World War and Popular Cinema, 1914 to the Present,* ed. Michael Paris (Edinburgh: Edinburgh University Press, 1999), 35.

107. Ibid.

108. Ibid., 37.

109. See Mary Cadogan, *Frank Richards: The Chap Behind the Chums* (Claverley, UK: Swallowtail Books, 2000), 131.

110. Cadogan and Craig, *Women and Children First,* 83.

CHAPTER 3: THE WAR IN THE AIR

1. Sir Edward Parrott, *The Children's Story of the War,* 10 vols. (London: Nelson, 1915–1919), 4:377.

2. Edmund Stedman, "Aerial Navigation" (1879), quoted in H. Bruce Franklin, *War Stars: The Superweapon and the American Imagination* (New York: Oxford University Press, 1988), 82.

3. Jules Verne, *The Clipper of the Clouds* (London: Sampson, Low, Marston, Searle, 1887); *Master of the World* (London: Grant Richards, 1904). On Verne's changing attitude towards technology see Kenneth Allot, *Jules Verne* (New York, Doubleday, 1954).

4. See Alberto Santos Dumont, *My Airships: The Story of My Life* (London: Grant Richards, 1904); Geoffrey De Havilland, *Sky Fever* (London: Hamilton, 1961). On Dunne, see Charles Turner, *The Old Flying Days* (London: Sampson, Low and Marston, 1927), 73–74.

5. G. Griffiths, *Outlaws of the Air* (London: Tower Publishing, 1895); E. D. Fawcett, *Hartmann the Anarchist* (London: Arnold, 1893); H. G. Wells, *The War in the Air* (London: Bell, 1908).

6. On the Zeppelin Menace see Alfred Gollin, *No Longer an Island: Britain and the Wright Brothers* (London: Heinemann, 1984); Michael Paris, *Winged Warfare: The Literature and Theory of Aerial Warfare in Britain, 1859–1917* (Manchester: Manchester University Press, 1992).

7. See, for example, serial stories, Andrew Gray, "Scourge of the Skies," *Boy's Herald* (July 1908–Jan. 1909): 267–90; Reginald Wray, "While Britain Slept," *Boy's Herald* (1910–1911): 383–406; John Tregellis, "Kaiser or King," *Boy's Friend* (1912): 555–84; Marr Murray, "The Flying Spy," *Dreadnought* (June 1914): 107.

8. On Harmsworth and Lanchester, see Reginald Pound and Geoffrey Harmsworth, *Northcliffe* (London: Cassell, 1959); Paris, *Winged Warfare.*

9. Turner, *The Old Flying Days,* 182.

10. On the Aerial League of The British Empire, see Paris, *Winged Warfare,* 88–100; Gollin, *No Longer an Island,* 454–57. On other air pressure groups, see Paris, *Winged Warfare,* 65–121.

11. See "Lessons of the War in Tripoli," *Aeronautics* 6, no. 60 (February 1913): 65. The War Office was well informed about the Italian use of aeroplanes and airships by their military attache in Rome; see *Report on Italian Aviation in the Turco-Italian War,* 1912, PRO AIR 1/576/625.

12. See Malcolm Cooper, *The Birth of Independent Air Power* (London: Allen & Unwin, 1986), 9.

13. George Scott, "With the Death or Glory Boys," *The Sphere* (8 July 1911), 52.

14. Editorial, *Boys' Realm* (26 June 1910), 421.

15. Field Service Regulations, Part 1 (1909, amended1914), 21, 127.

16. Ibid., 21, 165.

17. *Royal Flying Corps Training Manual, Part II* (Provisional) (June 1914), 49.

18. Lt-Col. L. A. Strange, *Recollections of an Airman* (London: John Hamilton, 1933), 75.

19. V. Wheeler-Holohan, "The Royal Flying Corps," *Boy's Own Paper Annual* 37 (1914–1915), 33.

20. Guy Thorne, *The Secret Sea-Plane* (London: Hodder & Staughton, 1915).

21. Claude Grahame-White and Harry Harper, *The Invisible War Plane* (London: Cassell, 1915), 129–30.

22. Percy F. Westerman, *The Secret Battleplane* (London: Partridge, 1916), 33–34.

23. W. H. Henry, *The Red Kite* (London: Ward Lock, 1916).

24. On Fokker supremacy see Cooper, *Birth of Independent Air Power,* 29–32.

25. John H. Morrow, *The Great War in the Air* (Washington: Smithsonian Institution Press, 1993), 33–34.

26. Henry Newbolt, *Tales of the Great War* (London: Longmans Green, 1916), 251. On other literary responses to air raids, see Laurence Goldstein, *The Flying Machine and Modern Literature* (London: Macmillan, 1986), 75–78.

27. On Warneford, see Neville Jones, *The Origins of Strategic Bombing* (London: Kimber, 1973), 64; see also the editorial in *Boy's Own Paper Annual* 37 (1914–1915), 671.

28. Parrott, *Children's Story of the War,* 4:386.

29. Newbolt, *Tales of the Great War,* 251.

30. Quoted in Louis Jackson, "The Defence of Localities Against Aerial Attack," *Journal of the Royal United Services Institution* 58 no. 436 (June 1914): 725.

31. H. G. Wells, "H. G. Wells asks for 10,000 Aeroplanes," *Daily Express* (23 June 1915): 1.

32. On German technical developments see John H. Morrow, *German Air Power in World War 1* (Lincoln: Nebraska University Press, 1982).

33. Parrott, *Children's Story of the War,* 4:380–81.

34. Rowland Walker, *Dastral of the Flying Corps* (London: Partridge, 1918), 146.

35. Ibid., 199–200.

36. Westerman, *Secret Battleplane,* 173.

37. Parrott, *Children's Story of the War,* 4:370.

38. Herbert Strang, *The War on Land* (London: Henry Frowde and Hodder & Stoughton, 1916), np.

39. Herbert Strang, *The Air Scout* (London: Henry Frowde and Hodder & Stoughton, 1912); *The Air Patrol* (London: Henry Frowde, 1913).

40. See Paris, *Winged Warfare*, 229–30.

41. Walker, *Dastral of the Flying Corps*, 10.

42. Raleigh to Mrs. M. Busk, 16 May 1919, in *The Letters of Sir Walter Raleigh*, vol. 2, ed. Lady Raleigh (London: Methuen, 1926), 507.

43. Sefton Branker's address to the Royal Aeronautical Society, 24 January 1917, quoted in Norman MacMillan, *Sefton Branker* (London: Heinemann, 1935), 142–43.

44. Denis Winter, *The First of the Few: Fighter Pilots of the First World War* (London: Penguin, 1983), 36.

45. Air Vice-Marshall S. F. Vincent, *Flying Fever* (London: Kimber, 1972), 22. See also Lord Balfour, *An Airman Marches* (1933, London: Greenhill, 1985), 45.

46. R. Wherry Anderson, *The Romance of Air-Fighting* (London: Cassell, 1917), 4.

47. F. S. Brereton, *Under French's Command* (London: Blackie, 1916), 163.

48. Captain Frank Shaw, "Join the Royal Flying Corps," *Chums* 23 (1915): 346.

49. "Getting His Wings," *Chums* 27 (January 1919): 238.

50. See Paris, *Winged Warfare*, 185–90.

51. Morrow, *Great War in the Air*, 104–5.

52. F. S. Brereton, *With the Allies to the Rhine* (London: Blackie, 1919), 203.

53. Morrow, *Great War in the Air*, 104–6, 148–51.

54. Walter Raleigh, *The War in the Air*, vol. 1 (Oxford: Oxford University Press, 1922), 204–5.

55. Ibid., 424.

56. See James McCudden, *Five Years in the Royal Flying Corps* (London: Aviation Book Club, 1930).

57. Morrow, *Great War in the Air*, 117.

58. See Peter Parker, *The Old Lie: The Great War and the Public School Ethos* (London: Constable, 1987), 200.

59. Wherry Anderson, *Romance of Air Fighting*, 3.

60. Major L. W. B. Rees, *Fighting in the Air* (London: Royal Flying Corps, 1916), 8.

61. Cecil Lewis, *Sagittarius Rising* (London: Peter Davies, 1936), 71.

62. Parker, *The Old Lie*, 200–201.

63. Walker, *Deville McKeene: The Mystery Airman* (London: Partridge, 1919), 236–41. On the Red Baron's death, see Peter Kilduff, ed., *Germany's Last Knight of the Air* (London: Kimber, 1979).

64. Newbolt, *Tales of the Great War*, 248–49.

65. Wherry Anderson, *Romance of Air Fighting*, 11–12.

66. Parker, *The Old Lie*, 201.

67. Mrs. Maurice Hewlett, *Our Flying Men* (London: Cassell, 1917), 37.

68. David Lloyd George, quoted in Goldstein, *The Flying Machine and Modern Literature*, 87.

69. Walker, *Dastral of the Flying Corps*, 247.

70. See, for example, *Le Matin*, 23 April 1918, and the newsreel coverage of Richthofen's funeral. See Michael Paris, *From the Wright Brothers to Top Gun: Aviation, Nationalism and Popular Cinema* (Manchester: Manchester University Press, 1995), 27.

71. Walker, *Deville McKeene*, 47.

72. Ibid., 10.

73. Morrow, *Great War in the Air*, 242.

74. See Claude Grahame-White and Harry Harper, *Heroes of the Flying Corps* (London: Cassell, 1916); Parrott, *Children's Story of the War*, 4:382–84, 9:49–53; T. W. Wilkinson, "Tales of the Air Service," a six-part series, *Boy's Own Paper Annual*. 41 (1918–1919); Eric Wood, *Thrilling Deeds of British Airmen* (London: Harrap, 1917); Herbert Strang, *Burton of the Flying Corps* (London: Milford, 1916); Walker, *Dastral of the Flying Corps*.

75. James Byford McCudden, *Five Years in the Royal Flying Corps* (London: The Aeroplane, 1918).

76. Percy F. Westerman, *Winning His Wings* (London: Blackie, 1919), 14, 59.

77. Ibid., 156.

78. Ibid., 97.

79. Ibid., 25. Sixteen years later Cecil Lewis would express almost exactly the same sentiments when he recalled his first flying experiences. See Lewis, *Sagittarius Rising*, 54–55.

80. Paris, *Winged Warfare*, 2.

81. Raleigh to E. V. Lucas, 22 September 1918, in Raleigh, *Letters*, 493.

82. Lewis, *Sagittarius Rising*, 45.

CHAPTER 4: SIDESHOWS: GALLIPOLI, MESOPOTAMIA, PALESTINE, AND AFRICA

1. Sir Edward Parrott, *The Children's Story of the War*, 10 vols. (London: Nelson, 1915–1919), 8:11.

2. Ian F. W. Beckett, *The Great War, 1914–1918* (London: Longman, 2001), 110.

3. Gerard J. De Groot, *The First World War* (London: Palgrave, 2001), 91.

4. Bernard Porter, *The Lion's Share: A Short History of British Imperialism 1850–1983* (London: Longman, 1984), 233.

5. Lord Hankey, *The Supreme Command, 1914–1918*, vol. 1 (London: George Allen & Unwin, 1961), 244–50.

6. Keith Robbins, *The First World War* (Oxford: Oxford University Press, 1984), 39.

7. Jan Morris, *Farewell the Trumpets* (London: Penguin, 1979), 160–61.

8. Parrott, *Children's Story of the War*, 3:264–72.

9. F. S. Brereton, *On the Road to Bagdad* (London: Blackie, 1916), 37.

10. See Sir Ian Hamilton, *Gallipoli Diary*, 2 vols. (London: Edward Arnold, 1920); John Lee, *A Soldier's Life: General Sir Ian Hamilton, 1853–1947* (London: Pan, 2001).

11. On the Gallipoli campaign, see L. A. Carlyon, *Gallipoli* (London: Doubleday, 2002); Peter Liddle, *Men of Gallipoli* (London: Allen Lane, 1976); Robert Rhodes James, *Gallipoli* (London: Pan, 1974).

12. Parrott, *Children's Story of the War*, 4:158.

13. Quoted in Peter Parker, *The Old Lie: The Great War and the Public School Ethos* (London: Constable, 1987), 217–18.

14. Percy F. Westerman, *The Fight for Constantinople* (London: Blackie, 1915), 18.

15. Ibid., 256.

16. Herbert Strang, *Frank Forrester: A Story of the Dardanelles* (London: Milford, 1915).

17. T. C. Bridges, *On Land and Sea at the Dardanelles* (London: Collins, 1915), 11.

18. Ibid., 100.

19. Ibid., 25.

20. Ibid., 31, 32, 34.

21. Ibid., 198.

22. Joseph Bowes, *The Young Anzacs* (London: Humphrey Milford, 1918), 101–2.

23. Ibid., 208.

24. F. S. Brereton, *The Armoured Car Scouts* (London: Blackie, 1915). Around the same time Brereton also published his Gallipoli novel, *At Grips with the Turks* (London: Blackie, 1915).

25. Anon. "A Good Word for the Turkish Soldier," *Young England Annual* 37 (1915–1916): 155–56. See also F. W. Martindale, "'Johnny Turk,' Sportsman," *Boy's Own Annual* 39 (1916–1917): 217–18.

26. Bowes, *The Young Anzacs*, 129. See also H. C. Buley, *Glorious Deeds of Australians in the Present War* (London: Melrose, 1915), and the same author's *A Child's History of Anzac* (London: Hodder & Stoughton, 1916).

27. Anon., "*The Clean-Fighting Turk*" *A Spurious Claim*, leaflet reprinted from *The Times* (London: Wellington House, 1917).

28. Guy Waterford, "Last Days at Gallipoli," *Young England Annual* 37 (1915), 235.

29. Ibid., 231.

30. John Masefield, *Gallipoli* (London: Heinemann, 1916), 3. See also Parker, *The Old Lie*, 228.

31. Parker, *The Old Lie*, 227.

32. Captain F. S. Brereton, *On the Road to Bagdad*, 19.

33. Morris, *Farewell the Trumpets*, 163.

34. Brereton, *On the Road to Bagdad*, 75.

35. Ibid., 283, 287.

36. Ibid., 312.

37. Ibid., 383.

38. Ibid., 313.

39. Alfred Miles and C. Sheridan Jones, *Heroic Deeds of Great Men* (London: Raphael Tuck, nd), 193, 196. For an assessment of the campaign and of Maude's contribution, see Arthur J. Barker, *The Neglected War: Mesopotamia, 1914–1919* (London: Faber, 1967).

40. Herbert Strang, *Carry On: A Story of the Fight for Bagdad* (London: Milford, 1917), 272.

41. Parrott, *Children's Story of the War*, 7:63.

42. Ibid., 74.

43. Joseph Bowes, *The Aussie Crusaders* (London: Humphrey Milford, 1920), 86.

44. Ibid., 158.

45. Lawrence's exploits were largely publicized by the American journalist Lowell Thomas, who had covered events in Arabia from mid-1917. However, it was Thomas's post-war lecture series, "With Allenby in Palestine and the Conquest of Holy Arabia" (soon changed to "With Allenby in Palestine and Lawrence in Arabia"), that made Lawrence into a public hero. See Jonathan Rutherford, *Forever England: Reflections on Masculinity and Empire* (London: Lawrence and Wishart, 1997), 70–103; Graham Daw-

son, *Soldier Heroes: British Adventure, Empire and the Imagining of Masculinities* (London: Routledge, 1994), 167–207. Post-war adventure fictions that made use of a Lawrence-type hero included Percy Westerman, "The White Arab," *Chums Annual* 40 (1932); W. E. Johns, *Biggles Flies East* (London: Oxford University Press, 1935); and Alan Western, *Desert Hawk* (London: Nelson, 1937).

46. F. S. Brereton, *With Allenby in Palestine: A Story of the Last Crusade* (London: Blackie, 1919), 238, 239–40.

47. Bowes, *Aussie Crusaders*, 211, 212.

48. Ibid., 216.

49. Brereton, *With Allenby in Palestine*, 243.

50. Bowes, *Aussie Crusaders*, 260.

51. Brereton, *With Allenby in Palestine*, 245.

52. Ibid., 286.

53. Parrott, *Children's Story of the War*, 8:207.

54. Brereton, *With Allenby in Palestine*, 285–86.

55. Mark Girouard, *The Return to Camelot: Chivalry and the English Gentleman* (London: Yale University Press, 1981), 291.

56. Vivian Gilbert, *The Romance of the Last Crusade* (New York: Appleton, 1924), 235. See also Parker, *The Old Lie*, 228–30.

57. See Bowes, *The Aussie Crusaders*; Strang, *Frank Forrester*; Brereton, *With Allenby in Palestine*.

58. See for example Argyll Saxby M.A., "The Black Lizard," *Boy's Own Paper* 39 (1916–1917).

59. Editorial, *Boy's Own Paper* 39 (1916–1917): 534.

60. See, for example, Brereton, *With Allenby in Palestine*, 159–60.

61. George Cassar, "Kitchener at the War Office," in *Facing Armageddon: The First World War Experienced*, ed. Hugh Cecil and Peter Liddle (London: Leo Cooper, 1996),44–45.

62. B. H. Liddell Hart, *History of the First World War* (London: Pan, 1975), 153–54; Gerard De Groot, *The First World War* (London: Palgrave, 2001), 96–100.

63. See Gail Braybon and Penny Summerfield, *Out of the Cage: Women's Experiences in Two World Wars* (London: Pandora, 1987).

64. Bessie Marchant, *A VAD in Salonika* (London: Blackie, 1916), 53.

65. Ibid., 88.

66. Herbert Strang, "The Watch-Tower" *Burton of the Flying Corps* (London: Humphrey Milford), 163–245.

67. See Melvin E. Page, ed., *Africa and the First World War* (London: Macmillan, 1987).

68. Captain Charles Gilson, *Across the Cameroons: A Story of War and Adventure* (London: Blackie, 1916), 153–54.

69. Lionel Warren, "Cutting the Eagle's Talons: The Diary of an Old Chum in German South-West Africa," reprinted in Philip Warner, *The Best of Chums* (London: Macdonald & Jane, 1979), 64–67.

70. Eric Wood, *How We Baffled the Germans* (London: Nelson, 1917).

71. See Page, *Africa and the First World War*.

72. Percy F. Westerman, *Wilmshurst of the Frontier Force* (London: Blackie, 1918), 16–17.

73. Herbert Strang, *Tom Willoughby's Scouts* (London: Milford, 1919).

74. Westerman, *Wilmshurst of the Frontier Force*, 98.

75. Strang, *Tom Willoughby's Scouts*, 240.

76. Westerman, *Wilmshurst of the Frontier Force*, 18.

77. "Our African Soldiers," *Young England Annual* 37 (1916), 140. In "The Middle Stump" (*The Boy's Own Paper* 41: 44–47), Soola, a native Askari serving the Germans, is won over to the British cause by the unerring bowling skill of a young Englishman, which the natives attribute to supernatural power. Captivated by the white man's magic, Soola eventually becomes a loyal servant of the empire.

78. Strang, *Tom Willoughby's Scouts*, 295.

CHAPTER 5: BRAVE SONS OF EMPIRE AND LOYAL ALLIES

1. Captain F. S. Brereton, *Under Haig in Flanders* (London: Blackie, 1916), 181, 264.

2. George Robb, *British Culture and the First World War* (London: Palgrave, 2002), 11.

3. Gerard De Groot, *The First World War* (London: Palgrave, 2001), 104.

4. Robb, *British Culture and the First World War*, 12.

5. J. Holland Rose, *How the War Came About* (London: Patriotic Publishing, 1914), 24.

6. Lauchlan Maclean Watt, "The Children of the Flag," *Boy's Own Annual*, 37 (1914–1915), 406.

7. "A Canadian Soldier's Story," *Young England Annual* 37 (1915–1916), 290.

8. Robb, *British Culture and the First World War*, 17.

9. De Groot, *The First World War*, 105.

10. See Peter Buitenhuis, *The Great War of Words: Literature as Propaganda, 1914–1918 and After* (London: Batsford, 1989), 98–100.

11. Talbot Mundy, *King of the Khyber Rifles* (London: Hutchinson, 1916); John Buchan, *Greenmantle* (London: Nelson, 1916).

12. *Third Report on the Work Conducted for the Government at Wellington House* (London: HMSO, 1916), 100. The cigarette card, the Report noted, "(made possible by the co-operation of the Ardath Tobacco Co.) is likely to be a particularly useful means of reaching the masses in an unobtrusive way." See also John M. Mackenzie, *Propaganda and Empire: The Manipulation of British Public Opinion, 1880–1960* (Manchester: Manchester University Press, 1985), but especially 74–76, 216–17.

13. Herbert Strang, *The Empire at War* (London: Henry Frowde Hodder & Stoughton, 1916).

14. F. S. Brereton, *A Boy of the Dominion* (London: Blackie, 1910), 29.

15. Ibid., 366.

16. The Canadians may have had few military traditions, but throughout the Victorian and Edwardian periods the martial spirit had been widely promoted among young men. See Mark Moss, *Manliness and Militarism: Educating Young Boys in Ontario for War* (Don Mills, Ontario: Oxford University Press, 2001).

17. Sir Edward Parrott, *The Children's Story of the War*, 10 vols. (London: Nelson, 1915–1919), 4:193.

18. Captain F. S. Brereton, *Under French's Command* (London: Blackie, 1916), 222.

19. Ibid., 226–27.

20. Brereton, *Under Haig in Flanders*, 159–60.

21. Parrott, *Children's Story of the War*, 8:68–69, 71. See also Captain Charles Gilson, "The Clearing Station: A Stirring Yarn of Canadian Pluck," *Chums* 27, no. 1378 (February 1919): 263–64, and concluded in no. 1379: 275–76.

22. See Tim Travers, "Canadian Film and the First World War," in *The First World War and Popular Cinema*, ed. M. Paris (Edinburgh: Edinburgh University Press, 1999), 96–114.

23. Buitenhuis, *The Great War of Words*, 153–54.

24. E. C. Buley, *Glorious Deeds of Australasians in the Great War* (London: Andrew Melrose, 1915), and *A Child's History of Anzac* (London: Hodder & Stoughton, 1916).

25. Parrott, *Children's Story of the War*, 4:277.

26. Herbert Strang, *Frank Forrester: A Story of the Dardanelles* (London: Milford, 1915), 220–21.

27. T. C. Bridges, *On Land and Sea at the Dardanelles* (London: Collins, 1915), 30.

28. Percy F. Westerman, *A Lively Bit of the Front: A Tale of the New Zealand Rifles on the Western Front* (London: Blackie, 1918), 9–10.

29. Ibid., 71.

30. Ibid., 80.

31. *The Times*, quoted in Jan Morris, *Farewell the Trumpets* (London: Penguin, 1979), 199.

32. Ibid., 213.

33. Ibid., 213–14.

34. Percy F. Westerman, *Wilmshurst of the Frontier Force* (London: Blackie, 1918), 17.

35. Harry Golding, ed., *The Wonder Book of Soldiers*, sixth edition (London: Ward, Lock & Co., c. 1919), 248.

36. See Herbert Strang, *Tom Willoughby's Scouts* (London: Milford, 1919).

37. Golding, *Wonder Book of Soldiers*, 257.

38. Parrott, *Children's Story of the War*, 3:81.

39. Ibid.

40. Bernard Waites, "Peoples of the Underdeveloped World," in Cecil and Liddle, *Facing Armageddon: The First World War Experienced*, ed. Hugh Cecil and Peter Liddle (London: Leo Cooper, 1996), 600.

41. Captain F. S. Brereton, *On the Road to Bagdad* (London: Blackie, 1916), 74.

42. Golding, *Wonder Book of Soldiers*, 264.

43. De Groot, *The First World War*, 110.

44. Percy F. Westerman, *Winning His Wings*, (London: Blackie, 1919), 93–94.

45. W. J. Gordon, "Coloured Troops of the Allies," *Boy's Own Paper Annual* 41 (1918–1919), 105–6.

46. Peter Parker, *The Old Lie: The Great War and the Public School Ethos* (London: Constable, 1987), 137.

47. Elizabeth O'Neill, *The War, 1914: A History and an Explanation for Boys and Girls* (London: T.C. & E.C. Jack, 1914), 27–30.

48. T. C. & E. C. Jack catalogue, 1915.

49. Ascott R. Hope, *The School of Arms: Boy Soldiers and Sailors* (London: Routledge, 1915), 130–85.

50. Herbert Strang, *A Hero of Liege* (London: Henry Frowde and Hodder & Stoughton, 1915), 71.

51. Henry Frowde and Hodder & Stoughton catalogue, c. 1909.

52. Parrott, *Children's Story of the War*, 1:239–40.

53. Escott Lynn, *In Khaki for the King: A Tale of the Great War* (London: W. & R. Chambers, 1915), 144; Percy F. Westerman, *The Dispatch Riders: The Adventures of Two Motor-Cyclists in the Great War* (London: Blackie, 1915), 15. On Westerman's views on race, see Cedric Cullingford, "'The Right Stuff': The Boys' Stories of Percy F. Westerman," *Children's Literature in Education* 24, no. 1 (1993): 53–71.

54. F. S. Brereton, *Foes of the Red Cockade* (London: Blackie, 1904).

55. Quoted in Caroline Playne, *The Pre-War Mind in Britain* (London: George Allen & Unwin, 1928), 117.

56. See Herbert Strang, *Fighting with French* (London: Humphrey Milford, 1915), 67.

57. Lynn, *In Khaki for the King*, 177–79.

58. Parrott, *Children's Story of the War*, 4:191.

59. "A French Boy Scout," *Young England Annual*, 37(1916), 38. See also W. E. Cossons, "Henri Does His Bit: A Tale of a French Boy Scout," *Boy's Own Annual* 41, (1918–1919), 293–97.

60. F. S. Brereton, *With Joffre at Verdun* (London: Blackie, 1917), 9–10.

61. Ibid., 11.

62. F. S. Brereton, *A Soldier of Japan* (London: Blackie, 1907); Herbert Strang, *Kobi: A Soldier of Japan* (London: Blackie, 1906) and *Brown of Moukden* (London: Blackie, 1907).

63. See John Tregellis, "Rule Britannia," a serial that ran in *The Boy's Friend* through 1905, or Captain Frank Shaw, "Perils of the Motherland," *Chums* 16 (1908).

64. Quoted in Niall Ferguson, *The Pity of War* (London: Allen Lane, 1998), 185.

65. Robb, *British Culture and the First World War*, 100.

66. Parrott, *Children's Story of the War*, 2:50.

67. De Groot, *The First World War*, 54–55.

68. Parrott, *Children's Story of the War*, 2:63.

69. See Norman Stone, *The Eastern Front, 1914–1917* (London: Hodder & Stoughton, 1975).

70. F. S. Brereton, *The Armoured Car Scouts* (London: Blackie, 1915), 182.

71. Ibid., 26–27.

72. Ibid., 189.

73. Captain Charles Gilson, *In Arms for Russia* (London: Humphrey Milford, 1917), 248–49.

74. Ibid., 67.

75. Ibid., 45, 102.

76. Ibid., 223.

77. Ibid., 221–22.

78. Ibid., 245.

79. Piers Brendon, *The Dark Valley: A Panorama of the 1930s* (London: Pimlico, 2001), 9.

80. Bessie Marchant, *A Dangerous Mission: A Tale of Russia in Revolution* (London: Blackie, 1918), 56.

81. Ibid., 244.

82. Ibid., 246.

83. Parrott, *Children's Story of the War*, 7:81, 89.

84. Ibid., 9:65.

85. Ibid., 7:65–70.

86. F. S. Brereton, *With Allenby in Palestine: A Story of the Last Crusade* (London: Blackie, 1919), 240–41.

87. Radcliffe Martin, "His Bit," *Chums* 37, no. 1376 (1919): 239–40.

88. See Ian F. W. Beckett, *The Great War, 1914–1918* (London: Longman, 2001), 126, 208–9; Martin Gilbert, *First World War* (London: Weidenfeld & Nicolson, 1994), 318–19.

89. Parrott, *Children's Story of the War*, 9:168.

90. Escott Lynn, *Knights of the Air*, (London: W & R Chambers, 1918), 48.

91. Ibid.

92. Ibid., 382.

93. Ibid., 47, 49.

94. F. S. Brereton, *Under Foch's Command: A Tale of the Americans in France* (London: Blackie, 1918), 13.

95. Ibid., 17–18.

96. Ibid., 281.

97. Ibid., 287.

CHAPTER 6: THE LAST OF WAR, 1917–1918

1. Captain F. S. Brereton, *With the Allies to the Rhine* (London: Blackie, 1919), 283, 288.

2. Allan Bishop, ed., *Vera Brittain's War Diary* (London: Little, Brown, 1981), 89.

3. Mary Cadogan and Patricia Craig, *Women and Children First: The Fiction of Two World Wars* (London: Gollancz, 1978), 59.

4. Cate Haste, *Keep the Home Fires Burning: Propaganda in the First World War* (London: Allen Lane, 1977), 56–57.

5. Jesse Pope, "The Call" in *Scars Upon My Heart: Women's Poetry and Verse of the First World War*, ed. Catherine Reilly (London: Virago, 1981), 88.

6. Such a view is perhaps most bitterly expressed in Richard Aldington's 1929 novel, *Death of a Hero* (London: Penguin, 1937), and Siegfried Sassoon's poems *Blighters* and *Glory of Women*, reprinted in *Men Who Marched Away*, ed. I. M. Parsons (London: Heinemann, 1965), 90, 97. But see also E. A. Mackintosh, *Recruiting*, and the comments by Michael Adams in *The Great Adventure* (Bloomington: Michael Addams, 1990), 128–30.

7. An excellent survey of women's war work is to be found in Gail Braybon and Penny Summerfield, *Out of the Cage* (London: Pandora, 1987).

8. See for example Vera Brittain, *Testament of Youth* (London: Gollancz, 1933) or Enid Bagnold, *A Diary Without Dates* (London: Heinemann, 1918).

9. Bessie Marchant, *A Girl Munition Worker* (London: Blackie, 1916), 133.

10. Ibid., 135.

11. Bessie Marchant, *A Transport Girl in France* (London: Blackie, 1918); Brenda Girvin, *Jenny Wren* (London: Cassell, 1920).

12. Hampden Gordon and Joyce Dennys, *Our Girls in Wartime* (London: John

Lane, nd), 7. See also *Our Hospital ABC* by the same authors (London: John Lane, nd).

13. Angela Brazil, *A Patriotic Schoolgirl* (London: Blackie, 1918), 135.

14. Ibid., 136–37.

15. See Cadogan and Craig, *Women and Children First*, 59–70.

16. Charles Gilson, *On Secret Service* (Oxford: Humphrey Milford, 1919), 10.

17. Ibid., 237.

18. George Robb, *British Culture and the First World War* (London: Palgrave, 2002), 163.

19. Cadogan and Craig, *Women and Children First*, 91.

20. Percy F. Westerman, *Winning His Wings* (London: Blackie, 1919), 90–91.

21. Correlli Barnett, *The Great War* (London: BBC Worldwide, 2003), 134–36.

22. Sir Edward Parrott, *The Children's Story of the War*, 10 vols. (London: Nelson, 1915–1919), 8:1–2.

23. Ibid., 16.

24. Barnett, *The Great War*, 158–60; Haste, *Keep the Home Fires Burning*, 140–78.

25. Ian F. W. Beckett, *The Great War, 1914–1918* (London: Longman, 2001), 110.

26. Siegfried Sassoon, *The Complete Memoirs of George Sherston* (London: Faber & Faber, 1937), 409.

27. Herbert Strang, *Fighting with French* (London: Humphrey Milford, 1915), 276–78.

28. H. G. Wells, "The Land Ironclads," in *Selected Short Stories* (London: Penguin, 1958), 84–105.

29. Ibid., 105.

30. J. P. Harris, *Men, Ideas and Tanks: British Military Thought and Armoured Forces, 1903–1939* (Manchester: Manchester University Press, 1995), 8–18.

31. Armoured cars provided the inspiration for Charles Gilson's *A Motor Scout in France* (London: Blackie, 1915) and F. S. Brereton's *The Armoured Car Scouts* (London: Blackie, 1916).

32. Harris, *Men, Ideas and Tanks*, 9.

33. Barnett, *The Great War*, 154.

34. *Daily Chronicle*, 18 September 1916.

35. *Daily Express*, 18 September 1916.

36. Parrott, *Children's Story of the War*, 6:209.

37. Lincoln Hayward, "Tanks and Caterpillars," *Boy's Own Paper* 41 (1918–1919), 161.

38. Parrott, *Children's Story of the War*, 6:224.

39. Ibid., 8:384–86.

40. Captain F. S. Brereton, *Under Haig in Flanders* (London: Blackie, 1916), 93–94.

41. Brereton, *With the Allies to the Rhine*, 255.

42. Percy F. Westerman, *To the Fore with the Tanks!* (London: Blackie, 1917), 131–32.

43. Ibid., 158–59.

44. Westerman, *Winning His Wings*, 134.

45. Ibid., 137.

46. Ibid., 128.

47. Beckett, *The Great War, 1914–1918*, 178.

48. Percy F. Westerman, "When Tank Meets Tank," in *The Secret Channel* (London: Blackie, 1918), 99–114.

49. Beckett, *The Great War, 1914–1918*, 178.

50. Harry Golding, ed., *The Wonder Book of Soldiers* (London: Ward Lock, 1919), 219.

51. Ibid., 221.

52. The following novels focused on tank warfare: Escott Lynn, *Tommy of the Tanks* (London: Chambers, 1919); Tank Major [pseud.] and Eric Wood, *Tank Tales* (London: Cassell, 1919); T. W. Corbett, *Marvels of War Invention* (London: Blackie, 1919). Interestingly, one of the very few juvenile novels published after the Second World War dealing with the Great War also focused on the war of the tanks; see David Welch, *Tank Commander* (London: Nelson, 1972).

53. Omer Bartov, *Murder in Our Midst: The Holocaust, Industrial Killing, and Representation* (Oxford: Oxford University Press, 1997), 21.

54. Ibid., 26.

55. Parrott, *Children's Story of the War*, 8:384.

56. Barnett, *The Great War*, 162–63.

57. Parrott, *Children's Story of the War*, 9:86.

58. Brereton, *With the Allies to the Rhine*, 132.

59. Westerman, *Winning His Wings*, 68–69.

60. Escott Lynn, *Knights of the Air* (London: W. & R. Chambers, 1918), 314–15.

61. Ibid., 317.

62. Ibid., 319–20.

63. Westerman, *Winning His Wings*, 79.

64. Ibid., 111.

65. Barnett, *The Great War*, 181–84.

66. Brereton, *With the Allies to the Rhine*, 247.

67. Ibid., 255–56.

68. Ibid., 257.

69. Westerman, *Winning His Wings*, 224.

70. P. J. Campbell, *The Ebb and Flow of Battle* (Oxford: Oxford University Press, 1979), 166.

71. Alan Bishop, ed., *Chronicle of Youth: Vera Brittain's War Diary, 1913–1917* (London: Gollancz, 1981), 114.

72. Ibid., 272.

73. T. P. Cameron to Mrs. Orpen, 3 May 1916, in *Letters from the Front, 1914–1918*, ed. John Laffin (London: Dent, 1973), 8.

74. Lynn, *Knights of the Air*, 318–19, 326, 355.

75. Westerman, *To the Fore with the Tanks*, 19–27.

76. Ibid., 43.

77. Percy F. Westerman, *A Lively Bit of the Front: A Tale of the New Zealand Rifles on the Western Front* (London: Blackie, 1918), 122.

78. Ibid., 147.

79. Lynn, *Knights of the Air*.

80. Westerman, *To the Fore with the Tanks*, 113–21.

81. *Boy's Own Paper* 41: 27–28.

82. W. E. Cossens, "The Giant's Robe: A Story of Football and Fighting," *Boy's Own Paper* 41(1918–1919), 23.

83. Owen Wheeler, "Great Britain's Record," in Golding, *The Wonder Book of Soldiers*, 83.

84. Brereton, *With the Allies to the Rhine*, 286–87.

85. See Bernard Porter, *The Lion's Share: A Short History of British Imperialism 1850–1983* (London: Longman, 1984), 242–46.

86. Harry Golding, ed., *Wonder Book of Empire* (London: Ward Lock, 1919), xii.

87. Cecil Lewis, *Sagittarius Rising* (London: Peter Davies, 1936), 207.

88. P. J. Campbell, *The Ebb and Flow of Battle* (Oxford: Oxford University Press, 1979), 161.

89. W. P. Shervill, *Two Daring Young Patriots, or Outwitting the Huns* (London: Blackie, 1919), 256.

90. Westerman, *Winning His Wings*, 253.

91. Jack Lindsay, *Wings Over Africa* (London: John Hamilton, 1937), 255.

92. Rowland Walker, *The Phantom Airman* (London: Partridge. 1920), 9.

93. Ibid., 205.

94. Quoted in E. S. Turner, *Boys Will Be Boys* (London: Michael Joseph, 1948), 182–83.

95. See Kirsten Drotner, *English Children and Their Magazines, 1751–1945* (New Haven: Yale University Press, 1988), 231.

CONCLUSION

1. Harry Golding, ed., *The Wonder Book of Soldiers* (London: Ward Lock, 1919), 83.

2. Robert Graves and Alan Hodge, *The Long Weekend* (London: Victor Gotlanez, 1940, Sphere Books, 1985), 26, 216; Samuel Hynes, *A War Imagined: The First World War and English Culture* (London: Pimlico, 1992), 424.

3. Lloyd Clark, "Civilians Entrenched: The British Home Front and Attitudes to the First World War, 1914–1918," in *War, Culture and the Media*, ed. Ian Stewart and Susan Carruthers (Trowbridge: Flicks Books, 1996), 38; see also Robert Wohl, *The Generation of 1914* (Cambridge, Mass.: Harvard University Press, 1979).

4. Philip Knightley, *The First Casualty* (London: Cardinal, 1991), 80–81; see also Philip Gibbs, *Realities of War*, 2 vols. (London: Hutchinson, 1938); and Martin J. Farrar, *News from the Front: War Correspondents on the Western Front, 1914–1918* (Stroud, UK: Sutton, 1998).

5. See Alan Borg, *War Memorials from Antiquity to the Present* (London: Leo Cooper, 1991); Catherine Moriarty, "Christian Iconography and First World War Memorials," *Imperial War Museum Review* 6 (1991): 63–75; Jay Winter, *Sites of Memory, Sites of Mourning* (Cambridge: Cambridge University Press, 1995); for valuable insights into how local communities remembered the war, see Mark Connelly, *The Great War, Memory and Ritual: Commemoration in the City and East London, 1916–1939* (London: Royal Historical Society/Boydell Press, 2002).

6. Quoted in Catherine Moriarty, "Private Grief and Public Remembrance: British First World War Memorials," in *War and Memory in the Twentieth Century*, ed. Martin Evans and Ken Lunn (Oxford: Oxford University Press, 1997), 128.

7. Gerard DeGroot, *Blighty: British Society in the Era of the Great War* (London: Longman, 1996), 286.

8. Omer Bartov, *Murder in Our Midst: The Holocaust, Industrial Killing, and Representation* (Oxford: Oxford University Press, 1997), 154–55.

9. See Moriarty, "Private Grief." Film is dealt with in Andrew Kelly, *Cinema and the Great War* (London: Routledge, 1997), and M. Paris, ed., *The First World War and Popular Cinema* (Edinburgh: Edinburgh University Press, 1999).

10. Brereton wrote only one war adventure story after the war, *Scouts of the Baghdad Patrols* (London: Cassell, c. 1920), a story of the British occupation of Iraq. He then seems to have turned to more peaceful themes, such as *A History of Travel* (London: Batsford, 1931).

11. Details from the author's collection.

12. See, for example, Siegfried Sassoon, *The Complete Memoirs of George Sherston* (London: Faber & Faber, 1937); Henry Williamson, *The Patriot's Progress* (London: Faber & Faber, 1930); Richard Aldington, *Death of a Hero* (London: Davies, 1929).

13. Aldine Library Catalogue, c. 1934.

14. See Bill Bradford, "George Ernest Rochester, 1898–1966," *Biggles and Co.* 29 (winter 1996): 33–35.

15. On Johns see Peter Berrisford Ellis and Piers Williams, *By Jove, Biggles! The Life of Captain W. E. Johns* (London: Comet, 1985).

16. Denis Butts, "Imperialists of the Air—Flying Stories, 1900–1950," in *Imperialism and Juvenile Literature*, ed. Jeffrey Richards (Manchester: Manchester University Press, 1989), 131.

17. See, for example, Cecil Lewis, *Sagittarius Rising* (London: Peter Davies, 1936); W. A. Briscoe, *Boy Hero of the Air* (London: Humphrey Milford, 1921); Lt.-Col. L. A. Strange, *Recollections of an Airman* (London: John Hamilton, 1933); or the stories of air warfare that appeared in air war pulps such as *Popular Flying* (Hamilton) and *Air Stories* (Newnes).

18. Editorial, *Boy's Own Paper Annual* 52 (1929–1930): 101.

19. Ibid., 73.

20. See Hynes, *A War Imagined*, 47–49; Ian Hay, *The First Hundred Thousand* (London: Blackwood, 1915 and many subsequent editions); Ralph Connor, *The Sky Pilot of No Man's Land* (London: McClelland and Stewart, 1921).

21. For Lawrence-type adventures after 1918, see chapter 4, note 45.

22. Anti-bolshevism and imperial adventure in 1920s/30s.

23. See George Rochester, *The Scarlet Squadron* (London: Hamilton, 1935); Michael Poole, "Emperor of the World," *The Boy's Magazine* (May, 1923), 204–24; John Sylvester, "A Planet at War," *Chums Annual* 38 (1930–31).

24. Herman Cyril McNeile [Sapper, pseud.], *Mufti* (London: Hodder & Staughton, 1919), 43.

Index

About the Author

MICHAEL PARIS is Professor of Modern History at the University of Central Lancashire and a Fellow of the Royal Historical Society. He specializes in the area of war and popular culture. His most recent book is *Warrior Nation: Images of War in British Popular Culture, 1850–2000*.